Gaming
the Game

Gaming
the Game

The Story Behind the
NBA Betting Scandal and
the Gambler Who Made It Happen

BY SEAN PATRICK GRIFFIN

Published by Barricade Books Inc.
185 Bridge Plaza North
Suite 309
Fort Lee, NJ 07024

www.barricadebooks.com

Library of Congress Cataloging-in-Publication Data
Gaming the game : the story behind the NBA betting scandal
and the gambler who made it happen / by Sean Patrick Griffin.
    p. cm.
Includes bibliographical references and index.
ISBN-13: 978-1-56980-444-5
ISBN-10: 1-56980-444-3
1. Basketball--Betting—United States. 2. Basketball—Corrupt
practices—United States. 3. Basketball—Moral and ethical
aspects—United States. 4. Battista, Jimmy. I. Title.
GV887.7.G74 2011
796.323'640973--dc22
                                                    2010045393
ISBN 13: 978-1-56980-444-5
1-56980-444-3

10 9 8 7 6 5 4 3 2 1
Manufactured in the United States of America

For Kelly and Connor

AUTHOR'S NOTE

AS AN AVID sports fan, I thought I was relatively familiar with the National Basketball Association (NBA) betting story when I decided to research this scandal in March 2008. Like most of the public, it seems, I had paid little attention to Jimmy Battista's role in the conspiracy. Certainly, media coverage was dominated by stories on Tim Donaghy, with an understandable preoccupation with the issue of the referee's influence on the outcomes of games. He adamantly denied fixing games, a claim which was supported by several media assessments and by an official NBA report. With that preeminent issue seemingly aside, at least as it pertained to Donaghy, I thought there was little point in focusing on him. The referee, of course, wouldn't be privy to the sorts of things that matter in a betting conspiracy such as this and I quickly discovered pro gambler Battista was far more noteworthy on a host of levels. Only Battista could discuss what he did with the information Donaghy provided, how much money was being placed directly as a result of Donaghy's calls, where that money went and why, and how this data affected international betting lines and related activities. The career hustler and bettor knew how everything in that universe worked, and could provide insights beyond what few people know about big-time sports gambling. Battista is also the best source to assess referee Donaghy's claims that he didn't influence NBA games he bet. Because of his role in the scandal, and as a result of his relationship with Donaghy and others close to him, the gambler is also someone who could discuss whether there were other referees involved. Furthermore, Battista would better know why he popped up in a Federal Bureau of Investigation (FBI) probe of New York City's Gambino crime "family," sparking the entire NBA betting fiasco. In fact, if my suspicions were correct, he would be able to explain the broader relationship between gangsters and the sports-betting community. Battista would also be a valuable resource to discuss what role inside information plays in gambling. If the man known in big-time gambling circles as "The Sheep" was willing to talk, in addition to setting the record straight on the NBA scandal, two topics of much conjecture could be examined ... *from the inside.* Jimmy Battista, I concluded, was the one who would best serve my interests, the one whose story would fill in existing gaps and others unknown.

* * *

At the urging of his wife, his family, and his close friends, Jimmy Battista entered the White Deer Run addiction treatment facility in March 2007 to conquer his long battle with drugs. He resolved not only to give up the cocaine and prescription pills, but the profession—the obsession—that precipitated his abuse in the first place. The feared and respected gambler was giving up betting for good, and his timing was incredibly fortuitous. Just weeks after his successful completion of the inpatient program and return home from the Lehigh Valley sticks, the FBI paid him a visit to disclose their interest in him regarding a variety of issues. Had he simply continued his normal and illicit activities, Battista would have unknowingly placed himself—and countless others—in more dire legal jeopardy than ultimately was the case. The uncanny combination of luck (or fate) and rehabilitation stirred Jimmy, and the subsequent court proceedings, media speculation, and imprisonment pushed him to the brink. The self-professed former bookmaker, bettor, and drug addict wanted and needed to tell his story.

* * *

As evidenced by its subtitle, *Gaming the Game* is essentially two stories in one: the life and times of pro gambler Jimmy "Baba" Battista; and the inside story of the NBA betting scandal (for which he was the architect). The former story entails Battista's rise within the sports betting world, and these narratives often include insights into the people, places, and things many of us never knew existed. Very little of this book's content is public knowledge, and individuals who have agreed to share details of their activities (often including hard data to support their tales) in order to explain the sociology of big-time sports betting have interests to protect. As such, certain names, dates, locales, and other identifiers have been altered, none of which takes away from our understanding of how this gambling underworld operates. Concerning the latter story (i.e., those narratives explicitly dealing with the NBA betting scandal), however, considerable effort has been made to offer the most detailed and accurate account to date. Thus, the scandal-specific characters and chronology are offered without alteration so that follow-up research can be conducted.

TABLE OF CONTENTS

CAST OF CHARACTERS

The NBA Betting Scandal

Judge Carol Bagley Amon—U.S. District Court Judge for the Eastern District of New York (EDNY) who oversaw the NBA betting scandal cases against Tim Donaghy, Jimmy Battista, and Tommy Martino.

Jimmy "Baba" "Sheep" Battista—lifelong resident of Delaware County, PA ("Delco"), just outside Philadelphia; architect of the 2006-07 NBA betting scandal; professional gambler; one of the world's most consequential movers; former bookmaker and runner.

Jack Concannon—Delco native; insurance company owner and recreational gambler who had known Jimmy Battista for years; placed bets for NBA referee Tim Donaghy on NBA games for a few years before Donaghy switched to betting with Battista in December 2006 after Donaghy was supposedly stiffed by Concannon on his winnings; returned to betting on NBA games for Donaghy in February 2007 (at which point Donaghy was also betting with Battista).

Gerard "Gerry" Conrad—Federal Bureau of Investigation (FBI) Special Agent (SA) who partnered with case agent Paul Harris; member of the FBI's Gambino Squad.

Tim "Timmy" "Elvis" Donaghy—Delco native; 13-year NBA referee at the time of the scandal; close, longtime friend of Tommy Martino; attended Cardinal O'Hara High School with Martino and Battista.

Jeffrey A. "Jeff" Goldberg—Assistant U.S. Attorney (AUSA) in the EDNY operating out of the Organized Crime and Racketeering Section (OCRS); assigned to NBA scandal case by summer 2007; took over as lead prosecutor in the case following AUSA Tom Siegel's August 2007 departure.

Jake Griffin—Philadelphia–based defense attorney for Tommy Martino; accompanied Martino to the grand jury in Brooklyn; ultimately replaced as Martino's lawyer by Vicki Herr.

Paul N. Harris—FBI SA who led the NBA betting scandal investigation; member of the FBI's Gambino Squad.

Vicki Herr—Media, PA–based defense attorney; succeeded Jake Griffin in representing Tommy Martino.

John F. Lauro—Tampa, FL–based defense attorney who represented Tim Donaghy; former AUSA, EDNY.

Thomas "Tommy" Martino—Delco native; Battista's lifelong friend and longtime "assistant;" juggled being a computer technician and small-time dope dealer; supplied Battista with his various drugs throughout the years; served as the intermediary between Battista and Martino's longtime pal (and fellow O'Hara grad), NBA referee Tim Donaghy, during the scandal.

Jack McMahon—Philadelphia–based defense attorney for Jimmy Battista; former Philadelphia Assistant District Attorney; ran unsuccessfully for D.A. in 1997.

Lawrence B. Pedowitz—New York City–based lawyer; former Chief of the Criminal Division in the U.S. Attorney's Office for the Southern District of New York (SDNY); represented the NBA during the betting scandal court proceedings; produced NBA-commissioned report in October 2008 examining the scandal and related NBA practices.

Pete Ruggieri—Delco native who attended Monsignor Bonner High School with Jack Concannon; professional gambler; Battista betting associate dating back years; piggybacked wildly successful betting picks first placed by Concannon and then by Jimmy Battista on games Tim Donaghy officiated; briefly served as an "out" for Martino and Donaghy when Battista entered drug rehab in March 2007, and soon refused to continue accepting bets when he realized what fools he was dealing with.

Philip "Phil" Scala—FBI Supervisory Special Agent (SSA) in charge of the FBI's Gambino squad; privy to much of the NBA scandal case; retired in 2008 during the sentencing phase of the case; lone FBI official who can speak openly about the scandal probe.

Thomas J. "Tom" Siegel—AUSA, EDNY, OCRS; led the prosecution of parties in the NBA betting scandal; left his post in August 2007 soon after Tim Donaghy pleaded guilty.

David J. Stern—NBA Commissioner from 1984 to present.

"The Animals"

"Bull"—named for his physical appearance; mover.

"Seal"—named for his physical appearance; mover; only Animal to remain with Mike Rinnier following the infamous split in the mid-1990s.

"Tiger"—named for his aggressive business demeanor; *de facto* "CEO/CFO" of all things Animals, including handicapping,

following the split with Rinnier; was among the most consequential sports bettors in the U.S.; mathematical and statistical
whiz; former bookmaker.

"Sheep"—Jimmy "Baba" Battista; named by his family for
his travails long before ever joining forces with The Animals;
in charge of managing "outs."

The Bookmakers

"Bluto"—big-time Jewish New York City bookmaker who was
allegedly connected to the Gambino crime family; longtime
friend and business associate of Joe Vito Mastronardo.

Louis "Lump" Lambrusco—legendary Delco restaurateur
and bookmaker; Battista mentor in the 1980s; associate of
Mike Rinnier.

Joseph "Joe Vito" Mastronardo—most consequential bookmaker in the Philadelphia region, and one of the most significant in the U.S., from 1980s through 2000s; associate of Mike
Rinnier; longtime associate of Battista and The Animals; also
a prominent pro gambler.

Ronnie Park—New York City bookmaker who started a
premier offshore sportsbook (All-Star Sports) in Curacao circa
2002/3 with the help of The Animals; returned to NYC after
All-Star Sports imploded.

Jimmy "Candyman" Pirollo—Delco-based bookie; was
murdered in December 1993, causing Mike Rinnier and The
Animals (with whom Pirollo dealt) to fear the Philly mob was
killing suburban bookies and bettors for not paying "street tax."

Michael F. "Mike" "Rug" Rinnier—prominent Philadelphia-area businessman who owned supermarkets among other legitimate investments; operated one of the region's largest bookmaking operations; employed The Animals in their formative years as bookmakers-turned-professional gamblers.

The Sharps

"The Chinaman"—Vietnamese-American; medical doctor; specialized in betting professional basketball and second halves of football; was also a fairly successful professional poker player.

"The Computer"—By far, the most successful and significant sports bettor in history; specialized in betting college and pro football; had unreal networks of individuals who provided inside information; widely credited with being the first bettor to employ a research team exploiting computer analysis applied to sports betting; renowned for his tenacity and business acumen; had numerous legitimate business interests.

"The Englishman"—specialized in betting soccer ("football") in England; prominent legitimate businessman; associate of The Chinaman.

"The Kosher Kids"—aka "The Koshers;" New York City–based, Jewish professional bettors legendary for successfully wagering on baseball.

"The Poker Players"—collection of some of the world's most prominent poker players who also wagered big money on sports (specializing in betting on baseball).

"Zorba"—One of the world's best-known professional gamblers; ran one of the most consequential off-shore sports betting sites; had close ties to The Computer.

Philadelphia's Organized Criminals

"Boys downtown"—also referred to by Battista and his suburban gambling colleagues interchangeably as "idiots downtown," "guys downtown," "mobsters," and "wiseguys." Each term is used to reference Italian-American organized crime figures who operated primarily out of South Philadelphia, and whose operations often extended into Philly's suburbs, into New Jersey, and into Delaware. Until the murder of mob boss Angelo Bruno in 1980, for decades the city's predominant organized crime group was called the "Bruno Family." Some referred to the syndicate as the "Scarfo Family" when Nicodemo "Little Nicky" Scarfo was head roughly from 1981 through 1991, after which he has effectively been serving a life sentence in prison for his role in various mob-related offenses (the 81-year-old Scarfo, who is incarcerated at the U.S. Penitentiary in Atlanta, is slated for release in 2033). Most have taken to simply calling the group the "Philly-South Jersey mob" ever since Scarfo's removal, and by 2010 the syndicate was barely a shadow of the organization Bruno led.

Jimmy Battista and his suburban Philly gambling associates, who operated in fear of a visit from this bunch, uniformly refer to Philly mobsters as some version of "boys/guys/idiots downtown." During the time Battista and The Animals were operating, their main concern was the ongoing (roughly 1991–1994) mob war pitting factions supporting Joseph "Skinny Joey" Merlino against those behind boss John Stanfa. The chaos in the underworld inspired the mob's greater extortion of bookmaking and betting operations like those run by The Animals. Threats and fear dominated this time, and greatly influenced the white-collar pro gamblers' move to Las Vegas.

PROLOGUE

AS USUAL, JIMMY Battista was the first to wake up. He got out of bed and rustled his wife Denise up and into the shower before heading down the hallway to the girls' rooms to get the day started for each of them as well. With Denise and their three daughters, whose ages ranged from six to eleven years old, getting washed and dressed, Jimmy ventured downstairs for what had become *his* daily awakening. "I did a line of coke on the computer desk downstairs in my office, popped two OxyContins, and had a cup of coffee. I was so strung out and that was how I kept going."

Why the forty-two year-old professional gambler—known in betting circles mostly as "Sheep"—was so strung out on December 12, 2006, would later become a national news story. For now, however, all Jimmy was concerned with was the morning routine. "It was a regular school morning. My wife was in cosmetology school, so she had to be out the door at eight-thirty to be there at nine. I got the kids breakfast, packed their lunches, and walked them to the bus stop. When I came back, I gambled through the morning session from like nine-thirty to noon. My main gambling headquarters was my office in my house."

Battista lived in a McMansion suburban development, the kind characteristic of the housing boom in the late 1990s and early 2000s. His home sat in Phoenixville, Pennsylvania, some forty minutes northwest of Center City Philadelphia and within walking distance of historic Valley Forge, famous for the brutally challenging encampment of George Washington's Continental Army during the winter of 1777. The neighborhood was populated with middle- and upper-middle-class types and overflowed with kids, whose swing sets and other playthings filled many of the groomed yards. The Battista's well-maintained brick face, with the trampoline in the fenced yard and the minivan and SUV in the driveway, did not stand out. Few neighbors—if any—had a clue about the chicanery that took place within the home's first-floor study. If they had entered Jimmy's betting lair, they would have immediately been struck by the thirteen computer monitors that covered the wraparound desk that had to measure fifteen feet in total. Each monitor served its own betting-related purpose. Some kept up-to-the-minute betting lines from sportsbooks around the world; others offered up sports injury and other news; and the remainder most often served as communication devices (via E-mail, instant messaging, and online phoning). The room also housed a large, flat-screen television placed strategically in the upper corner for best viewing. One oddity stood out, however. Amidst the computers and phones, and the sports-watching-driven technology, was a smaller VCR-TV combo which sat apart from the work trappings. This was exclusively for Battista's daughters, who got so accustomed to Dad's outrageous work schedule and long hours that they cherished just being in the room with him even if he was preoccupied and his attention was spotty. Often, as Jimmy was frantically phoning and clicking his bets and sensitive information around the world, his little girls would be there watching Disney tapes and Nickelodeon. Such was life in the Battista household.

"After the morning betting session, I walked the dog and then went over to Tommy Martino's house over in Aston. I always kept prescription pills and other substances there. I had a computer set up there, too, and I checked quickly to see if any of the games had moved. After popping some pills, I ran some errands and got back to my house in time to get the kids off the bus. I made chicken cutlets for dinner, which is what we ate pretty much every other Tuesday. When my wife got home at five o'clock, we all sat down and ate dinner.

I worked the night session from five-thirty to eight, which is when the basketball games would go off. I got in the car and drove to Tommy's house where I worked the late games until like ten o'clock. When the last games went off at ten, we got in Tommy's car and drove down to the Marriott at Philly International Airport."

Jimmy Battista and Tommy Martino were friends since they were boys playing stickball in the alley behind their row homes in Clifton Heights, another Philly suburb. On this uncharacteristically mild December night, Martino, as was the routine, drove as the two rode the twenty minutes up I-95 to the airport hotel. In classic Battista fashion, parking in the airport's garage like every other schmo was too much of a hassle, so he gave a valet twenty bucks to keep the car in the lobby entrance's curved drop-off area. Each man was dressed as they normally were wherever they traveled—Battista, with his shaved head, wore his standard sweatpants and sweatshirt; the more fit Martino sported jeans, a buttoned-down shirt, and of course perfectly maintained hair. The point of their trip was to meet Martino's good friend, Tim "Timmy" Donaghy, who had asked Martino if he could see Battista in person. By now, Donaghy was a twelve-year veteran referee in the National Basketball Association, and was staying at the hotel on the eve of the game he was slated to work between the Philadelphia's 76ers and the Boston Celtics. Though Martino was tight with Donaghy, Battista and Donaghy were only associates through their mutual friendship with Martino. If an occasion arose for them to cross paths because of Martino, Battista and Donaghy were careful over the years to remain out of each other's universe given the impropriety of an NBA referee mingling with a well-known professional bettor who had a rap sheet marked by gambling arrests.

"Timmy was a known gambler. People all throughout our lives knew he was gambling. He was getting football selections from other people I know pretty close. They weren't doing too good. I was working for the three sharpest guys in the country: The Computer, The Chinaman, and The Englishman. The Englishman was the world's best soccer handicapper; The Chinaman was pro baseball (MLB), pro basketball (NBA), and pro football (NFL); and The Computer was college sports, NFL, and NBA. It was the Harvard, the Yale, and the Penn when it came to gambling. This information was *incredible*. So I was moving sports bets on a daily basis for these guys, making a good living. Timmy was gambling but couldn't win because the guys he was getting his information from for college and pro football were choppy. Timmy and Tommy were close friends, and Timmy was getting drugs from Tommy when Timmy was in town, getting Percocet and weed and stuff like that. Tommy was also getting me all my drugs at that point. Well, Timmy used to call Tommy and say, 'Who's Sheep on?' because at that point my guys were having the strongest NFL season possible. Donaghy's guys weren't picking winners and my guys were crushing on weekends, going ten-and-two, eleven-and-four, whatever. We were beating the number. Tommy said Timmy wanted to meet with me to thank me for my football selections. I had heard that even though Timmy was now winning his football bets—because they were based on my selections—he was getting stiffed on his earnings. Timmy asked me if there was anything I wanted in return for the tips, and I said, 'We'll talk when we get together.'"

Until meeting in the Marriott lobby, the last time Tim Donaghy and Jimmy Battista had been in each other's company was when they appeared in Tommy Martino's wedding party. "I hadn't seen him in years but I recognized him right away because I saw him so many times on television. I bet basketball games and followed everything he did." The three men briefly exchanged pleasantries before walking into the adjoining upscale Riverbend Bar & Grill, a rather large and attractive airport meeting place. The vast restaurant seating area was empty, and the eight or nine patrons sat at the long bar with numerous televisions above carrying various sports programming, mostly West Coast NBA games. Aware that the impending conversation was likely to include some very sensitive—and incriminating—subject matter, the men seated themselves in the vacant dining area, out of earshot from the bar. Battista placed his phone bag, a draw-string-type carrier for his dozen or so cell phones—most of which were direct and exclusive lines from his biggest clients, on the seat next to him. "We met Timmy at like ten-thirty at night. We ordered our food and some drinks. Timmy was flirting with the waitress, who was a little older than us but cute. He was always a little arrogant and always trying to be sly, just like Tommy. I was very nervous because I knew I shouldn't have been doing this. I already had a couple of Percocets in me and maybe an OxyContin and went through like a bag and a half of coke before the meeting. I suspected that people were always watching me." As they finished their food and got through with the small talk, Donaghy asked Battista how his football picks were going. Battista replied that his bets—pro and college—were doing very well, and then caught Donaghy off-guard when he asked the referee how his NBA bets were doing. Clearly upset by the question, Donaghy stammered while denying he had been betting on pro basketball games. As an awkward silence surrounded the table, Battista got up.

"I excused myself to go to the bathroom, but just to do a few more lines of coke. I was a functioning drug addict. At that point I was doing drugs all day long. When I got back to the table, Timmy and Tommy went to the bathroom and I later found out that this was when Timmy told Tommy that I was right—Donaghy *was* betting NBA games as I suspected for a long time. I didn't want to discuss it further in the hotel because I was so fearful of people watching me. Timmy was as nervous as I was and we decided to leave. All three of us hopped in Tommy's car, with me in the passenger seat and Timmy in the back. We went to a gas station right near the airport to get rolling papers so Timmy and Tommy could smoke a joint. I was still on my own high from the blow and pills and when they were done smoking pot in the car, Timmy and I got down to business.

"He was bitching about Jack Concannon, the guy he was betting with. According to Timmy, even though Jack had a lucrative insurance business, he was a degenerate gambler. Timmy complained he had fifteen winners with Concannon that he didn't pay off. Jack supposedly owed Timmy forty thousand dollars, but told Timmy he didn't have the money because he lost it down at the casinos in Atlantic City. I wasn't sure if this was why Timmy wanted to meet with me, but I thought so. At least I hoped that was why, because I knew what it would mean if I had an NBA ref on my side. So, I said, 'Stop! Stop dealing with all these little fucking guys and come with me. How much do you want me to bet for you per game?' He said, 'Two thousand a game.' I told him I'd bet the two thousand a game but I didn't want him dealing with Jack anymore even though Jack still owed him money. The less people who knew, the better. We set the deal up. Tommy didn't say much. He was more concerned with looking at himself in the mirror. The whole time, I was looking around to see if anyone was following me.

"Before we dropped Timmy off, I asked him who he liked in the game he was reffing the next day and he said, 'Boston's gonna kill the Sixers.' So, I bet like sixty grand on the game and they won, they crushed. We met the next night, after the game, and I thanked him. There was part of me that said, 'You don't need to do this. Why are you fucking with this? You make enough money, you make a good living.' But, to me, what it came down to was the information. The information was key to me, and I wanted to control the information. As a gambler, having an NBA referee telling you what games he likes was like taking a kid into a candy store and saying, 'What flavor do you want?' I was thinking, 'This is going to go on for the next twenty years!'"

* * *

The hustle envisioned by Battista and Donaghy didn't last twenty *months*, let alone twenty years. During a routine probe into an organized crime family in New York, the FBI stumbled onto pro gambler Jimmy Battista. Members of the Bureau's "Gambino squad" could not have imagined what they were about to discover as their investigation spread to the Philly suburbs. What was originally a stereotypical organized crime case with a hint of money laundering quickly and loudly evolved into a probe of possible game fixing in one of the four major U.S. professional sports. Word of the investigation leaked in July 2007 and by September 2008 the three men were in federal prisons after pleading guilty to their roles in the conspiracy.

By dealing with Jimmy Battista, rather than with any number of other bettors or bookmakers, Tim Donaghy was unwittingly placing himself in harm's way. It is likely Tim did not know just how influential Jimmy had become since they graduated from Cardinal O'Hara High School in the 1980s, or how Battista's words and deeds now affected bettors and bookies worldwide. Jimmy was a self-avowed "white-collar" professional gambler who nevertheless prided himself on his low-key demeanor.[1] His semi-slovenly appearance and well-traveled minivan perfectly belied his significance and

---

[1] Among bettors and law enforcement officials, the term "white-collar" is often used to refer to professional gamblers who are not part of an organized crime conspiracy (i.e., not paying a "street tax" to a syndicate for "protection"). Battista's rather high-end clientele and his partner group each consisted exclusively of white-collar gamblers for whom sports betting was a profession.

standing in the international betting world. An affable man with remarkable communication skills and an uncanny ability to process numbers, he worked with and for the sharpest gamblers around the globe. For Battista, being a pro gambler meant that he purchased and sold highly sensitive inside information relating to sports events (e.g., injury information, referee assignments, etc.), and placed bets for several exclusive clients (in the U.S. and elsewhere) who often wagered in staggering amounts. His partners and clients were the ones sportsbooks feared most, and were such big deals they routinely altered betting lines with their plays. His work often took him to predictable places like New York, Atlantic City, and Las Vegas, and included forays in more exotic locales such as Antigua, Curacao, and the Bahamas. Battista was not among the world's top bookmakers or bettors or financiers, but he was arguably the key person in that universe who connected otherwise disparate (and oftentimes competing) parties and provided a multitude of services for all sorts of noteworthy figures. He served as a hub of activity with spokes ultimately leading to all sorts of characters, from hardcore gangsters to mob wannabes to heavy-hitting bettors and financiers to mid-level runners to stringers and edge players of all types, each of whom (even if unknowingly) relied upon him and his variegated expertise. It was this assortment of characters that attracted the FBI and which led them to Jimmy Battista and then to NBA referee Tim Donaghy.

Humble Jim

JIMMY BATTISTA WAS born and raised in Clifton Heights, PA, a white, ethnic, hardscrabble suburb of Philadelphia. Throughout his life, working-class Clifton was often regarded as the stepchild to its better-known (and -regarded) immediate neighbor, Springfield. "On the one side of Springfield Rd., there was Springfield and the other side was Clifton Heights. We were the blue collar side that lived in row homes, and the people in Springfield lived in single homes and lived a lavish life," says Battista. Some residents took pride in Clifton's edgy reputation and championed a comical, yet insightful, phrase for those who ventured into their part of the world: "Welcome to Clifton . . . now GET OUT!"

Battista's parents were representative of that era's Clifton: diligent, conscientious, hardworking folks who were church-going, "straight arrows." Larry and Connie Battista collectively worked three jobs throughout little Jimmy's childhood, which earned them their son's deep respect. "My dad was a saver, a grinder his entire life. He was the kind of guy who would drive four miles to get flounder on sale. My father was one of thirteen children to Cosmo Battista, who was an immigrant from Italy. Cosmo was born in 1895 and as a teenager was a window washer on the Statue of Liberty. My father would sell his soul to the devil if it meant his kids could go to school, have clothes on their bodies, have shoes on their feet, and have a better life. I respected him so much because he worked all the time and he was there no matter what. I loved his work ethic: 'You work hard, do the best you can.' He wasn't a fancy dresser, but he always provided for his family. My dad was kind of laid back, but my mom was a worrywart, really high-strung. My mom was a great lady growing up, very supportive, and preached the same messages: Work, get good grades. That's probably the thing I admire most about my parents, that they instilled a work ethic into me and my sisters." Battista laughs when he adds, "I didn't listen to them about *their other values* all the time, but they taught me nothing comes for free in this life. If you want something, ya gotta go get it."

Battista, who was born in 1965, considers his early childhood unremarkable, and looks back fondly on that time in his life. "I went to Holy Cross grade school, where I played football and basketball. I was manager of the basketball team and its best shooter. I was like 'Set Shot' Buford from *The Fish That Saved Pittsburgh*. I couldn't dribble, but I could shoot the lights out. I was a quiet kid and always kept to myself. My nickname growing up was Humble Jim, and some people called me 'Hummer' for short." The work ethic Battista speaks so admiringly of was soon passed on to him. "I always worked from the time I was about twelve years old. My father worked as a banker at Girard [later Mellon] Bank. He also used to work at a restaurant called the Clam Tavern in Collingdale and I would work bussing tables or in the kitchen three or four days a week. I then had a paper route and was a paper boy for the [now defunct Evening Philadelphia] *Bulletin* for a few years. To me, that was fast cash. It was fun. My friends and I would meet at the Getty station on Springfield Road and steal some papers and sell them, and then use the money to go play video games at the bowling alley. Even back then, I needed money in my pocket. I was so used to hustling and making money. We were, like, the lower side of Clifton Heights. My father had to work two jobs and my mom was working a job for my little sister and me to go to a Catholic grade school when my older sister was in high school. We were not 'the fortunate ones.' My dad would say, 'You are going to college. I don't want you working sixty or seventy hours a week like I do, just to get by.' As good as my parents were, I knew I had to fend for myself. I knew that if I wanted something, I had to work for it and go get it."

The working-class lifestyle in Jimmy's early life, complete with its many sacrifices and burdens, fomented disdain within him and impacted many of his decisions as he entered the world as an adolescent. Indeed, his childhood dramatically affected his view of the world and how he planned to move beyond his rather modest upbringing. Simple jobs performed by numerous teenagers were looked at by Battista as opportunities to exploit, as evidenced by his paper route. So great was his zeal to earn considerable amounts of money from an early age, he successfully manipulated several nondescript jobs into lucrative pursuits beyond their original purpose. Simply put, he was well on his way to a life of bartering and selling—and hustling—as a teenager in the late 1970s and early 1980s.

"As I got into adolescence, I was interested in ways to make a buck, fastlaning, and books weren't my thing. After a while, I learned how to open my mouth, and I got away with a lot of things. I also started getting in a lot of trouble. My cousin, Paul, was known as the Black Sheep of the family. He was always in jail, beating up kids, and stuff like that. Well, as I got older, I was known as Little Baba. Little Sheep. I kept getting in trouble and the name stuck. I wasn't Humble Jim anymore."

Baba the Black Sheep

THE NICKNAME BABA Black Sheep captured who Battista was, and foreshadowed who he would soon become as he entered Cardinal O'Hara High School. "I had a great high school career," Battista says. "All my life up until then, I was a short, chunky kid. In high school I got in really good shape. By the time I started junior year, I was five-eight and probably weighed a hundred and ninety-five pounds. I worked out a lot and was pretty strong. I worked out at Olympia Gym back when Arnold Schwarzenegger was involved and when professional wrestlers like Ivan Putski and Chief Jay Strongbow used to lift when they were in town. It was a well-known gym that people used to come to, and these guys were fucking animals. I played football my junior year and started for the junior varsity team, but got cut the next year and played rugby. Rugby was great because you didn't wear any pads and you could just hit people; it was my game. My rugby friends were big into drinking, but not into drugs. We would run five miles before practice, play rugby, and then drink our faces off. In the late 70s and early 80s, underage drinking and drinking and driving weren't the big issues they are today. We were regular high school kids who went to school, worked, played sports, and partied on weekends. I also played CYO [Catholic Youth Organization] basketball. My junior year, our CYO team was better than my high school team. In fact, we scrimmaged Monsignor Bonner the year they won the city championship and beat them. Our CYO team was that good. We were tough. We were Clifton kids, street kids.

"In high school, I had two loving parents who thought I did as I pleased. My parents were working so much and trying to control me as much as possible because they knew I was never satisfied and that I always wanted more. I wanted to do things at my own pace, and had a problem with being told what to do. I think they knew they had trouble on the horizon with me. Meanwhile, my sisters were scholar-athletes. My older sister was MVP of the Catholic League for softball and basketball for O'Hara and my younger sister was a pretty good athlete, too.[1] They were honor students, whereas I didn't give a fuck. I didn't want to apply myself. I just wanted to get by and enjoy life." For Battista, part of "enjoying life" in those days occasionally included hitting a local taproom before classes began. The outrageous routine caused him to engage in a gambit that piqued his interest so much that it foreshadowed a long and prosperous career.

"The first time I got into what you would call serious gambling was at a bar named Shields Tavern on Township Line Road in Drexel Hill, which we used to call Shieldsy's," Battista says. "My senior year in high school we would go in there before school and have a few beers and shots. There was this guy who challenged me to an arm wrestling match, and he told me I had to raise twenty-five hundred dollars to face him. My friends and I scrambled to get the money together, but couldn't raise more than a few hundred bucks. We were teenagers, we didn't have money. He still let me arm wrestle him, though, and I beat him. Just the process of trying to

---

[1] Battista's sisters each went on to graduate from Neumann College, after which they have had rather productive lives. Jimmy considers his sisters' accomplishments as further evidence of his parents' profound influence. His older sister still ranks among the career leaders in assists for Neumann College basketball, and according to Jimmy is now a commander in the U.S. Navy. His younger sister is a registered nurse who also happens to be married to a doctor.

get the money to face him, knowing that I was going to take him and win the bet, really got me going." Despite the rush of betting-related hustling, Battista didn't bet anything more than football pools in high school, and says he never placed bets with bookies on sports at that point in his life.

Up next was a brief foray in college. "I went to West Chester University and hated it," Battista says. "I went to college because my parents wanted me to go, and I chose West Chester because I was seeing a hot chick from high school and she went there. To me, college was just another opportunity to drink and party more. My freshman year in college was the first time I experimented with hard drugs. I tried coke. I thought it was pretty good, because the longer I stayed up the more I could party. Back then, I could just use it socially. I'd have some for a weekend and that was it." It was also during his freshman year that he became close friends with Tommy Martino, someone with whom Battista's name would be inextricably linked in the years to come.

"The first time I met Tommy was when I was five years old," Battista says. "I was going to kindergarten at Westbrook Park Elementary School. We both lived in Westbrook Park; he lived on Springfield Road and I lived on Westbrook Drive. His brother, Johnny, and I were good friends. We were the same age and went to kindergarten together and we were actually baptized the same day at Holy Cross church, on March 28, 1965. Me and Johnny were friends right through elementary school, even though he stayed at Westbrook Park for elementary school and I went to Holy Cross grade school. Well, Johnny had an older brother, Chuck, and a younger brother, Tommy, and we would all play together in alleys and stuff like that. Westbrook Park Elementary ends at fifth grade, and the Martino boys then went to Holy Cross grade school for sixth, seventh, and eighth grade, where I already was. We used to walk to school together on a daily basis. I'd walk down to the bottom of the hill, stop by their house, and call up to them, 'Hey, you guys ready?' and Mrs. Martino would yell back, 'They'll be right down.' We did that for all three years. We had a great childhood together, and hung out a lot. We played organized football and basketball together, and hung in the streets doing things like playing hockey and stickball. We were a pretty athletic bunch, and were playing sports year-round. We fought if we had to, like other kids, but sports were our thing.

"Me, Johnny and Tommy were altar boys together at Holy Cross Parish. Me and Johnny were best friends, and Tommy was always along with us. There were a few other friends that hung with us, but we were, like, the main core. Tommy was a year younger than Johnny, and Johnny and Tommy were great athletes. Johnny was the running back for our grade school team, and went on to play college football at Ursinus. From sixth grade through high school, Johnny and I were like salt and pepper, always together doing stuff with Tommy and a tight-knit group of guys from Westbrook Park. But, when Johnny went away to Ursinus, I was still at home and commuting to West Chester and started hanging out with just Tommy more during his senior year in high school. Tommy and I gelled pretty quickly because we both liked to party. We drank, smoked pot, did coke, and tried to get laid.

"Around this time, Mr. and Mrs. Martino were going through a divorce, so we would party at Tommy's house because there was so little supervision. Tommy's father had a best friend named Mark who was an engineer for a helicopter company. The guy was brilliant but he had some mental problems and his wife left him. He was like a stray dog and he used to hang with us. We were nineteen and twenty years old, and he was in his mid- to late thirties. He had an apartment that we would use to smoke pot, do drugs, and he liked that we always had girls hanging around with us, hoping that he could get some of the scraps. It was also great because if we didn't have money to buy drugs, he'd help us out. Tommy sold and smoked pot since early in high school. I smoked pot, but wasn't a stoner like he was. I didn't really like it because it put me to sleep. I was always on the go, and was always more into the speed and the coke. At that point, Tommy was selling weed just to put gas in his car and have some leftover for himself."

The lifestyle Battista so warmly and proudly recalls was not sustainable if he wanted to succeed in college. "I got kicked out of my dorm my freshman fall semester for partying so much," Battista says, "so I had to commute back and forth to campus, which was a pain in the ass. Clifton Heights to West Chester was a good forty-five-minute drive. I did that for a year and a half, and was working part-time. I kept thinking, 'This is getting old'—working late at night, waiting tables and stuff like that, and then getting up early to go to school. I didn't like it. It just wasn't for me. It also wasn't fun dating the girl from high school any longer, so I dropped out and got a job at a place called City Shoes.

"We were selling shoes for 'nine ninety-nine.' It was a great job to work because I got tons of women. Back then, I was fairly good-looking, in shape, and had long, curly hair. The place was like a fucking pussy factory! The owners loved me because women were coming in there and I was selling a lot of shoes for them. The people I worked for were so tight with bucks; they just wanted you to work like a slave, smile, and make that money, which I did. I also made my own money because I could move coke to other stores by putting it in the shoes. This is back in early 80s when drugs were pretty rampant. We had a way we took the silica salt out and put coke into the shoes. Silica was the salt packet in the shoes.[2]

---

[2] More commonly known as silica gel, these packets are often placed in shoes and other products to absorb moisture.

I was playing with drugs a lot, and there were other guys I worked with in the shoe business who were involved, moving shoes back and forth between stores and the warehouse. I would put maybe two or three grams in each shoe in place of the silica salt. That's how we sent the drugs. As much as I was using coke, I knew there was money in moving it. I never got hooked on the weed, but coke I knew people would pay for."

Battista's employer ultimately realized that numerous pairs of shoes were somehow being lost or stolen, and confronted their sales superstar. "There came a point where I stole more product than I was selling," Battista says. Fortunately for him, the owners had their own legal issues to address and didn't want an employee like Battista upset enough to assist authorities. His employers thus spared him further harm, provided he stopped whatever hustle he had going. "They got in trouble for embezzlement, and then I stopped dealing," Battista says. "I saw what kind of trouble was there if I didn't stop." He was soon rewarded for his decision, and especially for his loyalty. "They stayed with me because they didn't want to get into more trouble. They had me start opening franchises out in Monroeville, which is near Pittsburgh, for about half a year. To me, it was like their way of saying, 'We'll take care of you. Thank you for all the work you did.'"

Battista's adventure with City Shoes was about to come to a peaceful end, and was soon followed by another crude—and easily detectable—scam at his next place of employment. "When I got back from Pittsburgh," Battista says, "I left City Shoes and took a job at a BEST department store in the Springfield Shopping Center. There again, with my sales ability, I was their number one catalog seller. Well, I devised a scheme after about three months where I got every employee's social security number." The BEST computer system required employees to log in using their social security number, to which each sale would be logged. "I was working the pickup desk," Battista says. "I took everyone's social security numbers when they weren't working and plugged them in and ordered stuff so that I wouldn't get caught. I would tell kids when to show up, and the products would actually go through the computer system like it was a real sale for some employee, but I would just take the money. I would sell kids stereo equipment, video equipment. If something cost three hundred dollars, I'd sell it for a hundred and fifty. That was my thing. This went on for about a year before some girl ratted me out because I used her social security number to move some merchandise and she found out. The cops came to BEST to arrest me while I was working and caught me in the act. There were other people in the store doing similar things, but I took it to the extreme, like everything else in my life. By the time I got caught, they were missing thousands of dollars in stereo equipment.

"Around this time, I stopped playing with the coke, but I was drinking more. One night I got really fucked up and I was driving on the wrong side of Lansdowne Avenue in front of Monsignor Bonner High School coming home from one of the clubs downtown. When they pulled me over they got my license, which was fake. Back in high school, I dated this girl who worked at a photography store and I falsified a lot of licenses for teenagers and would make them twenty-one. They cost us like fifteen or twenty cents to make, and we would charge kids twenty bucks apiece. We probably did three hundred licenses at fifteen to twenty bucks apiece, which was good money. It was one of my first good hustles. She had all the equipment, and we typeset them, printed them, and laminated them. We had it down to a science. You couldn't scratch them or nothing. They were great. In fact, after I got locked up, they hung up my license in the Upper Darby police station. That's the way I was, though. I was always looking for an angle. I wasn't book smart but if I looked at something and studied it, I would find out a way to make a dollar off of it.

"Well, like a week later, I got caught underage drinking. I couldn't call my father to come pick me up because at that point my parents were pretty mad at me. I called Tommy Martino's dad and he bailed me out of jail. I'll never forget; it cost him sixty-seven dollars to get me out. He told me, 'You better wise up or you're going to get yourself into serious trouble.' So now, I had two drinking things lurking *and* the thing at BEST department store, which hadn't gone to court yet. I was facing charges of DUI, falsification of documents for the driver's licenses, taking BEST to the hilt, and under-age drinking. This was almost all at the same time. When we got to court, after they read all the things I had pending, the judge just looked at me and said, 'What is going on here?!'

"I'll never forget, BEST had, like, four lawyers. I had no money so I had a public defender. I made up a story that I owed somebody money and that he was threatening me and that was what made me steal and sell the stereo equipment. The judge bought it, and I'll never forget that since I was fac-ing jail time because of how much I stole. He let me plead to criminal mischief. With the other stuff I was charged with, the judge accepted that, although I had a good upbringing, I had just gone hog wild. I lost my license for six years. They dropped the charge of falsification of documents, and I got ARD.[3] I got no jail time, but had to do a lot of community service. I took that as a win. The Lord, Jesus Christ, was look-ing down on me! I got lucky."

Having been granted a remarkable reprieve, Battista was left to make something of himself at this crucial juncture of his life. The question as to whether he would ultimately revert back to his parents' beloved James Battista or continue on as the slick Baba Black Sheep would be answered all too quickly.

---

[3] ARD is short for Pennsylvania's Accelerated Rehabilitative Disposition, a one-time alternative to a trial, conviction, and possible jail sentence for first offenders. ARD is most commonly used in DUI cases. If an offender does not comply with the conditions set forth by the prosecutor (e.g., fines, community service, substance abuse counseling, etc.), charges are likely to follow. Successful completion of the ARD program results in the charges being dismissed and allows for the underlying record to be expunged.

Taking His Lumps

"**I** WAS STAYING WITH a friend of mine at his apartment and didn't want to go back home because my parents were furious with me," Jimmy Battista says. "I just got through this trouble and had to see my probation officer every so often. I had to get a job that I could walk to close to me 'cause I lost my license. My dad told me to go down to a restaurant called Spanky's and see the owner, Lou Lambrusco, who he knew from high school. So, I walked down from Westbrook Park to Spanky's to see if I could get a job as a waiter or a busboy. I said, 'Mr. Lambrusco, my name is James Battista,' and he said, 'You're Squarehead's kid! The only reason I am going to hire you is because you're Squarehead's kid.'" As Lambrusco says many years later, "His father was as straight as could be. I knew him from high school. We weren't friends, really, we just knew each other. People called him Squarehead because he was such a straight arrow and because he had a square head. When Baba came in that day, I hadn't seen his father in years." Battista was hired on the spot, and quickly discovered there was more to "Mr. Lambrusco" than met the eye. "I soon found out that he was a bookmaker who went by the name 'Louie the Lump,'" says Battista. "Most people only knew him as the owner of the restaurant. In no time, I got hooked into booking, betting, drinking, and drugging."

By the mid-1980s, Louie "The Lump" Lambrusco had already lived quite a life. Now in his late forties, the physically imposing Lump's days of football stardom were long gone but the tough reputation remained. Lump played football in high school, listed at six-three and two hundred and forty pounds, went on to play for the Marines at Parris Island, and even had a stint with semi-pro ball. A hard worker who liked to play just as hard, Lambrusco had become known throughout the area for his involvement with bars and restaurants. Though very much into the nightlife scene, Lambrusco never really did drugs. "I smoked pot a few times and tried to do coke once," he says, "but I couldn't snort because my nose had been broken so many times." He was also by now a fairly consequential bookmaker, taking in approximately ninety thousand dollars per week in betting action. He began booking back in his twenties when he was a bartender. "There was so many people coming in and betting," he explains. "They'd give me the action, and I was turning it in to somebody. I decided, 'Fuck it. I might as well take it.' I also used to do a lot of pools when I was younger."

Unlike many bookmakers, Lambrusco was not mentored into the profession. Rather, he figured out how to book just by personal, trial and error, experience. As he heartily says, "When you get beat up, you learn!" Lump had no "employees" in the beginning, and simply took the action himself. Over time, his clientele grew and he developed runners—who were responsible for collecting bets, debts, etc.—throughout Delaware County. Incredibly, Louie the Lump says he never took a pinch for gambling or bookmaking. As for the other possible risk to his operation, Lambrusco was never visited, much less threatened, by "the boys downtown" (i.e., Philadelphia's Italian-American crime "family"). It may have been that his book wasn't consequential enough to merit their attention, or that Delco bookies in general weren't mob extortion targets during the 70s and early 80s.

* * *

Lou Lambrusco had owned other establishments prior to the current effort with Spanky's, though none had earned him the acclaim and notoriety the new restaurant would. Just as Jimmy Battista was being hired as a waiter, Spanky's was undergoing a restoration and soon opened as Louis' Restaurant, with Lambrusco's hands-on management dictating things. Battista's introduction to Lambrusco's work ethic was immediate and made quite an impression. "He'd be working during the day renovating the restaurant," Battista says, "and by four o'clock he'd be back there 'behind the line,' as we called it, cooking. When I was a waiter trainee, he'd make us take classes. You'd say, 'Good evening. Welcome to Louis' Restaurant, my name is James and I'll be your waiter,' and Lou would sit there watching. If you reached across a table the wrong way, he would slap your hand and say, 'Don't do that! Serve from the left, take away from the right,' and stuff like that. He was dead fucking serious." As Lump puts it, "All the kids who worked for me knew if they didn't show up on time and work hard, I'd fucking kill them. If my own son ever showed up late, I'd punch him right in the fucking mouth."

Lump's manner of doing business was a hit with his twenty-something male waitstaff, who idolized their in-your-face boss. This was due in large part to his drinking exploits and his appreciation, so to speak, of women. Lump was a renowned drinker and was often the life of the party when the restaurant was about to close each evening. "For the waiters, when we would hang and drink in the restaurant after a night's work, watching Lump drink was a fucking show," Battista says. "I'd get my work done, go sit at the bar, and I'd get it moving," says Lambrusco. "If I bought six drinks, they might be a quarter a piece. If a customer bought six drinks, it might be thirteen dollars. That was the idea of getting everything moving. I'd sit and drink a bottle of scotch after work every night." Though Lump was approving—if not encouraging—when it came to drinking among his staff, he says, "I used to always tell the guys not to get into [hard] drugs. To me, it was such a waste of a person."

The combination of Lambrusco's experience, management style, go-getter service staff, and lively atmosphere would work well for the next few years. According to Battista, "Louis' was the place to go in Delaware County. We'd have bookmakers, politicians, and all sorts of people coming in and we were cleaning up. You couldn't get a table on a Friday or Saturday night. There was a bunch of guys my age who waitered at Louis' and we all busted our asses, but we loved it." "The place did a ton of business. It was the best restaurant Delaware County had ever seen," Lump fondly recalls. "You'd walk in and see tableside flames, bottles of wine everywhere. The food was good, the prices weren't out of line, and the service was excellent. I had six to ten young, good-looking guys in the dining room who were workers. We weren't cheap, but from hanging your coat to pulling out your chair, the whole thing was just class all the way. People still tell me it was the best restaurant they were ever in." Battista's assessment is, shall we say, less technical. "We were known for our work ethic, and people thought Louis' was a kick-ass restaurant. Our mentality was that you could come in, get a great dinner and a bottle of wine for a hundred dollars, and hopefully you were gonna get laid at the end of the night."

The outstanding service for which Louis' was renowned stemmed from Lump's nonstop pressure on the waitstaff, which served as an important lesson that Battista would exploit for many years to come. "You couldn't come in and just order an entrée," Lump says. "If one of the waiters came back to the kitchen with just an entrée on the order, they'd get their ass chewed out." "He'd make us compete for head averages on who had the highest check," explains Battista. "He'd be like, 'What the fuck?! You had a four head count and you can't get

two hundred dollars, you couldn't get fifty bucks a head?!' He'd
say to things like, 'The entrée alone is seventeen dollars. Did
you sell them a bottle of wine? Did you sell them a tableside
salad?' Battista sums up the broader significance of all this
as follows: "He was constantly showing us discipline and the
mind of a gambler, in essence, because what you learn is that
it all adds up."

Battista was learning all sorts of lessons during his valued
time with Lump and, according to Battista, not all of them
were what most would consider the right ones. "My dad was
real quiet, a good American citizen, and a great guy, where
Lump was the epitome of what you didn't want your kid to be.
But I liked him. There was something about him. He was a
hustler and a criminal. He had so many shady friends because
of his early days of bookmaking and other things he did. The
more I hung around with him, the more I learned. The state
of Pennsylvania was moving liquor trucks of wine and stuff
like that. Lump had these guys come to the restaurant and
would get the guys drunk in the bar. They'd have a trailer
full of wine and alcohol outside and we'd get bolt cutters, go
in the back of their truck and just fucking pilfer everything
we could. We would take like forty cases of wine, hide them,
and then go sell them. We'd take, like, a six-dollar bottle of
vodka and sell it for three bucks. So, my criminal activity
continued—and escalated, because I liked this guy! Then we
got into the betting. He was the first one who taught me how
to book.

"I was waitering throughout this time, and we used to do a
lot of tableside cooking. We worked our asses off, had to look
presentable, and had to know what you were talking about. But
when you were done you partied your ass off—you drank, you
drugged, and tried to get laid. One of the great lines Lump
used in the morning when we came into work was, 'Who
brought home the newspaper and who had breakfast with

somebody?' He made such an impression on me. He was one of these guys who had some of the funniest sayings, and I learned so much from him. He used to say, 'Baba, don't sell the steak, sell the sizzle.' At first I looked at the guy like, 'What the fuck are you talking about?' What he meant was, people are going to go to a steakhouse to buy the steak, so what you need to do is sell everything around it. Well, I applied those principles to my daily life." Lump obviously had his way of expressing his view on life and the impressionable Sheep took it all in. One last and great example offered by Battista involved Lambrusco's play on the popular Trix cereal commercial, featuring kids telling the product's trademark character, "Silly rabbit, Trix are for kids!" "Lump would say, 'Baba, every broad has a set of tits, but tits are for kids! Be an 'ass man' and you'll get more out of life.' His views on life and the things he said really set the precedent for a lot of the things I did.

"Even though I was a waiter, he taught me how to cook. I was joined at his side because me and him connected so well. He lived to teach kids his way of doing things. He was always against doing hard drugs, but he didn't mind drinking, smoking a little pot, and getting laid as much as possible. He thought they were the greatest things. He got hit with trip sevens on a St. Patty's Day. It was the last action he took. He covered the bets but got wiped out. He covered something like two hundred and fifty grand. He was always a man of his word. He was the one who always told me, 'If you take a bet, you better pay. If it takes you a while, you pay that bet off.' That stuck in my mind, like this is the way you have to be. Lump was everything I wanted to be. I wanted to own a restaurant, I wanted to be Mr. Nightlife, I wanted to stay out all night and go to work the next morning. I mean, Lump turned an after-hours place into a fine dining Italian restaurant with the mentality of drinking, numbers, gambling and everything else. A lot of people knew what was going on with the restaurant. One of [Philly mob boss] Angelo Bruno's good friends, who was a numbers man for the boys downtown, used to hang there. Other mob guys hung there, too, because the booze was good and the pussy was good. It was a place to settle scores and stuff like that."

As can be sensed by now, Lambrusco made quite an impact on the twenty-something Black Sheep. "Besides my father, Lump was the guy who kind of raised me. Now, it wasn't the right way to be raised, but he schooled me in everything. This guy was old school Italian, and people either loved him or hated him. Some people didn't like him because when he got drunk he told you if you were a fucking asshole, whatever. Back in the day, Louie the Lump was a fun-loving guy and an intriguing individual."

* * *

The introduction to the hyper-nightlife scene made possible by his relationship with Louie the Lump was the best and worst thing that could have happened to someone like Battista, who already had a fondness for forbidden fruits. "Soon after I started working at Louis' Restaurant my drinking and drugging escalated," Battista says. "I hooked up with this girl named Nina. I was about twenty-one, and she was twenty-eight and very attractive. When she came into the restaurant, she was always dressed to the hilt and everyone would look at her. She used to go out with the head of the Irish mob in Philly before he went to jail for life. Wherever she went, people stayed away from her because they feared who she was. When I moved in with her, I was in heaven. I was getting laid every night, and she was the hottest piece of ass walking around the neighborhood. We were into the drugs pretty heavy, though, because wherever we went people were throwing bags of coke at us and we didn't have to pay for any of it. Wherever we went, people were like, 'Nina is here, Nina is here!' and they took care of her. People were buying me bottles of Dom Perignon when I was twenty-one years old because I was with her. I was still working as a waiter at the restaurant and booking and betting, and Nina and I were out clubbing all the time. This went on for about eight months until we got into a fight one night when I was all fucked up. I went home to stay with my parents that night, and was so messed up I missed work the next morning. I had never missed work before. My mom came into my room to check on me and saw some coke I had. She called the local priest, Father Cassatas, and I went to a detox center at Delaware County Memorial Hospital.

"I knew I had a problem, and that I had to slow down, but I was just so into the nightlife. I got cleared up for two days in the hospital, and then went to Mirmont Treatment Center for twenty-eight days. I came out of rehab and went right back to work at the restaurant. Lump stuck with me when I was in rehab and made sure I got my act together. Even though I was just a waiter for him, he paid for my health insurance, which was great. I stayed clean for about three months, and then started drinking a lot of wine." Though things settled down for the moment, Battista's battle with addiction would be a recurring theme for the next twenty years.

* * *

Battista started getting interested in bookmaking soon after being hired at Spanky's (soon to be Louis') and seeing the lifestyle: sports, money, partying, women, and people constantly looking for—and being indebted to—you. "Because he knew how my father was, Lump wouldn't show me how things *really* worked and wouldn't allow me to get involved with *his* booking. Just seeing all the people come in asking for Lump and picking up on things really got me interested. I knew I wanted to do that, so I started booking for my friends." The miniscule, independent Battista gambling operation lasted throughout his years at Louis,' as he picked up pointers by watching Lump all the while. As he would for many years to come, Battista's close friend Tommy Martino remained on the periphery of the Sheep's operation. "Tommy wasn't into gambling, but he knew people who were and he would bring them to me. He was into selling weed, and I was into booking and betting with Lump. He would come into the restaurant with his girlfriends, but when it came to our own 'businesses,' we went our separate ways."

Battista's fascination with Louie the Lump's lifestyle was matched only by his curiosity regarding one of Lump's booking and betting pals. "There was a guy named Mike Rinnier who used to come into Louis' all the time, and was a big spender," says Battista. "He'd be drinking Dom; his table would have a bill of five hundred dollars like nothing." At the time, Battista didn't know much about Rinnier, but his boss surely did. "I met Mike back when I was selling bar supplies and I went into one of his places," Lambrusco explains. "It was just coincidence that he and I were both into booking and betting. He only went into booking because he lost so much money betting, and figured it would be smarter to book himself."

Mike Rinnier recruited Lambrusco to help open a restaurant called September's at some point in the late 1980s. The timing could not have been more fortuitous for Lump, who was having a falling out with his partners in Louis.' "Mike offered me a great deal," Lambrusco says, and within a few months the entire waiting crew, including and especially the burgeoning Sheep, left Louis' for September's to follow the now legendary Lump.

For the other waiters joining Lambrusco at September's, this was nothing more than a change of scenery. For Jimmy "Baba" Battista, it would be a life-changing event.

4

The Gambling Grocer

LOUIE THE LUMP and his cast of characters made the leap to join Mike Rinnier, fascinated by the prospects of Rinnier's next venture. "The Alpine Inn was supposedly run by a bunch of mob figures," Battista says, "and Mike Rinnier wanted Lump and me to come up and help him turn the Inn's restaurant into a place called September's. It was going to be a restaurant, nightclub, and banquet facility. So, I came up to work for Mike and his partner, Matt Brophy. Lump was at September's cooking, and I was there waiting on tables. I was also a small-time bookmaker, just with my friends. Well, Mike Rinnier was a bookmaker, and Lump did business with him in the early 80s." "Mike Rinnier was a ruthless, money-hungry motherfucker," Lambrusco says. "The dollar meant so fucking much to him. He was a good guy if he liked you. He liked Baba and he loved me. Mike took good care of me. But, I saw him chew people's asses out in front of other people, and if he had ever done something like that to me I would have punched him."[1]

---

[1] Within the first year of operation, Louie the Lump had a falling out with Rinnier's partner, Matt Brophy. According to Lambrusco, "It was a Saturday night and we were fucking busy working behind the line [in the kitchen], and [Brophy] came in and said, 'I got a complaint on a baked potato. It's not cooked.' I said, 'Are you fucking crazy. There ain't nothing wrong with that potato.' He said something back to me, and I handed him the tongs and said, 'Here, you fucking cook it. I quit.' He said, 'You can't quit,' and I said, 'Can't I? Watch me.' I went back to Louis' and bought out my old partners, but couldn't ever get the place back to where it was. The food was okay,

"Mike owned a few supermarkets and he was *great* with numbers and money," Battista says. "In my eyes, he was the greatest thing that came along since Lump. His work ethic was, 'You work hard every day, you party at nighttime,' but you had to clean up your act a little bit. He wanted you to wear a suit and be presentable. He was known as The Rug. He was afraid people wouldn't respect him in business because he was bald, so he wore a wig that was the worst you ever saw. In no time, I started to realize what a fucking monster Mike Rinnier was. He was heavy into booking and all sorts of people were turning their action into him." Battista was initially offended at the way Rinnier presented himself in common society. "At the time," he says, "I was thinking, 'Here he is, coming across as this restaurateur, Mr. Supermarket guy, always wearing suits, and meanwhile, he is a fucking bookmaker and bettor!'

"Out of nowhere, on a Friday afternoon, he said to me, 'I need a favor. I need you to go out to Vegas and bring out a package.' I asked him what he was talking about and he said, 'I need you to bring fifty grand out to Vegas.' I said, 'Sure!' Of course, I knew he was betting, but he never personally brought it to my attention. I think he was waiting to see how I was going to be with him. My thing was to just drop off the package, take my girlfriend out with me, and get the red-eye back on Sunday night to be back at work at the restaurant on Monday morning. Well, the kid I was supposed to meet out there was so fucked up that he made some wrong bets, and Mike said to me, 'Why don't you run around and pick up some of these numbers?' I said, 'Yeah. This is fun!' I was staying in a suite at Caesar's Palace [where Rinnier had predictably been comped] and I was eating and boozing like a king. He only had me do a little bit, but I got paid five hundred bucks on top of being set up with airfare, the hotel suite, and being taken

---

but you couldn't replace the dining room help." Despite no longer working together, Lambrusco remained a friend and mentor to Jimmy Battista for decades to follow.

care of everywhere my girlfriend and I went throughout the weekend. I was in hog heaven, and I liked being a runner."

It became a weekend ritual for Battista, and Rinnier's trust in his understudy continued to grow. Rinnier could "get down" bigger denominations in Las Vegas than in the Greater Philadelphia betting market. "I was tying or taping anywhere from fifty to a hundred grand to my body," Battista says, "flying out to the desert. The desert was always dry for money, and I became the money man. I was still getting paid five hundred a weekend, and me and my girl would get comped for everything; we got to see the best shows and sporting events. It was so much fun for me because I was in my natural habitat," Battista says. "Back home, I was working pay phones, getting and giving people numbers. This was before the gambling industry got computerized. It was like a sin because we knew the right numbers for the games from our connections in Las Vegas, where the sharp money was already altering the lines. It was like stealing money. The bookmakers in Philadelphia didn't know what they were doing. *It was just us against the bookmakers, and they didn't have a chance.*

"Mike had just gotten hooked up with some of the sharpest guys in the betting world. We knew he was getting great information because he was crushing bookmakers. At that point it was me and two other waiters who were turning in our books, our customers, to Mike. So, we were waiters in the restaurant, Mike and his operation were taking care of our customers—we couldn't go to the payphones while we were working, anyway—and we were betting on the games Mike was getting from the sharps. I was still working the restaurant, but I started going out to Vegas more often for him because he liked the job I was doing.

"Out in Vegas, I worked for a guy named Domino, who was from Havertown and ran Mike's operation out there. He had, like, seven runners who, depending on how trustworthy they were, would have between fifty and a hundred thousand dollars, and we'd run from casino to casino placing whatever bets Mike sent through Domino. We worked all day long, starting around five o'clock in the morning. You'd sit in a casino sportsbook, eat hot dogs or whatever you did, and bet all day. I'd watch sports all day long. I didn't just bet at one casino; I'd bet at six or seven. I'd carry a bag of money and chips and run from casino to casino. I was in heaven! I loved it because you could go out at nighttime and you gambled all day. We used to bet at Little Caesar's Palace a lot back then. That place was only as big as my house, but they would take a hundred grand a game, when the bigger casinos would only take big bets from squares, and even then they would only take, like twenty-five thousand. The owner of Little Caesar's was sharp. He would let us bet up to a hundred grand if we took the first number, the opening line of a bet. That way, he could factor it into what he was doing."

It was during his time as a runner for Mike Rinnier that Battista got his first taste of the grandest sports bettor of them all. If he was impressed by Rinnier's betting success, he was simply awed by the man everyone called The Computer, who was the first pro gambler to exploit the burgeoning technology's impact on sports betting. It would be years before Battista hooked up with The Computer, himself, but he immediately grasped his significance. "One of my jobs was to hang out in the Horseshoe Casino and follow The Computer's runners," Battista says. "I got such an education on The Computer doing this. When the runner would place a bet, I would give him a hundred bucks for The Computer's pick. I had made friends with his runners just so I could get this information. Well, I had this big-ass cell phone, the early kind of mobile phones, and I would call back East with the information. This is before there were online services tracking betting lines in real time, and our guys would take this information and whoosh! They were off to the races back home. We'd take the game off of our book's board so that no one could bet us. Then we'd spring into action getting as much down as possible on the right side with the right number, all before anyone knew what was going on.

"Some of the sharp guys like The Computer would send an old lady into a casino and have them bet good money, hoping the sportsbook would think she was a square and take her bet. Guys were always looking for people to go in and place bets for them. The sharps would set people up for a weekend in a hotel, and tell them to go play blackjack or whatever—like every other square—and then have them place three football bets for them on Sunday. They had it all set up, and that happened all the time. There was an art to that. Some of the stuff was so staged it was incredible. They'd send a guy in who looks like he's a drunk who doesn't know what the fuck he's doing, and meanwhile his bets were going to help set the lines around the world. Anytime a new sportsbook manager took over, he didn't know how or when he was going to get it in the ass, but it was coming.

"I did the Vegas stuff for more than a year. I was Mike's main man that went back and forth from Philly to the desert. In the meantime, I had become manager of September's. Mike's philosophy was, 'Work, work, work, work, work!' and that's what I did, which caused my girlfriend to break up with me. I worked so much that if my family wanted to see me, they had to come see me at work. I never had time for my mom, my dad, or my sisters because it was all work, gamble, work, gamble. That was the ethics I was taught. I had learned all this stuff from Lump, and Mike just brought it to another level—you know, put a shirt and tie on and you can do this on a daily basis. I said to myself, 'I like this guy,' because he was a maniac. He was nonstop, even more than Lump, and *he was brilliant*. He had supermarkets, he had restaurants, he had nightclubs, but it was never enough. He also had one of the biggest books in Delaware County."

Mike Rinnier was, indeed, an influential figure in the area, and Battista had heard numerous stories of Rinnier taking after people he deemed adversaries. The Sheep's personal and professional lives intersected at one point, and the result was an up-close view of Rinnier's ire. "The wife of Mike's business partner, Matt Brophy," Battista says, "had a sister named Mara who was divorced. We wound up dating for about a year and a half, and I got really close to Mara's little girl, Lori, who was about two years old. As this was going on, I moved back in with my parents for seven or eight months. They saw I was straightening my act out a little bit, trying to establish myself. I had just gotten engaged and was trying to turn my life around. My parents didn't know I was into the gambling, though; they just thought I made my money at the restaurant. This was 1989, things were going pretty good, and I got married to Mara that summer. I was twenty-five at the time, and we got an apartment in Drexel Hill. I was still managing the restaurant, but I couldn't gamble as much because now I had the responsibility of a stepdaughter and a wife and I wanted to keep everybody happy. She knew all about my gambling, though, because her brother-in-law was Mike's partner. Mara also loved the limelight and going out to Vegas. She liked going out and having fun.

"Well, at the time, Mike was being investigated for coupon fraud and bookmaking. He used to pay people to sit in an office above one of his supermarkets and clip out coupons, and he was somehow scamming with the coupons.[2] It was a Wednesday

---

[2] According to Battista, Rinnier had any number of hustles going on simultaneously. For instance, Battista says, "He was such a fucking unscrupulous businessman. Mike stiffed half the purveyors he had. His thing was to work up bills in the hundreds of thousands of dollars and then approach the person he owed and say, 'So, I owe you four hundred thousand dollars. I'll pay you fifty cents on the dollar in three installment payments over the next six months.' And he would just drag people along."

night, and Mike wanted us to go to one of his supermarkets when the bar closed and run all the files out because he was fucking nervous the feds were following us everywhere we went. Well, my old girlfriend from high school was a Miller Lite girl who was working a charity event that night at September's. It was like quarter of two in the morning, and we're all meeting to go do this for Mike, but she was hammered drunk. She got all fucked up and I wanted to make sure she got home safe—I had to choose between driving her home or going to get rid of all the files. I remember them saying to me, 'Mike is going to be mad if you don't show up,' but I couldn't just leave her there at September's Place all fucked up after we worked a benefit. I drove her home and dropped her off, and didn't go to help them with the files. Mike was pissed at me for such a long time; he couldn't believe that I chose to help a girl over him. I wasn't manager of the restaurant after that for like six months; that was my punishment.

"If people didn't do what Mike wanted, he would fuck with them, and that's the way he ran his businesses. He was such a control monger. He'd control your work and your personal life. It was just like the movie *The Firm* except he didn't kill anybody. He'd move you to another store or give you another job that wasn't as much money. He was so convincing in the way he did it, too; he made you feel like a piece of shit. Mike told his partner, Matt, and my wife Mara (Matt's sister-in-law) that I was more concerned about other things than the 'Rinnier way of living' and questioned my work ethic. Mara and I got married on July 6, 1989, and six months later to the day, she walked out on me and handed me divorce papers. I was heartbroken because even though I loved Mara, I had gotten really attached to her daughter. I had been trying to change my life around, and I thought I was a great father figure in her life. Her real father was still around, but me and Lori became really close. I took her to school, and did other things like that with her. Other than that, the thing that made me mad the most was the way they portrayed me, like I was the bad seed in the whole thing. But, even with my personal situation, Mike couldn't get rid of me because we had the gambling together.

"As I was going through my divorce, the boys downtown—the Philly mob—were shaking down all the bookmakers in the Philadelphia area. Well, this was right around the time we got hooked up with a bookmaker downtown and were beating him for a lot of money. The boys downtown got wind of it, and we were told they were seeking me out. I left the restaurant so I was out of the limelight, and worked at the seafood department of one of Mike's supermarkets. The mob was after Mike's operation because we were taking so much money out of the market. They wanted to get to Mike and they figured the way to get to Mike was to come after me, for some reason—maybe because I was the one out there traveling all the time. It might also have been because I worked a lot on the phones dealing with bookmakers for Mike. So, now, I didn't have my wife, I was working in the fucking seafood department, and I was left gambling just at nighttime. I'd work all day, come home, take a shower, go to the gambling office and work the five o'clock session until about eight-thirty at night.

"Around that time, Mike recruited a guy named Tiger, who was an up and coming bookmaker, to be partners. Mike knew Tiger was sharp and a much better handicapper than he was. His nickname was Tiger because he was always on the hunt! He was so fucking aggressive as a bettor and as a businessman."

"I had been bookmaking for a couple of years before Mike Rinnier had one of his people start betting me," Tiger says. "I heard Mike was a big businessman, owned supermarkets, and that he was a genius. Everybody who worked with him or for him knew he was a huge gambler and bookmaker. I was a young, independent bookmaker and Mike probably thought I didn't know what I was doing and that he could make good money betting me. He was wrong, of course, and he found that out in time. When I was young and just starting out, I used to do studies on how often games would fall on certain numbers, on certain point spreads. I'd calculate those percentages and then assess the value of certain line moves, and how certain moves would increase your chances of winning. Very few people were doing that back then, and nobody in the Philadelphia area that I knew of was. Being young and raw in the business was my biggest asset, because I didn't accept any of the old norms of the bookmakers in the neighborhoods. Everything they learned their whole lives was working against them because they were all told that bettors couldn't win, that everybody was a sucker. *I knew that wasn't true.* Mike Rinnier ended up getting all their money, but he didn't get any of my money.

"So, Mike and I started dealing a little with each other, and we'd help each other in different ways, until he heard I was putting people in Vegas. When he realized I was going to have my own crew of runners out there, and that I would be getting the best numbers out there and having them sent back East, he asked me to go full partners with him, fifty-fifty. It was a great deal for me because Mike was betting in such volume compared to me, but he wasn't as sharp. Mike and his people weren't real good handicappers, and they were just getting information from other bettors.

"When I took over the office, there were guys betting their own stuff with the office's money, and there were guys who were so fucking slow adapting to the changes in betting lines. I changed all of that and we started crushing pretty soon after I got involved. There were some serious problems, though, because when I started with Mike, I started at the top. I was in my early twenties and pretty much everyone was older than me, and here I was ordering them around. Mike had recruited me to run the betting side of the office because the last two or three guys didn't work out. Well, when I was betting, I didn't fuck around. When it came to running a betting office, I was a little bit of a tyrant. If I told somebody to go get 'minus two-and-a-half' and they came back with a card—a betting slip—that said 'minus three,' I would be furious and they'd know about it. I don't think Mike had any of the guys in the office ready for somebody like me, so it was not an easy transition for any of us.

"They also didn't know anybody who handicapped like me, meaning using probabilities, value-based decision making, arbitrage, all that sort of stuff.[3] I think they were mostly used to old-school bookmaking and betting, relying more on trends and instincts which said that nobody can bet and win in the long run. I knew already, at that age, that you could absolutely win in the long run as long as you took it seriously and didn't get caught up into it emotionally. The beauty of the situation was that most bookmakers and sportsbooks at the time still held the same belief—that you couldn't win consistently over time. Well, that was great for me because I was going to fucking crush them one by one."

---

[3] This area is remarkably complex, involving sophisticated mathematical calculations and statistical probabilities. I have opted not to get into this analysis and discussion here as to not distract from the focus on Jimmy Battista's career, but will almost certainly be revisiting the art and science of high-end sports gambling and will present my findings in a suitable forum. In the meantime, interested parties may wish to consult the source notes for suggested readings.

Eye of the Tiger

"I WAS IN MIKE'S office when I first met Jimmy," Tiger says. "I heard people talking about Baba or Sheep before I joined with Mike, but nothing more than that, really. I just knew Jimmy was a clerk and that Mike liked him. Well, three weeks into me working with Mike we had a really good week, so he and I went out with our wives to September's for dinner. Well, Baba came over as our waiter, and said, "Good evening, my name is James and I'll be your waiter . . ." and I was thinking, 'What the fuck is this?! This is the guy who sits across from me every day in the betting office, and he's not going to say, "Hey, what's up Tiger?" "How's it going guys?" or something informal like that?' Meanwhile, my wife could see that I was freaked out and she asked me what was wrong after Jimmy took our drink order and I told her, and Mike just said, 'Yeah, that's Baba. He pretty much stays on routine.' That was what Mike loved about Jimmy; he did what he was told and he did it well, no matter what it was."

"Pretty soon after he joined us, Tiger and I really started to hit it off," Battista says. "He was a very hard worker, and he knew I was the 'time to make the doughnuts' guy—I'd get up by eight o'clock, go to work, stay all day, and show up the next day. I knew there was money to be made, and he knew he could count on me." "When Jimmy started working with me," Tiger says, "it was a rough marriage at first because Jimmy didn't understand what I was trying to do. I would be yelling at him, 'I want you to say *this* exactly *this way*' and stuff like that. And yet, within a short time, it was like he knew what I was thinking. We used to fight a lot at the start, but it wound up like he could read my mind and he was fast and sharp. He became so instinctive that it was extremely valuable to me that he was working with me."

"I was one of the better clerks in the office because I was always fast and furious," Battista says. "I would always get the right numbers, and I wouldn't mess anything up. This is before the Internet, back when you had to get 'rundowns.' My specialty was being able to call our network of books—sportsbooks and bookmakers—and get the day's games and lines read to me—a *rundown* of the lines, and relay that information quickly to Tiger, who would tell me and everybody else what numbers to get, what to bet. People—our outs—knew me and liked me, and would get me that info fast. I developed such a good relationship with our outs that a lot of times when I would call for a rundown, they would just give me the latest changes, which is all I was calling for anyway.

"So, the way we had everything set up, to us, was like stealing money, because we were always getting the best numbers. A lot of times we weren't really handicapping; we were just picking the information [betting line moves] from all of our outs. We were like a human version of what some online services were years later. I'd call a bunch of bookmakers, including some out in Vegas and a lot of guys up in New York. New York was the big spot other than Las Vegas, and they had sharp guys and guys who were piped into sharps out in Vegas. During November, we had three sports going on at the same time: pro basketball, and college and pro football, so I was managing a shitload of numbers over and over again. We had these sheets that listed all the day's games and we would constantly update the lines with each rundown. If me or Tiger heard a line on a rundown that was a move or that was a line Tiger had said to look out for, we'd click our fingers up in the air which meant all the movers in the office had to pick up their phones and get ready for Tiger's orders on what numbers to get. The guys in our office had outs in the local area—Montgomery, Bucks, and Delaware counties, Allentown, the outskirts of New York, in Vegas, and all the way down to Florida."

"Jimmy was so fucking good at rundowns," Tiger says. "He'd be on the phones *nonstop* for three hours every night during the week. He'd be getting the rundown and yelling to me what the numbers were and I'd be checking them against the last rundown for any changes. Depending on what had changed and what I wanted, I'd be yelling to all the movers in the office to go to their outs and get X number on Y game. Each and every time the movers would get money down with their local bookmakers, we'd have to update the chart with what action we had. As that was going on, Baba would be rattling off the next rundown. It was fucking frantic in that office, and we were on top of the line moves because of all the rundowns. This was all before computers and services that could track all of this stuff for you, and we were ahead of a lot of people with this system."

In addition to the actual handicapping and mathematical analyses he performed, Tiger also excelled at exploiting his knowledge of the sports betting market. "Baba was key because he was so fast with the phones," Tiger says. "If I would ask him for a rundown after we had already heard the lines from before so I knew the last lines, he'd be ticking off the lines—by book, 'four-and-a-half, six, seven,' and I'd be like, 'Wait! Seven, with Junior?! Holy shit, that line was five-and-a-half with Junior last time.' I'd click my fingers in the air and yell right then, 'Everybody go lay six-and-a-half and five-and-a-half over the Spurs' because I knew Junior took big bets and I knew The Computer was betting him and that's why Junior moved his lines. I didn't need to know who the teams involved were, or anything like that. It was just a matter of getting constant rundowns and knowing who bet where and why.

"A professional gambler—whether you're a bookmaker or a bettor—has to have the ability to look at a lot of different things all at the same time. You have to watch a lot of different numbers, watch them move, and know what it all means. If you have football and baseball, or football and basketball, going on at the same time, you have to have two pages up at the same time. As you're watching all the numbers move and trying to process what all that means, people are giving you orders for specific games and you have to go bet them and turn in the orders, change the chart that tracks how much money we have and where our bets are placed: 'Oh, we've got this bet minus six for ten grand and the line is up to seven-and-a-half, that's a good thing, but we've got another bet at minus six for twenty-five grand and the line is down to six, fuck, maybe we followed a phony bet and we should take some seven-and-a-half and get off this game.' You were always jockeying for position based on which way the lines were moving.

"I had the bookmakers ranked based on sharpness, knew who took big money bets, and factored that into my decision making when I was looking at the lines. So, if a sharp bookmaker had a different line than some other guys, I'd immediately tell everyone to go to those other bookmakers and get what I needed because those other guys had the wrong line. Back then, the market was so slow and so weak; those local bookmakers didn't get updates on the lines. They'd get their lines at five or six o'clock at night and took bets until the game started at seven or eight. Well, the sharp money out in Vegas and other places was moving the lines in Vegas, but the local bookies were still using whatever number they started with that night. It was stealing money."

"There were two of us who were doing the rundowns," Battista says, "and we each had fifteen stores. So, Tiger was processing the lines for around thirty books, looking for certain changes and numbers. We were constantly updating our charts, tracking all the line changes, our bets, and how much money we had in play. Years later, all those sheets and charts would turn into computerized screens and they'd change themselves, but back in the day, we were doing all that by hand, over the phone, with hundreds—maybe thousands—of phone calls every work shift. Back then, bookmakers weren't fast enough to get the line changes. These were all old-timers, and they'd be like, 'Sure, I can give you that number,' not having a fucking clue why we wanted that number. The technology that evolved later made our lives easier, obviously, but it also hurt us because it took away one of our key advantages in the rundowns. Nobody did what we did, and computers eventually allowed everyone to have all that line info that we used to hustle to get. Back then, we had one guy assigned to update the chart. He had a tough fucking job, because we were *constantly* handing him our cards—the tickets for our bets, and he had to keep everything straight. His job was made even more difficult because you had a bunch of guys writing fast and a lot of the tickets were tough to read, but he had to get everything right or we would have been fucked.

"I am telling you, people couldn't believe what the office activity looked like. It was fucking crazy. We really should have filmed our outfit, especially on a football Sunday, because anybody who ever saw it was blown away by what we were doing. That's why people respected us so much, because we knew what we were doing and we worked like fucking dogs. We were beaten down after a shift of betting—totally exhausted, but we were in it for the kill and that's what it took. I honestly think we were the best in the country at what we did back then. We were on top of everything and we were so hungry. In the last ten minutes before a kickoff, I'd call fifty to sixty times for rundowns because numbers would be popping and there were earners all over the place. The only break we got on a football Sunday was just after the one o'clock games kicked off, when we would have food ordered in. Once we got done eating, though, we got geared up for betting the second halves of the one o'clock games and for the four o'clocks. There was such an art to what we were doing. I still get chills thinking about those times, they were so fucking exciting.[1]

"There was no such thing as being late for work, especially in the morning on a Saturday or a Sunday during football season. You had to be in that chair and ready to go. You better have eaten, gone to the bathroom, everything, because you couldn't leave the chair and miss the right numbers. Some of the old school bookmakers in New York would use the line that they went to bed with the night before. Well, they didn't know that The Computer fucking destroyed the market out in Vegas since then, so we were there first thing in the morning to sap up the changes.

"We were a herd of young, hungry Animals. It didn't take long for people to realize that we weren't fucking around, and that they better respect us or they'd get burned. The other thing that distinguished us from other gamblers and bettors was that by the time the day was done, we were dead tired, and didn't go out much. Other guys would be partying all the time, hungover, whatever. We weren't into burning hundred dollar bills and acting like big shots in bars or strip clubs. We were focused on being productive the next day, which meant

---

[1] During what little down time existed in the office, the Animals ate—a lot—and bet on anything and everything. Often, the wagers centered on eating and other contests involving bodily functions among the staff. Revisiting these events many years later evokes laughter and remains a source of pride for The Animals, who were each rotund to some degree in their booking and betting heyday because of their career-dominated lifestyle.

being on time and ready to go, and you couldn't do that if you were out late every night.

"I learned a lot from Tiger, and with him more in charge of the betting, we were putting a lot of books out of business. We were sucking big money out of the market, because we had Tiger's handicapping and we had all kinds of inside information. The inside information was always the key. So, whether that meant buying someone or being someone's friend and being there for them, that was the business of getting the right information. Our information was coming from all sorts of people all around the country, whether it was about the betting lines or sharp bets in Vegas, or inside stuff about players, coaches, or refs and stuff like that.

"We really started developing a network of people giving us information, especially people who owed us money. A lot of times you'd have somebody owe money who couldn't pay off their debt in cash, so they'd offer something else instead. So, if somebody owned a restaurant or a bar, they'd take care of you in some way relating to their establishment. Caterers would take care of special functions for free, people would give us tickets to events, stuff like that. We started getting all sorts of stuff as currency for bets. Sometimes, people could help us get inside information, like this guy who delivered food into Veteran's Stadium. His way of paying us back was relaying back certain information from inside the stadium. Another time, we had this guy who owed us money report to us just before a Chicago Cubs baseball game at Wrigley Field. We needed to know whether the wind was blowing out or blowing in before the first pitch, and that was his only job—call us with a report about the outfield flags and the wind.[2] Shit like that was pretty common after so many people owed us money."

---

[2] The wind reports from Wrigley were useful in betting the over/under on total runs scored in a game. If the wind was blowing out, for instance, this would often dictate a bet on the over.

With Tiger at the helm, Rinnier's operation was a well-oiled betting machine. Their main office was located in an apartment complex directly across the street from the popular Lamb Tavern in Springfield. It apparently never dawned on the other complex residents what activity was taking place above them. Populated exclusively with hyper-aggressive young men, the office operated much like the infamous penny-stock boiler rooms of the same era. "We rented out the entire top floor," Battista says. "It was a wraparound, which was really three apartments that we connected. Between booking and betting, there were always twenty to thirty of us working in the office. There were work shifts for everybody that depended on what betting season it was.

"There were four rooms total. The main room had sixteen to eighteen people, including me and Tiger, then two offices off of that, then a bathroom and another long office with 'floaters' in it. The floaters were pretty much there for low-level booking and betting from different neighborhoods; they worked in the office and turned their action in to Mike. One of the other offices was essentially a bedroom that had four desks and phones and was used by a group of movers who were betting with local bookmakers who didn't know about Mike or Tiger. The movers had to be alone in that office off of the war room [main office] so that all the fucking noise wouldn't be heard on the other end of the phones, because if those bookmakers heard all the commotion they would have realized they were dealing with something bigger than just Joe Schmo calling in a bet, and who knows what they would have done. At a minimum, they would have stopped taking the calls and the bets.

"I sat at the main, really long desk directly across from Tiger, because I was the fastest and the one who could help him the most. There were workstations for most of us, each of them with their own phone, and I took mine pretty seriously. I had my sheets, which were college and pro football schedules with my handwritten betting lines from different books. I did everything by hand. We subscribed to the sportsticker that came from a sportsbook and we would take the sports form sheets off the ticker so that we would have the same game number as everybody else. When you bet a game, you didn't just say 'I'll take the Eagles minus five' or whatever. Every bet had a number, so the 'Eagles minus five' might have been number 'three-sixty-nine,' and for clarity you'd say, 'Give me three-sixty-nine, Eagles minus five, for ten dimes.' They would then repeat that back to you so there was no confusion. So, on my desk, from left to right, I would have the ticker sheets for pro football, college football, and the NBA [if these were in season, say in the fall or winter]. I'd have three or four Ticonderoga number two pencils with good erasers, and some Bic number ten blue pens, because they were the sharpest and quickest pens to write with. I'd have about four hundred three-by-five index cards in front of me for my tickets. There were always three phones on my desk; I worked all of them all the time, and sometimes I'd have one in each hand and one hanging from my neck.

"We had Bell Telephone hook up something like twenty-five lines for our phones that were on speed dial to our outs. Time was money, and you didn't want to miss line moves and all the earners sitting there to be had. We taped all our phone calls and almost all of the books taped their calls, so that there was never a debate about a bet. The moment you picked up a phone in our office, it was taping. Obviously, we weren't doing this to take people to court or anything like that, but in our business your word was key and you didn't want people bad-mouthing you that you didn't pay, that you fucked people over, whatever. We had three or four televisions back then, all connected to the best sports packages we could get on satellite or cable. The other rooms were quiet, but our room was usually pretty loud, depending on what was going on. Sometimes it was pretty quiet, but on a football Sunday up until one o'clock, it was fucking loud! All our offices were sound-proofed, and there was never an open window, so that nobody outside could hear us. Our betting sessions were loud and violent, and we didn't want anyone to know what we were up to.

"We had thirty clerks going out and tormenting the market, invading America's bookies and bettors and they didn't even know what was happening. Mike was making so much money booking and betting that he was feeding his other businesses like restaurants and hotels. The gambling operation was making him millions and millions of dollars in cash. He claimed it on his taxes, though; he didn't screw Uncle Sam. Now, I don't know if Uncle Sam got the right number, but he paid taxes on his gambling earnings! He used to tell anyone who worked for him that they had to pay gambling taxes. That advice saved me when I got busted several times through the years because you can take a gambling charge, but tax evasion is a whole different thing.

"Meanwhile, the Philly mob was really trying to get into us. They were trying to shake us down for money and for our information, because they knew we were destroying all their local outs. I got sent out to Las Vegas because the situation with the mob was so hot. They were looking all over for me. Mike and Tiger put me up in hotels out there, and I was running around again in my heaven. I was partying and having a good time. One night, I got done my shift and I was out drinking and started playing blackjack. I blew out—I lost thirty-eight grand of Mike's and Tiger's money in a few hours. They were really mad at me—for good reason, but they couldn't bring me back to Philly, so they sent me down to Santo Domingo.

"At roughly the same time, Mike and Tiger realized they had to get out of the Philadelphia area because the boys downtown were trying to shake them down. Everyone agreed that we had to keep a really low profile around the city. This was in the early 90s, and Santo Domingo was where everyone was going. The Dominican Republic was where people were opening up offshore book joints. The water was blue, the food was terrible, and we booked. There were ten or fifteen of us, all working for Mike and Tiger. We were treated like kings. We booked all day, and gambled at nighttime. Six or seven months into it, though, the Dominicans started shutting all the sportsbooks down. We had to get out of Santo Domingo because if you went to prison down there, you didn't know if you were getting out!

"We came back to the Philadelphia area, but had to stay almost in hiding because we didn't want anyone to know we were back. We were really worried about the Philly wiseguys. There was a mob war, and there was a lot of shit going on. It was so bad that we were taking bets in the office on who was going to be killed next. I was back in the gambling office working for Mike and Tiger as a clerk, but Mike was starting to get pissed because more and more I was showing my allegiance to Tiger. I saw that Tiger was much more brilliant than Mike was. Tiger was also very street-savvy and wasn't going to let anyone take advantage of him. He knew that Mike could never survive because he wasn't a handicapper or a sharp bettor; whatever success Mike had was because of who he knew and he was just copying other bets. It was obvious that Tiger would be breaking away from Mike sooner or later."

It was Battista's relationship with Mike Rinnier, however, which introduced him to a burgeoning gambling superstar who would be a key part of The Sheep's story for decades to come.

6

Sharpening Up

JOSEPH "JOE VITO" Mastronardo was a legend among bookies and bettors in the Greater Philadelphia area, and would be among the most consequential bookmakers and pro gamblers on the East Coast for three decades. On this, bookmakers, bettors, and law enforcement officials are in universal agreement. Like many of his big-time betting peers, he came from a middle-class environment and was considered a "white-collar" bookmaker. In fact, Mastronardo's defense attorney once famously called him a "gentleman gambler" in reference to Mastronardo's nonviolence policy for deadbeats (who were simply cut off from further action). Joe Vito's exploits dated back to the mid-1970s, but he rose to the top of the Philly bookmaking scene in the 1980s by exploiting his brilliant mind for numbers and for business. He was also known for honoring his "action" and for employing cutting-edge technology ahead of his competitors. In sum, he was "it" when it came to booking and betting by the time he turned forty. Adding to his fascinating story, in 1978 Mastronardo married Joanna Rizzo, the only daughter of Frank Rizzo, who had served four years as Philadelphia police commissioner before being elected mayor in 1971.[1] Mastronardo's marriage created more than a few street rumors over the years when it came to his ability to stay out of prison, despite being so widely known as the area's booking big shot.

---

[1] Rizzo was re-elected mayor in 1975.

"A bunch of us in the office were booking and turning our stuff in to Mike Rinnier," Battista says, "so in essence he was controlling a pretty big part of the market. Mike had us as his warriors to go get the customers, get the outs. Well, Joe Vito was the biggest bookmaker in Philadelphia at the time. Even though Joe controlled Philadelphia, which was a big market, we controlled South Jersey, Delaware, and a lot of the Philly suburbs. Mike and Joe weren't really competitors. Joe Vito was The Prince of the City, and Mike just wanted to grow and control more of the market outside the city. I had heard about Joe, simply because he was such a big deal. He was extremely—*extremely*—bright. Of all the people I have met over the years, Joe Vito is easily one of the five sharpest guys. Not just in math and in sports, but business-wise. A lot of people didn't like him because he was opinionated and spoke his mind, but he was usually right." "Joe Vito was a pure genius when it came to gambling," Tiger says, "and he taught me a lot. I used to sit with him for hours drinking coffee, just picking his brain and listening. Being around Joe so much brought me to another level. His respect for math affirmed much of what I already believed, and now I *knew* I was right."

"Word on the street was that the mob was always after Joe," Battista says, "but that Rizzo always protected him. Joe and his brother, John, hooked up with Mike Rinnier in the early 80s.[2] Mike always wanted to be Joe; Joe had the street sense and was smart. Well, we heard that Rizzo always wanted Mike to take Joe and make him into a businessman, but Joe didn't want that at all; he was a gambler. Mike was a good businessman, and I thought he was good with numbers, but he was just stealing all the numbers. *It was Joe who knew the right*

---

[2] Interestingly, John Mastronardo starred for the Villanova University football team before being selected by the Philadelphia Eagles in the 10th round of the 1977 NFL draft (overall pick 259).

numbers, and Mike was just taking the information, giving it to us, and we'd be taking all the right numbers elsewhere."

Joe Vito's bookmaking operation was described in a 1988 Pennsylvania Crime Commission (PCC) report as "strong" and "independent" of Philadelphia's predominant Italian-American crime syndicate at the time, the Bruno/Scarfo family. Mastronardo, then in his late thirties, lived just outside the city in Huntingdon Valley and headed the operation with the assistance of his brother, John (who was six years younger) and their father, Joseph Mastronardo Sr. John ran the ring's Philadelphia office, which was located in a lower-middle-class neighborhood, while Joseph Sr. oversaw an office in Boca Raton, Florida. As the PCC noted in 1990: "The Mastronardo bookmaking operation was a credit business. Bets were taken over the telephone on a toll free number, and all calls were recorded by the organization. Computerized statements or billings were prepared for clients (bettors) every few days. Strong-arm tactics or violence were not used to collect debts. If a client reneged on a bet, Mastronardo would no longer do business with the bettor." In this regard, the Commission added, "[Mob] member Nicholas "Nicky Crow" Caramandi bilked Mastronardo out of thousands of dollars. Caramandi refused to pay his gambling debts because Mastronardo was not one of the 'mob's protected bookies.' The Mastronardo operation apparently did not pay 'street tax' to the Philadelphia Family."

Mobster Caramandi later explained that he was actually trying to extort Mastronardo, but failed, noting that a "partner" of his named John Pastorella knew Mastronardo and started betting with him "fifty thousand, sixty thousand on ten or fifteen games each weekend. But I was also trying to smoke [Mastronardo] out, because I wanted tribute money off of him, shake money, because we'd heard this guy did real well, taking one hundred, two hundred thousand a game. I figured once we lose I'll meet this guy and read him his rights, that he has to pay." Caramandi's plan worked like a charm to start, as he said, "Well, the first week we win, like, fifteen thousand . . . But the second week we lose fifty-two thousand. And Mastronardo's on the phone looking for his money. So now I switch everything around and I tell him that he owes *me* fifty thousand. I tell him Pastorella made a mistake betting the games. I say Pastorella was betting with my money and that Mastronardo's responsible and I wanna meet him. He says, 'I don't wanna get involved with no gangsters.'" As was the case in the very near future with Battista and his gambling pals, Mastronardo carefully avoided the harm that awaited him if he was ever to cross paths with Philly wiseguys. "And he would never meet me," added Caramandi. "He musta gone underground or something, 'cause we could never find him. And so eventually we boxed a draw there and forgot about it."

Authorities estimated that Mastronardo's operation at the time grossed approximately fifty million dollars annually. The Mastronardos were the targets of a high-profile 1987 federal prosecution which also involved a stockbroker at Shearson Lehman Brothers who, according to the PCC, "played a significant role by converting profits of the operation into bonds and securities. Thus, illegal money was converted into legal assets and income taxes were avoided . . . Initially the profits were converted to treasury or cashier checks and money orders in amounts under ten thousand dollars to circumvent the requirement of filing an IRS Currency Transaction Report." The checks and money orders were then used to buy bonds and securities using nominee accounts at Shearson Lehman. Each of the Mastronardos was convicted in February 1987, with Joe Vito being sentenced to two years in prison and receiving a fine of two hundred and fifty thousand dollars.[3]

---

[3] Joseph Mastronardo actually served 18 months in prison, and John Mastronardo served 3 months.

As a sign of things to come, the Mastronardos continued to operate even during their federal trial, and the next couple of years would yield millions of confiscated dollars on repeated occasions relating to their massive sports bookmaking and betting enterprise. Law enforcement intelligence disclosed Joe Vito's national prominence emanating from the Philly suburbs, and locales from Los Angeles to New York were found to be part of the grand Mastronardo enterprise.

Battista and The Animals had much to learn from the legendary Joe Vito, including how to avoid the numerous pitfalls awaiting pro gamblers—especially those operating in the Philadelphia area.

* * *

One of the most consequential events in The Sheep's betting career took place toward the end of 1993. Battista, consumed with his work for Mike Rinnier, was always on the lookout for law enforcement and, more importantly, for Philly mobsters who were not pleased with the lack of respect shown by Rinnier's operation. At the time, Philly's underworld was in turmoil. Infamous, hot-headed mob boss Nicodemo "Little Nicky" Scarfo was convicted of racketeering in 1988 and sentenced to life in prison. Following Scarfo's precipitous downfall, the predictable struggle for power ensued with flashy up-and-comer Joseph "Skinny Joey" Merlino and the more seasoned and staid John Stanfa leading rival factions in the early 1990s. The streets of South Philly weathered the internecine warfare, while the area's bookies wound up with their own related problems. Rather than paying one entity—the Scarfo mob, area gamblers now had *two* groups demanding protection money. Rinnier's crowd and some of their suburban betting pals were already on bad terms with the "boys from downtown" either because they hadn't been paying enough tax or because they were crushing some of the mob's bookies with their betting, and now there was the added underworld bravado and hysteria emanating from the Merlino-Stanfa battle. If Mike Rinnier was paying a street tax to the mob, word was that his offering was insufficient and that he or one of his surrogates should expect a visit to address the matter. In fact, this was the case with many suburban bookies throughout the fall of 1993, and one in particular experienced considerable problems.

Jimmy Pirollo was a short, balding, gray-haired figure in his fifties who was known for his easygoing disposition and his professional manner. "One of our local bookmakers and a good friend of ours was a guy named Jimmy Pirollo," Jimmy Battista says. "Everyone loved him because he was one of the most generous guys I ever met in my life." Louie the Lump was among those who benefitted from Pirollo's generosity. "One day," he says, "I was walking around with a puss on my face, and Jimmy asked what was wrong. I told him I was broke. He came back the next day with two brown bags with thirty thousand dollars in cash and said, 'Pay me back when you can.' He was a good guy, Jimmy Pirollo."

Good guy or not, Pirollo was apparently not paying a cent to either Philly mob faction, and received the attention of an extortion crew sent on behalf of John Stanfa. Jack Manfredi, a pest exterminator who also happened to be a mob shakedown artist, visited Pirollo in September of 1993, and told him, "Stanfa sent me up here . . . [and] wants money from every bookmaker in the city and he wants anybody that's doing business in the city to turn it into him, or give him a piece because, you see, the difference between him and the other guys [is that] when he says something he backs it up and he does something." The thirty-five year-old Manfredi also told Pirollo, "I work for somebody just like you do. This business is our business, okay? You're part of that business, you gotta do the right thing. We're not out to hurt you. Everybody's gotta do the right thing." Manfredi, who was also trying to muscle money out of a few other local bookies and the owner of a popular high-end strip club called Delilah's Den at the time, said he wanted three hundred dollars per week from Pirollo. If Pirollo was petrified of Manfredi, it was with good reason. Not long after these exchanges took place, Manfredi was arrested by police investigating another sports bookmaking operation. As police approached Manfredi, he tossed an unregistered gun under a parked car, and later surrendered two other guns. He also had a set of throwing knives on him.

What Jack Manfredi and his mob associates didn't know when they visited Jimmy Pirollo was that the diminutive bookie was wired for sound by the FBI. That criminal case, however, wouldn't be sufficiently developed until the spring of 1994, and not even Mike Rinnier and his colleagues knew of the federal investigation, much less of Pirollo's role.[4] As such, the mob shakedowns continued throughout the fall, and the area's gamblers operated with trepidation. In any illicit business, paranoia is common, as are numerous myths and conspiracy legends, in large part because there is no means to validate most of what is rumored. Whispers of threats, real or imagined, alter all sorts of activities even when there is, in fact, nothing to fear. The numbers of underworld actors who have volunteered information to authorities out of irrational concerns are considerable, and what occurred next in the careers of Rinnier and his crew is a routine exercise among illicit entrepreneurs.

---

[4] Manfredi was indicted along with twenty-three others, including mob boss John Stanfa, in March 1994. Twenty-two teams of FBI agents and local law enforcement officers arrested the gangsters early in the morning hours of March 17th as part of a large federal investigation into extortion, loan-sharking, bookmaking, and murder. Manfredi later admitted to being part of a shakedown crew that collected the street tax on behalf of John Stanfa. Though Manfredi pleaded guilty, he did not cooperate with the government. The large Stanfa racketeering case eventually resulted in twenty-six of twenty-nine defendants pleading guilty or being found guilty at trial. The U.S. government identified the remainder of Manfredi's crew as Sergio Battaglia (convicted), John Casasanto (pleaded guilty), and Herbert Keller (pleaded guilty).

"Jimmy Pirollo was affiliated with Mike Rinnier book-ing and betting, more booking." Battista says. "He was a close friend of ours, and we all worked together. He lived in Glenolden and owned a mom-and-pop bar supply company, and sold things like coasters, napkins, straws, little treats, pretzel sticks, munchies and candies people would put on top of a bar. Stuff like that. That's how he got the nickname The Candyman, because he always had sweets on his truck. But his main thing was booking. He was the only person in Glenolden living in a row home that was driving a brand-new fucking Mercedes. Jimmy P was the greatest!

"He booked anybody and everybody; he didn't care. 'Just give me a yellow pad and a pencil' was his philosophy because he knew back then, before we all got so sophisticated, that no one could win in the long run. Well, Mike Rinnier and Tiger started betting him and beat his brains in, and that's how they became partners." "When I went partners with Mike in the early 90s," Tiger says, "we were betting and booking, and we would bury the bookmakers; we would bet them and bury them. They'd owe us so much money that they'd have to come work for us. So, we'd run their books. We would call them and give them what lines to use. We were using these bookmak-ers to actually get down on the right sides. We manipulated the lines in the market to try and control the way people bet so we would be on the right sides. Jimmy Pirollo was one of those bookmakers that we used."

By the fall of 1993, Pirollo's involvement with Mike Rinnier was a subject of interest for Philly's mobsters. "Jimmy wasn't paying anything to the guys downtown," Battista says, "and they knew Jimmy and Mike were now partners. They came into Jimmy's house and robbed him twice that I know of. One time, they dressed up like cable company guys, came in, duct-taped him up, bitch slapped him, pistol-whipped him, and said, 'You're gonna fucking pay.' They wanted like a fifty dime payment or something, but he just told them he'd take care of it, and they left. He was lucky, because he used to hide bricks of money up in his basement ceiling." With mob events such as these swirling in the air, an otherwise irrelevant local bettor sent everyone hiding for cover on a Saturday morning that December.

Jimmy Pirollo's son, Jay, was a small-time bookmaker whose betting clientele was a far cry from his father's substantial book, and which included a man named Charles "Chuck" Giordano who owed him seventy-five hundred dollars. Giordano had made several appointments to meet with Jay to pay off the debt, but never showed up. Finally, Giordano promised to appear at Pirollo's father's home on December 18th to settle the matter. Unfortunately for Giordano, he also owed another group of bettors around thirty-five hundred dollars and—unlike Jimmy Pirollo—they had the muscle and the apparent motivation to use it to get their money. Three hulking men visited Giordano at midnight on December 17th to make their displeasure regarding the outstanding debt known.

Jimmy Pirollo had another Saturday of booking football action ahead of him on December 18th, but his first stop was Philadelphia International Airport. Jay was heading to the islands for a scheduled vacation and Jimmy was dropping him off. When Jay hugged and kissed his father goodbye, he likely could not have imagined what the day would hold for the admired Glenolden bookmaker. At approximately quarter after eleven that morning, Dave Segich, a friend and colleague of Jimmy Pirollo's, showed up at Pirollo's house to handle that day's bets. Segich, who earned a hundred bucks a day for the task, started setting up a table in the basement betting office when a knock on the door came. Chuck Giordano had finally honored his promise to appear at Pirollo's home. When Jimmy Pirollo opened the door to his home, he didn't recognize Giordano at first. Only when Giordano identified himself as

"Chuck" did Pirollo acknowledge him and bring him inside the home, suggesting he was expecting him for a meeting.

As the men entered the basement, they chatted about Christmas while Pirollo sat behind his desk. Just as Dave Segich reached down into his briefcase for a pen, he heard Pirollo scream "Oh my God!" Giordano had pulled out a nine-millimeter gun and, as Pirollo screamed, shot The Candyman in the face, killing him. Segich was shot next, with the bullet tearing into his face below the nostril and exiting behind an ear. Segich was nevertheless able to use a chair as a shield to get up the stairs and out of the basement and out of the home. He ran through the front yards and bushes of neighbors, bleeding profusely from his face all the while. Segich finally collapsed next to a neighbor's steps and watched anxiously as Giordano fled Pirollo's home, speeding down the street in his Ford Bronco. Concerned neighbors rushed to Segich's side, covering him in a blanket and trying to stem the bleeding.[5] Roughly half an hour after fleeing the Pirollo scene, Giordano paid off the thirty-five-hundred-dollar debt that had been owed to a betting group for several months. It was determined that four thousand dollars was missing from Pirollo's basement following the shooting.

Of course, this level of detail wouldn't be known fact for some time, and for now Jimmy Pirollo's colleagues were about to receive the dire—and chilling—news. "It was late on a Saturday morning and we were in the gambling office betting," Battista says. "The phone rang and someone in the office said that Jimmy Pirollo, The Candyman, got killed. A Pennsylvania state trooper who had arrested us before called Mike from Jimmy's house, and I remember the look on Mike's face when he heard Jimmy got killed. He was really scared. We

---

[5] Though Segich survived, the shooting left his face scarred. Giordano, despite claiming he shot Pirollo and Segich in self-defense and denying he stole from the bookie, was convicted of first-degree murder, robbery, and related charges and sentenced to life in prison.

already knew about the war Merlino and Stanfa and all those guys were having. Well, they were also trying to shakedown all the bookmakers from Delaware County. We immediately thought it was the mob that did it. Mike was panicking because he thought they would be coming after him next. They had already warned Mike about not paying the protection tax, and they sort of knew we were destroying their books.

"I was in the middle of getting a rundown, and Mike said, 'Sheep, come here. I need you to go over to Candy's house. He got shot and was killed.' He sent me over to Jimmy's house to get a feel for things. I *wanted* to go because I felt so bad; he was a good friend of mine. I knew him for about five years and we did a lot of stuff together. I saw all the police there, and them taking the body out. It was a sin. We were trying to find out the basics of what it was." It wasn't long before Battista and Rinnier were hearing more about the recent extortion threats. "We all thought, 'Oh my God, it's the mob. They went in and fucking killed him.' They were there just a few weeks before shaking him down." To make the organized crime paranoia more gripping, the alleged shooter was named Chuck Giordano. When Rinnier's crowd heard the killer's name ended in a vowel, it confirmed for them their worst fears of a mob hit. "It freaked us all out," Tiger says. "*Giordano*?! We were thinking, 'Alright, we're all gonna get killed.'"

"Because Mike thought the boys from downtown were after him, he asked me to move in with him and protect his family," Battista says. "At the time, I didn't have a gun or a permit, but I started carrying guns to protect Mike and his family." "When Jimmy Pirollo got murdered," Tiger says, "they thought it was a mob hit and the next thing you know Baba was walking around with a shotgun under a trench coat! Baba was Mike's right-hand man at the time, and was in Mike's house with another guy, just sitting in his living room with shotguns because we thought it was the mob. Baba was with him everywhere he went. When Mike would go down the casinos, he would rent, like, five limos and it was like a caravan so no one would know which one Mike was in. It was like a shell game going down the Atlantic City Expressway because there were rumors Mike was going to get kidnapped and stuff like that. At the time, which we later realized was just a coincidence, the dagos from downtown were shaking Mike Rinnier and Jimmy Pirollo and all those guys down. I didn't even know because I wasn't in that part of the organization. I was just the gambling part, and we were betting our asses off. We were pretty secluded from the outside world. We didn't even know how bad they were getting shaken down. Well, they were getting shaken down pretty fucking bad."

Sheep and Tiger were immersed in a subculture that included many undesirable characters. The relatively humdrum, straight-shooting pro gamblers and their crowd thus had immense appreciation and respect for a class act like The Candyman. Indeed, Tiger still pauses when he thinks about Jimmy Pirollo, and says, "He was a really good guy. God, what a great fucking guy. The first time I met Jimmy, he was driving a red Corvette. He lived in the nicest row home on the fucking planet. The neighborhood wasn't the greatest but the place was real nice inside. The basement was the betting office. The only thing noteworthy about his betting office was that he took bets out of a desk and he had a drawer with a pile of hundreds in it. He would be like, "Oh, I owe you ten grand. Hold on a minute. He'd take out like sixty grand, and pull ten out and put the fifty back in the drawer. That was stupid, and that's what got him killed. Somebody saw that and wanted that money."

As someone with particularly keen insight, Battista offers his reflections on Pirollo's slaying. "Jimmy's son had a reputation for being a degenerate gambler who was booking people on his own," Battista says. "He had some kid who owed him money, and he was supposedly threatening to sic some guys on him if the kid didn't pay up. We heard that Jimmy's kid was saying, 'My dad is going to come after you. You don't know who my father is, blah, blah, blah," shooting off his mouth, where his father was actually the nicest guy in the world. Jimmy Pirollo wouldn't shake down anyone. He'd say, 'When you get the money, you pay me.' But, his kid was apparently trying to make a name for himself being a tough guy. Well, that, in essence, got his father killed. The kid who owed the money went over Jimmy's house, and instead of paying him went over and shot him. Among our crowd, Jimmy's kid was just a fucking asshole, and most of us looked at it like he got his father killed." The area's gamblers were none too fond of Pirollo's son, even before the slaying.[6] "I didn't like Jimmy's kid that much," one says. "He took advantage of Jimmy, I thought." Never one to hold back, Louie the Lump is a bit more emphatic and cutting when he says, "Jimmy's kid wouldn't make a pimple on his father's ass. He was a jerkoff. Jimmy didn't deserve him."

* * *

The Pirollo slaying only aggravated the preexisting and omnipresent fear suburban gamblers had of the Philly mob, and until things calmed down Mike Rinnier employed a host of tactics to ensure his safety—and the viability of his organization. According to those close to him, this meant somehow ingratiating himself with law enforcement authorities and local political figures. It is unclear what, if any, political protection Rinnier enjoyed and how he benefitted from this or from his supposed role as an informer.

"In time, the Pennsylvania State Police helped him hook up a monitoring system for him because they knew the mob

---

[6] Though certainly not fans of Jay, area gamblers like Battista nevertheless felt awful for him because of how close Jay was to his father.

was after him," Battista says, "but Mike still kept me close at his side. Guarding Mike and his family became the way I paid back the thirty-eight thousand I lost out in Vegas playing cards; Mike paid off my debt. I was working all day in the supermarket, and gambling all night in the office for Tiger and Mike. I was making pretty good money—putting all the money I made at the supermarket in the bank, and living off the cash from the gambling. I lived a pretty good life. Around this time, I met a girl named Denise who was going through the beginning stages of a divorce. She was just a beautiful, sweet woman. She was a bartender at Club Manhattan, one of the places I used to stop in when we were done gambling. I used to stop in on Tuesday nights, which were 'Country and Western' nights, and she would be bartending. This was one of the clubs Mike owned, and he soon asked me to start bartending there. Well, Denise and I became friends and then started dating after hours, but she was going through a divorce and had two little kids. Mike got mad at me and was like, 'What are you doing? This girl's still married.' So, he said, 'We're sending you out to Vegas. Ya know, you can't be fucking up someone's life.' I said, 'Listen. If they're gonna get divorced, they're gonna get divorced.' So, I went back out to Vegas, stayed out for the whole football season, but she and I still kept in contact. She used to call me from the bar when her shift was done. I came back from Vegas right after the Final Four. Right when I came back, Mike and Tiger were ready to split.

"Over the next year, I split from Mike to work for Tiger. The two of them were still sharing the betting office, but they were working out the parameters of who was going to have who and what. I started working for a seafood company driving a truck. I was running seafood for them, but my thing was to be booking and betting still and just using their trucks and phones. I'd ship seafood during the day and work in the betting office at night. Denise and I were getting close, but one day I told her, 'We've got to stop this, because people are getting pissed.' Soon she left her husband, and asked me if I wanted to get married after she was formally divorced. We moved in together, and rented a house in Havertown. I was working with Tiger a lot, and I started working with a guy who worked under him named Bull. He was built like a Bull—stocky, no neck. Now, Tiger was the boss and Bull and I were his two clerks. Bull and I became really close friends, we spent so much time together. When you're sitting next to a guy that's two hundred and eighty pounds and likes to eat cheesesteaks and hoagies just as much as you do, and you're farting on each other and gambling all day long, you develop a relationship!

"Mike and Tiger were through, and Tiger wasn't paying anybody a street tax even though there was still this mob war on the street for who was going to control everything.[7] We were betting full force with Tiger, and a really sharp guy that worked with Mike named Seal decided to come with us. He was actually shaped like a seal. He had the small head with the awkward body shape of a seal. He had had enough with Mike because he knew Mike couldn't pick winners. Well, Seal's deal was based on a percentage of Mike's winners. Tiger was a proven winner and used more math and fundamentals in his gambling. Now Tiger was the boss, and it was Tiger, Sheep, Bull, and Seal. Some people started calling us 'The Animals' and the name stuck."

---

[7] Regarding why he split with Mike Rinnier, Tiger says, "There were a lot of reasons Mike and I parted ways, mostly over serious business matters. The easiest way to explain it is that I was a numbers guy, and Mike was a people guy. He never really understood what I was doing, in part because he was so consumed by his other business interests which distracted him from the betting office, that his business model couldn't survive as people like me, Joe Vito, and especially big-time guys like The Computer, got sharper and sharper. Deep down Mike was a good guy, even though he was a ruthless businessman. He was the one who taught me a lot of what I used for the next twenty years, like paying taxes on your gambling. That saved me, because we got raided a few times over the years and the authorities realized I always paid taxes."

The Tiger-led Animals also altered their operation and were exclusively professional bettors for the rest of their careers. "By now," Battista says, "the police and the feds knew all about us, *and* the Philly mob was still trying to get into us, so we started to get away from booking to focus more on betting. We wanted to have a better lifestyle and not deal with all the hassles from bookmaking. We knew that law enforcement fucked with bookmakers but they didn't really fuck with gamblers. Since we had each been arrested a couple of times, we figured it was a good move to just bet. Besides, we were sharp enough by then that we could make good money betting without booking. It was also nice not having to try and beg people to pay off their bets and stuff like that. You always had so many customers who owed you money when you were booking. A guy would owe you 'X' amount of dollars, but he only made 'Y' amount of dollars and he had a house, car, wife, kids. We got stiffed a lot, like most bookmakers, so we were pretty confident we could make as much betting.

"Seal was doing the baseball, and Tiger was doing the pro football. College football we could never pick anything good. Seal got us hooked up with a guy named Dinky, a Jewish friend of his who got us piped into some sharp guys for betting baseball—a really famous card player, and The Kosher Kids. The Kosher Kids were Jewish guys out of New York, and they were *the* best in baseball. We got hooked into them, and they asked us to move games. We were another out for them, using our markets. We would be handicapping baseball, moving baseball, and we were stronger than ever. We were dictating the numbers, and The Koshers were just fucking destroying people. They wouldn't let anyone know what they were doing, and they'd bet all 'dogs.' They had inside information and knew the numbers. They'd work six or seven weeks, take millions out of the market, and then just quit and walk away. Our deal with them gave us a healthy living, but we had to keep moving from place to place because more and more people knew what we were doing."

As Battista and his Animal pals saw their stature rise, they were absolutely convinced Mike Rinnier would stop at nothing to exact his revenge for pushing him out of the area's gambling hierarchy, where he had resided for years. According to Battista, their suspicions were realized not long after the acrimonious split. "In the mid 1990s," he says, "we were about a month into baseball season, and the police came in with sledgehammers, broke down the door, and we got busted.[8] They had been following me, Tiger, and some other guys. We later heard that Mike Rinnier was an informant and had given us up. We thought something was up because the next day we met with him and all of the people he dealt with had been arrested, *but not Mike*. We were fucked; they had our computers and everything. Within two days, me and Tiger got into his Ford Explorer and took off for Vegas. We didn't know what was going to happen back home, but we couldn't miss baseball season."[9]

Jimmy Battista had just married Denise, and now had two little kids to take care of and provide for—all from a distance.[10] The heat-of-the-moment Vegas relocation and the ensuing increase in stature within the betting world assured The Sheep some interesting times as he continued his rise to the sports gambling summit.

---

[8] Tiger offers some comical insights into such police activities when he says, "When you're in the gambling office and you hear the wood cracking on the door, you are hoping it's the police! They don't knock, and you are praying it's the cops. You are *fucking scared shitless*! That is just an awful feeling."

[9] Battista ultimately received ARD and was sentenced to probation and community service (not unlike the outcomes for his other skirmishes with the law relating to his gambling activities).

[10] As a sign of things to come, Jimmy Battista worked the afternoon shift on his wedding day. "Denise and I got married on a Thursday morning in Elkton, Maryland, which was about forty-five minutes away. We came back and I got changed to go to the gambling office to work the afternoon shift at three o'clock because there was college football that night. After I got off work at eight, we had a big party to celebrate our marriage."

7

Go West, Black Sheep

THE TRYING COMBINATION of Mike Rinnier's vindictive actions, related law enforcement heat, and Philly mob extortion prodded The Animals to relocate in Las Vegas. "We feared what Mike Rinnier had done to us," Battista says. "You also had the war on the streets between Stanfa and Merlino. They were beating up and shaking down bookmakers and bettors, and making everybody pay street tax. It was nuts. So, because of all of that, we went out to Vegas." Though Seal opted to stay with Rinnier in the Philly suburbs, his loyalties remained with his Animal pals and the men afforded each other various betting-related services—all without Rinnier's knowledge.

In Las Vegas, they operated out of, and lived in, a large five-bedroom house not far from The Strip. The gambling office was located downstairs in the living room, where there were a bunch of desks and phones. The room also housed fifteen TVs, which were connected to the various satellites being used to exploit different sports packages. The Vegas office, which afforded them vital, comprehensive and real-time information, was representative of the several betting locations The Animals would utilize in the coming years.[1] Typically, there

---

[1] While Tiger and Sheep were in Las Vegas, they were visited by a mutual friend who expected to go out and party all night in Sin City. After all, he knew his pals were among the most consequential bettors in town and figured they'd be up for showing him around what he considered "their" town. The friend was dismayed to find that Tiger hadn't been down to The Strip in six months—despite living within walking

were at least two offices in operation at the same time, with
one in Philadelphia and one in Sin City.

"We chose to work in Philly because booking was just
a misdemeanor and they didn't really care," Battista says.
"In Delaware County, bookmaking was a big deal, whereas
in Philly you'd get a slap on the wrist. We weren't actually
bookmaking then; we were only betting, but our reputation
was booking and I'm sure the police would have assumed we
were booking." The Animals worked in various offices in the
city's revitalized, yuppie Manayunk section in the late 1990s.
Battista's favorite was in The Mill Studios, where artists had
dozens of studios to paint and sculpt, no doubt unaware of
the illicit and often immature operations going on beneath
them. "It was just me, Tiger, and Bull in an office with a TV,
computers, and a bathroom," Battista says. "The bottom of
The Mill had a real dusty basement, with great open space.
The owner had it all partitioned, and we had an office down
there. You had to go down twenty-five steps and through two
locked doors to get down to our office, and no one even knew
we were down there. We had a great setup. We had a kitchen
area, sofas, a treadmill. Plus, you could yell, scream, fuck
around. We used to say you could kill somebody down there
and nobody would know. If there was a fire in the building,
we would never have known! The only problem was that there
were no windows and you never knew what time it was. It
was also tough in winter because you'd either freeze or cook
like a steak. There was no heat, and when the furnace for the
building would kick on the flames would shoot out at us. Those
were some crazy times. We did well there, though. We were
winning in that basement and didn't want to fuck with the
gambling gods by moving. Baseball was good and we had a

---

distance, and that these gamblers lived amidst pizza boxes and fast-food wrappers in
an around-the-clock betting office. His hopes of partying it up big-time were dashed,
and he wound up seeing the sights by himself. Such was the life of this cast of pro
gamblers in Las Vegas.

great NFL preseason. We worked there straight through the NFL season." To make matters even better for the food-loving Animals, there was a Greek restaurant right across the street. "We would just sit in that basement and eat greasy Greek food all day and night. We had so much fun—three guys in an office eating, burping, farting, playing cards, and betting," Battista says. "Running a gambling office and controlling the numbers while staying under the radar was incredible."

Staying under the radar would be a key to The Animals' success and longevity. Ever aware that their activities were always in danger of being discovered by competitors, hustlers, mobsters, and law enforcement officials—each of whom had their own motivations to target The Animals' betting operation, office locations were changed every so often as a routine course of business. "We tried to be careful with everything, moving offices every so often and not trusting other people to help us," Battista says. "It was a pain in the ass, but it was all worth it. When we broke from Mike Rinnier, we lost his political protection. Even though it was better in Philly as far as police goes, we had to make sure nobody knew we were there so that the 'boys downtown' wouldn't bother us." Out of necessity, to capitalize on time-sensitive matters, each of the pro gamblers also had to work out of their homes on occasion. This was kept to a minimum, though, because, as Battista says, "We all had kids and didn't want to bring the heat on our homes and families."

By the late 1990s, The Animals were well established in the big-time sports betting world, and had a sound business model, complete with a betting schedule, risk assessments (within betting decisions and vis-à-vis law enforcement matters), profit margin analyses, and most especially a clearly defined division of labor with Tiger at the helm. "We'd bet preseason and regular season NFL, college football, and pro baseball," Battista says. "Football was our thing, and we'd pay attention to what the Koshers and the Poker Players did," so that their baseball wagers could be mimicked. "At the end of every football season in February, we'd go through the company's business expenses and pay everyone their share. We considered baseball season the start of the new betting year, like a warmup for the real season: pro football. We used to always look at baseball season as grinding pennies. The pennies added up, a few thousand a week, and hopefully by the All-Star break, we'd have a nice bankroll to keep going. We always hoped to have a nice amount of money built up before preseason football got started." Because they didn't bet basketball at the time, The Animals very much looked forward to the break between the Super Bowl in late January and the start of baseball season in early April. It was essentially the only time each year they could spend with family without being affected by the hyperactive and demanding sports betting business.

Battista proudly explains that the foundation for their success was laid immediately following their split with Mike Rinnier, and it required rational, sober decision making and an ability to defer to others. "Believe it or not, we never really argued with each other. Tiger knew pro football like nobody else. Bull dealt with college football totals. I knew all the outs and knew how to get and move the money. Everyone had their niche. There were no egos. We only cared about dollar signs, and that meant accepting what each person did well and letting them do it. The only real debates were over who we should be dealing or betting with, because some people didn't pay well or didn't give us good deals.

"The thing that separates people from being successful or not is that sometimes you just have to sit and listen. You have to look at people as dollar signs. If someone knows more than you, or has better connections than you, accept it and figure out a way to make that work for you. The key to being above everybody else was sitting back and taking everything in. I have seen so many people in that business who thought they knew everything. Meanwhile, people like me would be saying, 'You're a fucking idiot. You don't know what you're doing. And, you're done.' They'd be bragging about all sorts of shit and they'd be dead fucking broke and out of the industry in months."

The arrangement with his partners suited Battista well, allowing him to exploit his considerable talents, offering him a great income, and affording him much-desired anonymity. "One of the things I liked about Mike Rinnier is that most people didn't know how much shit he was doing with booking and betting," Battista says. "I wanted the same thing. I wanted nobody to really know everything I was doing with gambling, but I wanted all the things that went along with being a big-time gambler." Included among "the things that went along with being a big-time gambler" for Battista was exploiting inside sports betting information.

"When I used to work for Mike," Battista says, "there was a college coach he was friends with who would give us what we called our 'Big East Game of the Week.' We'd give him the point spread on a game to pick once a week, and he'd tell us who he liked, taking into account the spread. He had such incredible insight on stuff we couldn't have known. That was the first time I knew inside information was being transferred between parties. You always heard stories, but I thought a lot of that was bullshit. I started realizing that there was *so much* inside information being traded. We had a bookmaker friend of ours who had a college basketball ref that bet games with him. One time, the bookmaker called and asked us if we could get three hundred thousand down for him on Georgetown plus-seven because the ref was on the take. No matter how good you are with numbers, you're not going to win more than fifty-five to fifty-eight percent without inside information.

"Sportswriters—journalists—are really the key. There are so many variables into a team that guys like journalists who are around the team can help a bettor understand. It could be the mood of a team, and whether or not they are tanking the season late in the year because they're already out of the playoffs. It could also be access to a team trainer, who is giving more detailed information than the public has. The reporters look like they're gathering information for stories, but some of that stuff is being transmitted to big-time bettors. I used to deal with a guy who used to routinely get into a certain locker room all the time, and let me know what was going on with that team. He was in there on a day-to-day basis, and the information was incredible."

A bookmaker or bettor might pay a reporter in cash for his services, but they are most commonly paid in bets or excused from prior betting losses. Battista developed relationships with reporters and with trainers, expressly to groom them as inside sources. The Sheep offers a tidy example of how these shenanigans manifest in betting circles. It involves a Philadelphia Eagles game in which star running back Brian Westbrook's injury status was not known until just before kickoff. "He was questionable but we got a call out of the locker room before anyone else that he wasn't playing," Battista says. "The Eagles were favored by ten points, and the over/under was something like fifty-two. Well, Westbrook being out of the offense was a big deal. The total moved like six points. We bet the dog and buried the under. The under hit and the dog covered."

The inside information didn't have to come directly to Battista or his partners for them to benefit. The Animals often knew who among the world's bettors possessed such knowledge and piggybacked bets accordingly. "We were trying to pick everyone's pocket," Battista says. "The Poker Players were picking sixty to sixty-five percent in baseball. We knew they had inside information, and these guys were con men at their best. They weren't just conning people at the poker table. Those guys had bundles in their pockets and friends everywhere. If they bet a baseball game, there was a reason why. We found out later that they also had handicappers working for them, but their success had a lot to do with the inside information they were getting. They contacted us to move games for them because they heard we were dependable, our money was good, and we worked every day. They were Southern guys and we developed a good relationship with them. We moved their baseball games for a few seasons, and they were monsters, just like they were at the poker table.

"We also moved baseball games for a guy named Doc Johnson, who was The Computer's handicapper back in the 1980s. During football season, Doc would have his 'Big Ten Game of the Year' and the line would move like six or seven points, because he had inside information. If the quarterback was out the night before a game, or if he had gotten in a fight, Doc fucking knew. Some of the things he knew were ridiculous."

Notwithstanding their access to inside information and the betting successes that resulted from it, The Animals were still just below the premier echelon of sports bettors. That realm consisted of just a handful of sharps, headlined by The Computer, who did all he could to keep the competition down. "Once we got established, people started following us and jumping on our games. Well, we would use that to our advantage," most commonly to manipulate betting lines to suit their wagers, Battista says. "Meanwhile, as we were doing that, The Computer was putting ten times as much as we were into the market to put us on Queer Street. We were young and aggressive, and he would use that against us. He had better information than we did, had more money, and more people working for him. If he wanted to manipulate the lines and get us on the wrong side, he could." That is, unless The Animals were really confident in what they were doing and thus would not be influenced by the line moves dictated by The Computer. "We didn't find out until years later just how influential he was, and how much he was fucking with people like us," Battista says.

Sheep, Tiger, and Bull were rising in stature, and their number of outs grew significantly. More importantly, they were increasingly finding and exploiting bookies who would take ever larger bets. A great example of a major out for them was a New York–based bookie named Bluto. "He was a loud, obnoxious, arrogant motherfucker, who told it like it was," Battista says. "I loved the guy. He was a great bookmaker. If he spoke, people jumped. He knew we had people behind us who would stand for the money if we lost, and he would let us get twenty thousand on baseball games. We developed a relationship with him and pretty soon he let us get fifty thousand a game. We heard rumors that he might be connected to the Gambinos up in New York, so we would only meet up with him in Atlantic City or in Las Vegas. We didn't want to get involved with any wiseguy nonsense up in New York. We were just gamblers—short, fat, bald gamblers, family guys with kids in the backs of our minivans with buckets of sand from the shore! We bet with him until he got pinched, when his clerk ratted him out. He went to prison for a few years, and was out of commission. We had to move onto other people like him. The thing was, anyone could bet the big places online. We did that, too, but we wanted to find big books in the U.S. who had deep pockets that we could take on."

Battista liked it when serious online/offshore betting took off because he no longer had to spend the time getting rundowns. A simple check of lines on the computer ended the hassle of numerous tedious phone calls, even though the actual bets in the early days were still placed by phone. "We were using a bunch of offshore places, and there was a big sportsbook in England that we absolutely destroyed. They didn't think we were sharp at all and they'd let us bet again and again," Battista says. "They didn't respect us, and wouldn't even move a number when we bet it. We had so many accounts with them, and we'd nickel and dime them. It was great because we could get good money down without affecting the lines in Vegas or offshore. After we took them for a few hundred thousand, they finally realized who we were." According to Battista, when it came to wagering with offshore sites, "The betting was the easy part. Getting paid was the problem, because of the illegality of everything. You had to develop relationships with the right people in the United States to be able to get the money back from offshore. Moving the money became so important. There was someone whose nickname was 'Little Guy' who drove for UPS during the daytime but was the money man for the East Coast. He got paid a thousand dollars a trip to move money, and would do eight or nine trips a week. He was good, carried a piece, and you could trust him."

In addition to the more consequential online sites and the volume of local bookmaking outs throughout the U.S., the traditional Las Vegas market remained. Regardless of where they were living or working, The Animals employed a cadre of full-time runners to get down as much money as possible in Vegas casinos. "Some runners got paid a salary and others got paid on volume. They usually got paid twice a year—at the Super Bowl and during the All-Star break in baseball," Battista says. "There were so many variations. Runners just had to cut the best deal they could with the bettor or the mover. The problem with using runners was that you really had to stay on top of them. They'd fuck up the bets, take the wrong teams, get the wrong numbers, and you had to cover the losses. You'd have to worry about them stealing, selling your information, worry about them getting robbed." As for who was recruited for this fairly important part of a major betting syndicate, Battista says, "Runners could have been anybody. We had drop-outs, retirees, people with all sorts of backgrounds. Ideally, you'd have people sent to you from family and friends, so you could trust them. We'd shuffle them around from casino to casino so that they wouldn't draw attention to themselves in the same day. The next day, they'd be stationed somewhere else. The key was always keeping them running."[2]

Though the betting operation was in high gear and more profitable than they ever expected, the traveling back and forth between Las Vegas and Delaware County got to be too much after a few years. For the three men who each had wives and little kids back home, the profits gained by being physically present in Vegas didn't offset the travel hassles and time away from family. The Animals returned to the East Coast for good, though they retained a presence in Vegas with their group of runners.

By this point, the immaturity and brashness that characterized a good portion of Battista's early gambling career was long gone, replaced by a more serious and inward-disposed persona. "Mostly, I stayed out of the limelight," he says. "I didn't want to be known for anything. I wanted to be Plain Jane and fit in; the 'family guy.' Because after my years of living the life, I wanted to be able to gamble without anyone knowing what I was doing. The more I did that, the better my life was. I was an 'everyday' father and husband, and could still control the numbers gambling. That was the greatest high in my life. I didn't

---

[2] Regarding the issue of runners carrying such large amounts of cash around Las Vegas, Tiger says, "In some casinos they had lock boxes, so the runners were always told not to go home or come back to the office with the money. They were just supposed to leave the cash, chips, and tickets in the boxes. As for taking money from the office or someplace to the casinos, which really only happens at the beginning of a betting season, I would tell my runners, 'Always pay the "dollar." There's always somebody willing to park your car for a "dollar." Valet park, and you alleviate the only way you're going to have trouble, which is being carjacked on the streets away from the casinos. Once you're out running from casino to casino, there is really no worry because there's security, police, and cameras everywhere.' Tourists were walking past runners who were carrying hundreds of thousands of dollars on them all the time, but they just didn't know it."

have to be twenty-one again." Though The Sheep's partying days were long over, and although he was physically present more than he had been in years, his ridiculous work schedule still caused grief at home. Battista rarely had time for his wife and kids, even during otherwise routine gatherings and celebrations. This was particularly the case during the Thanksgiving and Christmas holiday seasons, when college and pro football were in full swing. "Those holidays were tough. I brought stress into the picture because I was always working," Battista says. "I'd bring my laptop everywhere. We couldn't eat until after the fucking game kicked at four o'clock on Thanksgiving! It was always an argument, "Why can't we eat before then?!'"

If Battista's family matters at home were taxing, the ties to his parents were even more strained. "My relationship with my parents wasn't super tight because they always knew I had something going on," he says. "They were always unsure of what I was going to do next, because it was never like, 'Hey, mom, I got a job here!' at some legitimate place. I thought it would be best if I didn't tell her what I was doing as I got older. My mom didn't like the choices I made. She didn't like my chosen lifestyle. She wanted me to finish college. She didn't like the restaurant business, because she knew that was another world. She also didn't like that I was involved with gambling. She never understood why I couldn't just work a normal job. She was very bothered by what I was doing. If friends would ask about what I did for a living, she would say, 'I don't know what he does' or 'He works in the restaurant business.' She was also very religious and I wasn't. There was one time where I was asked to be the godfather to one of my nephews and I had to get papers from the Catholic Church. At that point, though, my first marriage wasn't annulled. The priest told me that if I paid the parish fifteen hundred dollars, they'd let me be the godfather. I told the priest, 'I can get a cheaper deal from the boys downtown! This is extortion!' I figured I'd give them two to three hundred dollars, give the altar boy ten bucks for doing the service, and make everyone happy. My mom was upset and couldn't believe the way I spoke to the priest and the way I handled myself. She knew, though, that I always speak my mind."

As he grappled with his myriad family matters, Battista had work-related concerns to address. "Life was good, but we were always on the run," he says. "You never knew what was going to happen. You always had to worry about the idiots downtown coming out to shake you down. Then you had the police and the FBI always looking for people like you. And then you had all the squares trying to find out what you're doing. So, you were constantly on guard to remain low-profile, work hard, and get in and get out of whatever you were doing. It wasn't fear, really, it was just that you never had time to rest. And, you always had to deal with stiffs. At the end of the 2001 football season, a big guy at a major online sportsbook stiffed us for eight hundred and eighty thousand dollars. To make it worse, we had a hundred thousand on the Patriots in the Super Bowl with him.[3] I can remember being out in Vegas sitting in the Bellagio waiting to meet the guy, and he never showed. I kept calling his cell phone, and when he wasn't answering I kept hoping he was in a car accident or had some other emergency, because otherwise I knew we were getting fucked. It turned out the sportsbook fucked a lot of people, and owed a total of something like thirteen million dollars, including seven million to The Computer. They just took the money and ran. Shit like that happened every few years. It was the nature of the business. Nobody ever figured out whether they just took the money and ran or if they just didn't know what the fuck they were doing. There were some years we didn't get stiffed,

---

[3] The New England Patriots, who were two-touchdown underdogs, beat the St. Louis Rams 20-17, and thus Battista et al. would have won their Pats-plus-fourteen bet, aggravating the theft.

but on average you expected to get burned for a few hundred thousand one way or another."

One way pro gamblers like The Animals offset such predictable and expected losses is by simultaneously entertaining more traditional business ventures. In Battista's case, this typically meant being involved with nightclubs and restaurants, like Marina's, a sports bar that was located in Havertown, PA. "I was approached in the late '90s to manage Marina's because I had a background with restaurants," he says. "I liked it because people knew I was a gambler, and now I had something that looked more legitimate. I could run the place and still gamble, but it meant really long days starting with prepping everything in the restaurant early each morning. I'd be down there by nine or ten in the morning, and wouldn't get home until around midnight. I would stop into the betting office off and on during the day. Marina's opened around St. Patrick's Day, which was good because I didn't bet basketball that year and could spend the time between the Super Bowl and baseball season working on getting Marina's ready."

The Marina's gambit also allowed for an experience that captured The Sheep's multi-faceted persona. During the 2001-02 Eagles season, Battista often listened to 610AM WIP sports radio when he was in the kitchen overseeing things. One day, he says, co-hosts Mike Missanelli and Howard Eskin "were talking about what the Eagles record for the last five games of the season would be. Well, I called in as 'Jim from Havertown' and bet them the Eagles would close out stronger than they expected. If they won the bet, my restaurant, Marina's, would cater an event for WIP up to a thousand dollars. If I won the bet, they would have to come and work for me at a benefit I was organizing for the family of Timmy Soulas. Timmy Soulas and I played rugby together in high school, and he was one of the people killed in the September 11th World Trade Center terrorist attacks a few months prior. I was trying to raise money for his wife, who had five kids and another one on the way. I had five kids and I knew what she must have been going through, and all of us were devastated. So, if I won the bet, Eskin and Missanelli would have to bartend at Marina's during the Soulas benefit. Our bet came down to the Eagles' last game of the season against Tampa Bay. Tampa Bay was favored by three. If the Eagles won, Howard and Mike would have to come work for me at Marina's. At the same time, though, the guys I was moving for were on Tampa Bay, and had Tampa minus two, two-and-a-half, and a little three, for something like twenty thousand dollars total. I didn't know which side I wanted to win more. The Eagles won in the last few minutes of the game, so I lost the bets with my guys on Tampa, but won the bet with Eskin and Missanelli. They honored the bet, and we wound up raising a few thousand dollars for the Soulas family, which was nice.[4] Howard and Mike had no idea who 'Jim from Havertown' was, and even when we got together, I don't think they knew what I did for a living or who I was connected to."

After about four years, Battista's venture with Marina's came to a necessary end. "It was just too much on me," he says. "It was forty-five minutes away from my house and between that and the twelve-hour-plus workdays, I was never home. It also wasn't worth it because by then I realized how much more money there was to be made gambling full-time." And this was before an offer was made to Battista that he and his Animal pals simply couldn't refuse.

---

[4] WIP co-hosts Howard Eskin and Mike Missanelli honored their bet by working the bar at Marina's on February 28, 2002. Battista, an avid sports fan and listener of talk radio, got a kick out of meeting Eskin, then and still one of Philadelphia's most controversial commentators. "Even though Howard comes off as a jerkoff on the radio, he has a good heart. He cared about helping people. He reminded me of Tommy Martino, though, because he was in love with himself and how he looked. I don't think there were enough mirrors in his Lexus for him." Contacted in March 2010, Mike Missanelli says he doesn't recall the event or meeting Battista, and thus never realized throughout the more than two years of NBA scandal coverage that he had actually bartended alongside the scheme's architect.

8

Shady People in Sunny Places

WHEN THE NFL season ended in February of 2003, The Animals couldn't believe how poorly the past five months had gone. "It was our worst football season ever," Battista says. "Normally we'd be up a few balloons, but we weren't close to that." Their fortunes were about to change, however, if they were willing to take a chance—and a journey. Battista received a phone call from a colleague who suggested The Sheep should meet with a guy in New York named Ronnie Park who was known for taking bets of more than a hundred grand. Park was a bookmaker who supposedly got his start working with the Kosher Kids, and who had big clients. "He was about ten years or twelve years older than me and was a sensational salesman," Battista says. "He was given a lot of money by members of his family and used this as upfront money for a third of his bookmaking business. So, I went up there to meet with Ronnie and he said, 'I hear a lot about you guys, and want to know if you'd be willing to move some stuff for me.' We were interested because it would generate exposure and create revenue. Ronnie told me that he was going to open an offshore sportsbook and wanted to know if we would help him run it. He knew we had booked before and that we were doing well betting by that point."

A follow-up meeting was set for a month later for this fairly consequential negotiation, to be held at a McDonald's of all places. "Tiger and I were sitting there in the McDonald's waiting to meet with him, and a limo showed up with a driver," Battista says. "The driver opened up his door and let him out, and we were already thinking, 'Okay, this guy's a fucking idiot.' When we finally got down to business, Ronnie was a smooth talker. He offered us salaries, a percentage of his whole operation, and would cover the expenses of us traveling back and forth and things like that." It all sounded great, but The Animals had families to consider. "We always wanted to go back to the islands, because we saw what we could have done before and we didn't exploit it," Battista says. "The only reason we didn't was because we all had kids. It was tough saying, 'Honey, here's the money, so pay the bills, change the diapers, cook dinner, and walk the dog. I'll be in Curacao for a few months!'"

Even though the betting crew had families to think about, the offer was appealing because they still lived in fear of the FBI, the Pennsylvania State Police (who were far more willing to go after gamblers than were Philly cops), and of Philly mobsters. The Animals eventually agreed they should pursue Ronnie's offer.[1] "We made the deal, and the plan was for me to go down a couple of weeks before Tiger and Bull," Battista says. "The goal was to be up and running for baseball season."

When Battista arrived in Curacao, he was picked up at the airport by Ronnie and his driver, who whisked him off to the lavish Floris Suite Hotel, where he'd be staying. Park was staying at another plush beachfront hotel nearby which was right next to Paramount Sports.[2] "Ronnie had a

---

[1] Technically, Ronnie Park cut distinct deals with each Animal, and Battista doesn't pretend to know the particulars of the other offers.

[2] "Paramount Sports" is a pseudonym for what is likely the world's most consequential offshore sportsbook. Paramount typically takes the largest bets and has considerable influence in adjusting the world's betting lines, in large part because it is widely acknowledged that the top sharps wager with Paramount most frequently. "Paramount's line was the bible of the gambling industry," says Battista. "They paid almost no attention to the other lines. They didn't care. If you were going to move their line, you were betting serious money. They also knew, though, that the sharp guys might invest a few hundred thousand to put people on Queer Street and to move the lines."

bungalow right on the beach," Battista says. "The Floris was gorgeous, and had this really prominent clientele. It was all too good to be true. I was going to be staying there for the first six weeks as we got everything started up. Even before Ronnie and I got started opening up his online sportsbook, All-Star Sports, I realized how important it was going to be for Tiger and Bull to get down to Curacao.[3] There was so much shit going on there at that time with other offshore books, and we had no idea."

Ronnie Park already had a staff working on getting the office and computers set up, and it was going to be Battista's job to develop customers. Though that would eventually occur as planned, it was immediately sidetracked when the computer system was activated. "As soon as we turned the computers on, we started gambling," Battista says. "Even though we were supposed to be working on developing the business, we couldn't see the numbers without booking and gambling ourselves!"

At that time in the development of offshore gaming, bettors in the U.S. still had to phone in their bets, even though they could now track betting information online. The Animals were about to benefit in ways they could never have imagined simply by monitoring the phone calls pouring into the new sportsbook, and their rise to the betting summit would be all but complete. "I was the one in charge of the phones," Battista says. "As soon as I listened to the phones and I realized who was calling us down there, I called Tiger and Bull and said, 'You guys gotta get down here right away.' I knew practically all the guys calling to place bets with Ronnie's new offshore book, and they were some of the world's sharpest bettors. These were people we had heard about but who would never do business with us. Now, we were receiving their bets! It was unbelievable. They were calling Ronnie to place bets, move games, everything. There was no way we could wait

---

[3] The offshore sportsbook name "All-Star Sports" is a pseudonym.

for Tiger and Bull to join me like we originally planned. If *I* was foaming at the mouth, I knew they would go fucking crazy when they saw and heard what was going on. Instead of coming down in a few weeks, they came down a couple of days after I called them. They got set up in the same hotel as me, and we were ready to go. The first day I brought them into the office, we each sat at different desks. I had them pick up phones to listen to the calls coming in. We were all just looking at each other listening silently to these sharps and their movers calling down to Ronnie's new book. Tiger just stared at me across a desk with his mouth and eyes wide open as he heard call after call coming in from these guys we had been competing against, and gave me and Bull a thumbs up as he mouthed, '*Oh my God*.' We knew right then that this was going to be unreal for us."

Don Best is an extremely important Web site that offers real-time odds and line moves from sportsbooks around the world. A subscription to the site has long been a must for professional gamblers, who treasure the one-screen snapshot of consequential betting line information. Bookmakers liked the arrival of Don Best because people no longer had to keep calling for rundowns. It saved bookies money in manpower and it helped them with their phone bills, even if they had "800" numbers. In large part because of his established New York clientele, Park had a solid customer base to get All-Star Sports off the ground. Importantly, though, sharp guys heard about Ronnie Park's new All-Star Sports by seeing it listed on Don Best, which had just started becoming popular. "So, the sharp guys had all this information and were betting serious money with All-Star Sports," Battista says. "We were just taking it all in. Even though we were pretty sharp and ahead of most of the people we dealt with, this was another level for us. Ronnie had agents in the U.S. who had to stand for the money. I got to know the agents really well, which meant I got to know who their clients were." It was all coming together for Park and his Animal colleagues.

"We worked every day, seven days a week, eight to twelve hours a day," Battista says. "It didn't matter that much to us because we were used to working our asses off. When we were down there we were all away from our families, and we worked around the clock so that when we came back to the States we wouldn't have to work at all. We each had our own deals with Ronnie: salary, percentage of the business, food and living expenses. And, we were getting an education you couldn't get anywhere else."

After a few months, All-Star Sports had approximately fifty employees, and Battista moved from the Floris to a rented five-bedroom house. By then, he had taken over the company finances at Ronnie's request. "I got hooked up with the biggest agents in the world. These guys also had actors, movie producers, presidents of big companies, all betting big money. I was so focused on developing relationships with these people for whenever we would be leaving offshore. I was dealing with people on a daily basis, and got introduced to the sharpest guys in places like Poland, Russia, and Taiwan. Now I knew who the big guys were all around the world, and how they were moving games. Before I went to Curacao, I thought there was just Vegas and offshore. I thought I always knew how money was moved around, and that I was good at it. But, when I got down there, I was like, 'Jesus Christ!' It was so overwhelming. Now I knew why Uncle Sam was so eager to stop those sportsbooks, because you were talking billions of U.S. dollars flowing through those places that the government couldn't touch."

Battista was suddenly at the center of the big-time sports betting universe. "We were partners with the Kosher Kids that baseball season," he says. "Ronnie had been a clerk for the Koshers back in the 1970s, and now we were moving their games. We worked with them for seven weeks, and they made something like six million dollars in that short period of time. I was also talking to The Computer, and especially his movers, a lot. I also developed a relationship with another one of the world's main sharps—Zorba the Greek. Zorba owned his own sportsbook, and would partner up with The Computer all the time to control the market. The Computer knew it was a nice thing to have a sportsbook in your pocket, and Zorba could move numbers and money around for him. They would move games together. It saved The Computer a lot of time, and made both of them a lot of money. Zorba was one of the few guys offshore who could pull off booking and betting at a high level." Just as The Sheep strengthened his ties to Zorba and The Computer, another of the world's top handful of sports bettors came calling—literally.

"There was one afternoon when Ronnie was out partying and I was left to run the office," Battista says. "The Chinaman called and asked to speak with him, but he got me. He was furious about a line move on a baseball game and was screaming at me that he told Ronnie not to move the number. I was thinking, 'Who the fuck is this guy to be telling us what the line should be?!' I explained to him that we got so much action on one side of the game that we had to move the line, and he said he would have bet enough on the other side if we had just told him. He wanted to keep the market sound until Asia and Taiwan opened up. The Chinaman controlled the markets in Taiwan and Asia. Whereas we would give him fifty-dime bets, his connections there would let him bet hundreds of thousands. Before that conversation, I kind of knew how big he was, but after that call I really started grasping what a fucking monster he was. That was my first time ever speaking to him, and I had no idea then that I'd be working for him down the line."

Unfortunately for The Animals, and especially for Ronnie Park, the burgeoning offshore sportsbook was about to crash and burn in less than a year. "All-Star Sports was doomed from the start," Battista says. "Ronnie cut such bad business deals with so many people. He also spent so much money on unnecessary overhead, like expensive furniture and shit like that. The expenses were so out of hand, and the deals he cut with people were too good to last. He had too many friends and he couldn't say 'no' to anybody. I thought he had oodles of money, but it was all just on the sheet. After working for him a few months, I realized his finance sheets—where you list assets and liabilities—weren't real. All I thought was, 'Oh my God. We're fucked.' A lot of money was owed to him and people wouldn't pay. Sixty or seventy guys owed him money, and they were never going to pay.

"He was sitting on a gold mine, but didn't know what he was doing. When you're down there, you have to choose—either you're going to book, or you're going to bet. He tried to do both, and it destroyed him. Only a select few people could do both down there. Ronnie's lifestyle of spending money was also ridiculous. He would blow money on drugs, women, plastic surgery, all that stuff. He'd bring people down from the U.S. and wine them and dine them. He played the role as good as anybody, even though he had a wife and kids back home. He was so different than we were, and that was part of the problem with his business. Nobody outside the company knew about any of this, though, and people were flocking to his sportsbook.

"By the start of summer, Tiger and Bull had gone back to the U.S. because they saw that the house was going to cave in. They got paid, and went back with their families. I stayed down there though, because we were hoping to get to football season where they could call down to me and I would be able to get big numbers without affecting the market. Even though I was working for Ronnie, the interests of The Animals were way more important.

"When preseason football started in August, Ronnie was trying to recruit legitimate businessmen to come down and invest in his company. Once they visited and looked at everything, they all said they weren't interested because they saw what we did. This thing couldn't survive, and Ronnie owed so many people money. It was like a massive pyramid scheme that didn't make any money for the head of it. I went to him in October and told him I was going home. Anyone with half a brain would have known his business model couldn't work, and none of us—me, Tiger, or Bull—wanted to be there when Chernobyl happened. I could have justified being away from my wife and kids if the business model and profit margin were different, but none of this made sense.

"When I told Ronnie I was leaving, he begged me to stay and offered me a bigger portion of the company. But, there was no way I was staying on that sinking ship. I told him my concerns about the financial situation, but he tried to tell me he was going to turn it around. He may have been a master manipulator, but I wasn't falling for any of his bullshit. As I was getting ready to leave, I went over the company's finances with Ronnie's secretary so that someone could know what to do when I was gone. She was blown away by how fucked up everything was. When I left, I went around to all the people he owed money to let them know I had nothing to do with what was going to happen. I planned on dealing with these people in the future, and I didn't want them pissed at me or The Animals for what Ronnie was trying to do. Ronnie's partner in All-Star Sports was a guy named Chinese John, who controlled a lot of Chinatown in New York. I never even knew his last name or if 'John' was his real name, but when he went back to New York, he became another one of my outs."

More important than simply having another quality out was the prospect of working for a bettor Battista considered among the top three in the world. "When I told The Chinaman I was leaving the sportsbook, he asked me what I was planning on doing," Battista says. "I told him about heading back to the U.S. and working with The Animals again. He asked me to consider moving for him, and I told him I'd think about it." Especially grateful to Tiger for his steadfast leadership and support, Sheep remained with his longtime betting pals—at least for the moment.

Battista reflects on the rise of The Animals through the short-lived yet invaluable All-Star Sports effort, cognizant of how naïve they were at the start. "In the mid-90s, we were learning and attacking," he says. "We graduated betting college in the late 90s. Going to Curacao in the early 2000s was like getting an MBA in betting, and we realized how little we knew before and how much shit was going on with The Computer and a few other guys. We just didn't realize how many resources there were to get money down around the world."

As if the incredible offshore experience wasn't enough already, a bonus awaited The Sheep. Before leaving Curacao, Battista was presented with a veritable money-making machine in the form of nine-year NBA referee Tim Donaghy, by way of two longtime Battista associates.

Jack Concannon graduated from Cardinal O'Hara High School rival Monsignor Bonner in 1983. Concannon, a basketball star who led Bonner to their first Catholic League championship since 1960, was a six-foot-six forward who went on to play for nearby St. Joseph's University. Concannon later coached Bonner for five seasons ending in 1996, and by 2003 he was part owner of a Delaware County insurance agency. The public image of Concannon would be sullied in a few years, but for now he was largely known as just another guy. "Jack really played the role—good Catholic family guy, successful businessman," Battista says. "Meanwhile, he had a reputation among my crowd for being down Atlantic City losing his shirt and betting all the time. I knew Jack fairly well, going back to when we were kids. We're the same age, and I've known him since fifth grade when we played football against each other. He was the quarterback for St. Lawrence, and I was a lineman for Holy Cross, and we played against each other in CYO basketball, too. Concannon actually sold me my life insurance back in 2000."

All of this would be Delaware County trivia if not for Jack Concannon's betting relationship with his friend Tim Donaghy. "Jack was friends with Pete Ruggieri, going back to high school at Monsignor Bonner, and they played golf together," Battista says. "Pete was a pro gambler like me, and we were friends for years. Jack always wanted to know what football games Pete was on because he knew Pete was sharp. Well, Jack used to play golf with Pete and would use Pete to get his sports bets down; Pete was Jack's agent. In 2003, Jack was betting NBA games for two thousand dollars per game, but started betting some games for five thousand, and those five grand games were *crushing*." For pro gamblers, such curiosities typically don't go unnoticed, much less without further inspection.

"It didn't take us long to figure out what was going on once we looked into those games—they were games Timmy Donaghy was reffing," Battista says. "Nothing was ever spoken between Jack and Pete about Timmy, but Pete and I just put two and two together. We knew that Jack and Timmy were friends, so we figured that Jack had some arrangement with Timmy. We couldn't fucking believe it. Here we were, professional gamblers, being provided with an NBA referee's picks on the games he was reffing! So, we started copying Jack's bets on games Timmy was reffing, and we did that for about thirty games that year. Pete and I gave Timmy a nickname, "Bingo," and when Pete would call down it was me asking Pete, 'Who is Bingo on tonight?' Timmy had no idea Pete and I knew what he was doing, and neither did Jack." As for Concannon's wagers on games Donaghy officiated, Battista excitedly says, "Timmy's picks were great. In fact, I started calling Timmy 'Elvis' because he was The King. He was *unbelievable*."

If it wasn't ridiculous enough that Donaghy didn't know his bets were ending up with Battista, whom he knew for years, and with whom he had partied on occasion, there was an incredible footnote to the already surreal, two-degrees-of-separation story. Tim Donaghy was close friends with Jimmy Battista's lifelong pal, Tommy Martino, and the last time all three men were together was at Martino's wedding. Nevertheless, Battista says he never let his buddy in on the remarkable situation. "Even though I talked to Tommy every once in a while from Curacao, and even though he was probably talking to Timmy all the time back then," Battista says, "Tommy didn't know what Timmy was doing with his betting, and he didn't know what I was doing with Timmy's bets. Obviously, I wasn't going to tell Tommy. This was incredible and I wasn't going to fuck it up by telling anybody."

Ever the savvy business entrepreneur, for whom "less was more," secrecy was key, and such sound business acumen allowed him to mimic Donaghy's bets unfettered for the next four NBA seasons. It also helped that Battista was so consumed by his hyperactive betting career, of which the Donaghy discovery was a bit part.

9

Parting Ways, Glory Days

AS JIMMY BATTISTA returned from his rather eventful stint in Curacao, those outside of his immediate circle still knew little about what he was really up to. Though now living in an upscale neighborhood near Valley Forge, Pennsylvania, The Sheep consciously maintained a low profile. This included driving a rather modest 1998 Dodge Caravan with more than 100,000 miles on it. "Could I have afforded a Mercedes or some other nice car? Absolutely, but I dressed like a slob, wanted to look like a slob," Battista says. "There was no need to advertise. Less was more: the less people knew about me, the better it was for me. In my early days, my twenties, I was flamboyant, running the streets, and drove a Mercedes 190. As I got older, probably by my late 20s, I realized how stupid all that was." Now among the best movers in the pro gambling world, Battista had the proper perspective to exploit his earned standing. "The guys I was working with in the Philly suburbs were very successful," he says. "They looked at the gangsters downtown—who were so flashy and were always getting their names in the papers, always drawing attention to themselves, walking into bars and dropping hundreds—as fools. We had a different mind-set: 'You're with your wife. You're with your kids. You work all fucking day long. You make the doughnuts. You work your ass off.' We didn't want to be known. Why would we? We didn't want anyone to know that we were the ones who were going to take all that money out of the market. As far as everybody knew, we were just 'everyday guys.'

"It was a great business model. We all dressed in shorts and T-shirts. When The Animals got together, people had no idea who we were or that we were the big money behind certain things. I think if people would have seen us, these three fat slobs, and were told about all the shit we were doing, they would have said, 'Get the fuck out of here!' I never felt the urge to tell somebody who I was or what we were doing, to impress them or whatever. Only a fucking idiot would want to tell people what we were up to."

Sheep, Tiger, and Bull were now all back in the U.S., with Seal still just a call away within Rinnier's operation. All four men once again lived and operated within miles of each other in Delaware County, and it seemed these were the best of times. Back in comfortable surroundings with their families near, they continued exploiting the outs and the insider lessons resulting from the All-Star Sports venture in Curacao. The years of priming the world's sportsbook pumps were paying off, and The Animals never had so many means to get big money down.

"With some of the offshore places, we dealt through agents in New York, Vegas, or Florida," Battista says. "With others, we dealt directly with the owners. They didn't do that with most people, but they knew us. We bet all over the place in Vegas, too, but some places took bigger bets than others. The Coast Casinos were great, and we'd also use Bellagio, Mandalay Bay, and others." Success oftentimes has an adverse affect on betting operations, depending on the fleeting needs and motives of sportsbooks. This was particularly true for The Animals in Sin City. "There were plenty of times we got flagged by different casinos from betting, and they knew our runners," Battista says. "Even though we'd try and rotate the runners from different casinos, it was tough because people would find out who they were working for. There were times when our runners couldn't place bets that we had to send a different person right off the street every day into a casino just to get a bet on a game. If they could get a ten thousand–dollar bet, we'd pay them fifty bucks."

The Animals were firing on all cylinders almost immediately since Battista's return to the U.S., but their decades-long run of booking, betting, and brotherhood was about to come to an end.

"The Chinaman asked us to move some games for him," Battista says. "Within a few weeks, we were up *big*, but then he and Tiger had a falling out. When he and Tiger wanted to take the same side of games, it was a matter of who was going to get more on those games. The other problem was that there were times when Tiger and The Chinaman were against each other on their picks." The irreconcilable problems were obvious to everyone, and soon The Chinaman asked Battista to come work exclusively with him for the purpose of moving games. "The Chinaman loved the fact that I worked so much and was there all the time," Battista says. "He wanted to go for the kill when it came to betting, and that took being available around the clock, every day. Tiger was against me leaving because he and The Chinaman were essentially competitors. Tiger and I had worked together for years, but this was an incredible opportunity for me. With The Chinaman, I could still work out of my house most of the time, and then travel to Vegas and other places some of the time. Tiger was an incredible handicapper, but The Chinaman was operating at a level just above him. So, I accepted the offer."

Battista's split with his longtime partners and pals was unthinkable to those in their broader crowd. Their ties extended beyond the betting business, and Tiger was especially off-put by Battista's decision given all he had done for The Sheep over the years. Further, there were technical matters with which

Tiger and Bull would now have to contend. "By going with The Chinaman, I was causing some problems for The Animals because I was the one with the outs," Battista says. "I couldn't handicap anywhere near as good as Tiger, Bull, or Seal, but I was the one on the phones and meeting with people for the numbers, the money and everything. Even though I left The Animals on bad terms, I still kept in touch with them because now I had the information. They wanted to know what The Chinaman was betting and how he was moving games, and I needed them to help me move games and stuff like that. So, even though they were pissed at me, we still talked a lot after I split with them."

The Sheep's new partnership would flourish for the next few years, all the while accompanied by anxiety caused by a host of factors, not the least of which was the illegality of what he was doing, now on an even grander scale. The fear of getting caught and what that might mean was offset by Battista's validation within the international sports betting crowd's most exclusive club. Throughout, the logistics of Battista's betting operations were largely unchanged following the jump to his new partner.

"The Chinaman was out in Los Angeles, and I was in my house outside of Philly," Battista says. "At first, working with just The Chinaman was great. He was paying me a salary and a percentage of his winnings. The setup for me was unbelievable, except I was working all the time. I was at home, but I was buried in that box—my office, and I was on the phone *all the time*. He was a very demanding person to work for, but at least it was worth it. We worked the end of the '03-04 NFL season, and then started to focus on baseball. The Chinaman *owned* major league baseball when it came to betting. Pretty soon, the people offshore where I was placing his bets were giving me kickbacks to bet with them because they wanted The Chinaman's action. They all knew me from when I was working the sportsbook in Curacao." Battista didn't have long to get accustomed to his new arrangement with The Chinaman before yet another opportunity arose.

The Chinaman called Battista and asked him to do a favor for Zorba, who asked The Sheep to move a game for him. In no time, Battista was moving numerous games for Zorba, and for The Computer, who was a partner with Zorba on a host of things. "They liked that they could trust me, that I had the outs that paid, and that I was working all the time," Battista says. "For a gambler, this ultimate echelon of betting was a market you dreamed of. These guys were just incredible."

Moving for three of the world's most influential bettors quickly brought other rewards. "Pretty soon, word on the street was that Sheep was moving for all these guys," Battista says, "and I started getting phone calls with people offering me deals to give them the sharp bets. I never even thought of this happening when I first hooked up with The China-man. It was a nice bonus to working with them. Sometimes, I would sell the picks, as long as it didn't affect the bets I was placing for my clients. I actually told The Chinaman I had been offered for some of his games by The Englishman, who might be the world's best soccer handicapper and bettor. He had no problem with me giving The Englishman his picks because we needed access to parts of the European market, and The Englishman could give it to us. From then on, I moved games for The Englishman, too." The introduction to The Englishman opened Battista's eyes and expanded his betting enterprise still further.

"One of The Englishman's partners, this guy named Peter, gave me a trip to the Bahamas as a way of showing his appreciation for me giving him the sharp bets," Battista says. "My wife and I couldn't go, so I gave the trip to Tommy Martino. He went to the resort Atlantis in the Bahamas with his girl-friend, his brother, Chuck, and his guest. Everything was taken care of, soup-to-nuts, and that trip had to be worth twenty thousand dollars. They would have given me anything at that point because our picks were worth a small fortune. Peter was connected to high-ranking people in British government and had places in Florida, Amsterdam, Dubai—all over the world. Peter wanted to meet, so he and I flew into Orlando and we met in a hotel lobby. He was an older guy, and when I got up to shake his hand, he slapped my face like a grandfather would, smiled, and said [in his polished British accent], 'My son, we're going to make lots of money together.'

"One time, I was on the phone with Peter and he was in Russia at some charity event with [then-U.K. prime minister] Tony Blair. Here I was giving him what games to bet on the phone just as he was sitting at a table with Tony Blair!" On another occasion, Peter was going to the Super Bowl and was expected to be sitting with former U.S. President Bill Clinton in a box. "Peter invited me and my wife to go," Battista says, "so we give them our social security numbers for the background checks. He called me two weeks before the game and told me that I didn't get the security clearance to be in the box, and that I'd have to sit in what he called 'the grandstand.' It was a nice offer, but we declined. We would have gone if we had gotten in the box with Clinton." If the perks that went along with having Peter as a client weren't enough for Battista, there was an important and yet unknown benefit that only a major pro gambler could appreciate—and exploit.

"At first, I didn't know that one of Peter's good friends was Harry at Paramount," Battista says. "Peter said to me, 'Harry will give me anything I want. He'll give me half a million dollars if I ask.' Inside, I was like, 'Yes!' Harry feared us and wouldn't take big action, so now I looked at Peter as the ultimate out. I felt like I was running the circus, though, because I was now doing big-time deals with The Chinaman, Zorba, The Computer, and The Englishman and his pal, Peter. The

Chinaman was using my connections with all these guys to his advantage and we had more ways to get big money down. It was easier for us to get millions of dollars down without affecting the market. My family life was nonexistent, even though I was in the house pretty much the entire time. I'd be in the office with all my computers and all my phones firing away all day and night, every day of the week. That escalation from one to four or five major bettors all took place within a year. By 2005, I was getting mentally destroyed."

If The Sheep was struggling at that point in his life, he no doubt couldn't handle what was on the horizon. His decision to split from his Animal pals had, indeed, brought him the expected wealth and then some. Battista, however, had vastly underestimated what he was getting himself into, and had little if any time to appreciate his newfound standing in the sports betting world.

10

Standing on Top of the Sports Betting World

HE HAD REACHED the sports betting summit. Now working with the world's sharpest bettors, Jimmy Battista's day-to-day activities would soon become the subject of considerable scrutiny. The Sheep's betting operation, among the most significant in the industry, was something to behold.

LOGISTICS

"In my home gambling office, I had a bunch of laptop and desktop computers, and a few TVs," Battista says. "I had at least ten computer screens live at all times, and they were essentially stacked three high by four wide. If it was, say, October and basketball season was just beginning and football season was five or six weeks in, my first screen to my lower left would have pro football from the Don Best. The second screen [vertically] would be college football. The top screen would be pro basketball. Those Don Best screens would tell me all the lines from around the world—the casinos, the offshore sportsbooks, and other books. Those screens would change all the time and if a line moved it would show me with a black mark on the screen. If it was a major line move, I had my computer set up that it would actually announce [in a computerized human voice] 'Major Line Movement.' That would happen when every bookmaker was getting hit at the same time. So, when I was going out on a game and hitting fifteen to twenty bookmakers at once, the Don Best would notify people like me. On the far right of my desk would be screens showing my main offshore accounts, where I had the big numbers, so I could see my accounts as I was processing everything going on. You could have sites set on 'auto-pilot' so that it updated itself with any changes automatically. Just to the right of the Don Best screens, I had my Zorba's offshore sportsbook site up. His site routinely took games off the board, which let people like me know that someone like me was betting something. Because of my deal with him, I could contact him and bet on whatever he had going on with those games.

"Other screens were for sportsbooks in Asia, Taiwan, and England. I actually had another computer on my main offshore account that was hooked up with a different Internet router just in case my main router got messed up. My other computers were all set up for communication. I'd use them to chat, talk through Skype, to set up moves, send out orders, all that stuff. I used to speak to other bettors and movers through the computer using Skype because we believed that was a way to avoid being traced. Even though there was a delay of a few seconds, it was worth it so that your conversations weren't tapped.

"Eventually, I started working in different spots, constantly moving to avoid the authorities. I didn't want to be locked into one place in case someone was onto me. I worked a little at Tommy Martino's house in Aston, and had a place in Manayunk, a spot in Vegas, and at my house. I even took my laptop and my phones and went to different parks. I'd sit in my car or on a park bench, and work from there. I never worked more than a few days in a row at any one spot. There were times where I'd work at one spot one day, another the next, another the next.

"Each of my clients got their own phone so that I would talk to them and only them on their phone. I also had phones just for other purposes. I didn't want to confuse people on the phones. I always brought my 'phone bag' with me, which was a little black drawstring bag. I used to carry all the cell phones in it. At night, I would have anywhere from fifteen to twenty phones charging in my house. None of them were in my name. T-Mobile was a gift from Heaven. When you bought a phone with them, you could just make up a name. You didn't need a driver's license or anything. I registered them all in the names of actors from my favorite TV show, *Everybody Loves Raymond*: Ray Romano, Peter Boyle, Brad Garrett, Patricia Heaton, Doris Roberts, and so on. I would pay cash each month for like a hundred minutes on each phone. You could go to any T-Mobile store in the country and just keep adding minutes.

"T-Mobile was great because you could call anywhere in the country and overseas. You were paying for it, ten cents a minute, but it was fucking worth it because your name wasn't attached. You don't want it anymore? Take out the sim card, destroy the phones, and you're done.[1] I'd throw the sim cards out in a different place than the phones so that no one would ever connect the two. Usually, I'd put the sim cards in some river or creek or whatever. I was spending thirteen or fourteen grand on 'disposable' cell phones. I had a friend who owned a restaurant that had an acid dip tank, for cleaning the grill.

---

[1] According to wisegeek.com, "sim" stands for *subscriber identity module*, and "is a portable memory chip used in some models of cellular telephones. The SIM card makes it easy to switch to a new phone by simply sliding the SIM out of the old phone and into the new one. The SIM holds personal identity information, cell phone number, phone book, text messages and other data. It can be thought of as a mini hard disk that automatically activates the phone into which it is inserted."

Well, he would let me come over and throw the phones in the acid so no one could get a hold of them. I'd leave them in there for fifteen minutes, and then break them with a hammer. I would do this on a monthly basis. It was a hassle but it had to be done. Every month, I re-did the phones."

THE MARKET

"I controlled a large part of the market. I knew what the sharpest handicappers were doing," Battista says. "These weren't like those fucking shitheads out in Vegas with their bullshit tout services. The guys I moved games for, they were the big swinging dicks of the sports gambling industry. They'd say, 'Go get me half a million a game,' or 'I need three hundred thousand a game,' or whatever. That was the true money. It wasn't like they were appearing on a bullshit sports syndicate show every weekend saying, 'Well, I'm going with so and so.'

"I knew I had the information—the right sides and the right numbers on the games—but you still needed to have the people to get big money down and to get it down with people who would pay. I had outs at a bunch of places online, a bunch out in Vegas, all over the world. Online sportsbooks would usually only take a hundred grand a game, and my thing was to make deals with Vegas books and local stores to get down on the games in fifties, forties, thirties, and twenties, and others for even less. I was routinely meeting people in Vegas, meeting people in New York, in Alabama, in Florida.

"I used to hope I would lose around twenty thousand dollars to bookmakers, so they would see that I paid—my money was good. I knew that in a few months time, I was gonna take them for *ten times* that amount. There was a bookmaker in Philadelphia—I was betting him for about five thousand a game. I lost thirty-two thousand dollars to him in the first three weeks. A few weeks later, he paid me four hundred and forty thousand dollars and said, 'I don't know what you did. I never saw someone who would take twelve games a day and consistently go eight-and-four, seven-and-five.' That is how strong the information was from my handicappers on college and pro football, baseball, and basketball. I would find guys who were taking between one and five thousand a game. It was going to be over for them in a matter of time, and they didn't even know it. They were like, 'This guy's paying me. He owes me twenty-five grand and bang, he pays.' I'd tell them, 'Remember this when I win. I want it back right away.'

"The new casinos in Las Vegas were so corporate and, even though they kept their sportsbooks, they didn't take big numbers anymore. They would take five or ten thousand dollars from a sharp guy, and let a big spending sucker bet fifty or a hundred grand because they knew he couldn't pick his nose. They needed those big spenders to pay for people like me and the guys I worked with and for all those years. The Computer used to use big-time celebrities, especially actors, to bet for him in the casinos. One time there was a movie producer who made two-point-eight million betting college and pro football in one weekend, and the sportsbook manager refused to pay him because he was convinced The Computer was behind his bets—and he was right!

"I had two crews out in Vegas running around getting numbers in casinos like the South Coast and the Gold Coast. The smaller casinos took bigger bets than most of the larger casinos. They were monsters, and would take fifty to a hundred thousand, whereas the Mirage or Caesar's would only take ten or twenty. They had so much action coming in that they could offset our bets."

MONEY MATTERS

On Keeping Records Of Betting Transactions

"When I moved for the four guys, they gave me a straight percentage of the volume of placed bets—win, lose, or draw," Battista says. "These were guys who bet a few hundred thousand per game, easy. Twice a year they had to pay me a percentage of their earnings. I also bet a little on my own. I wrote most of my bets on three-by-five index cards. I also used some triple-ply forms in case I had to split up the work. I never put stuff on the computer if I didn't have to. I had two shredders at home, and once all the bets had cleared, I would shred everything. It was a pain in the ass, but it was worth it. Joe Vito thought I was crazy, but there was no way I was putting all that I was doing on hard drives. These were not little figures. The government would have been very interested in that sort of stuff, and I was never going to take that risk.

"When you used to bet offshore before computers, everything on the phone was recorded. So, if there was a dispute, you could pull the tape. I used to always have them repeat my bet back to me so there were no problems. Also, my voice was so well known that people would say, 'Sheep is on the phone.' They knew who I was, and there was a mutual trust for the most part. Even if there was a misunderstanding, all the offshore stores had claims departments, and you could call and have them pull up the tapes. There were times where an offshore book would have a new clerk who would take a thirty thousand dollar bet from me, let's say. Well, the clerk would hang up and be asked by a superior about who had just placed the bet. When the clerk would say, 'Sheep,' the manager or whoever it was would scream, 'What?! Call that fucker back and tell him he can have three thousand, that's it!' And I'd say, 'No fucking way! The clerk took the bet. Pull the tape.

You honor the bet!' As time went on and people started betting online, there was no debate about what or when you bet.

On Moving Money

"Moving money within the U.S. meant moving cash,' Battista says. "At least twice a week, I was traveling somewhere to pick up or drop off money, usually on Tuesdays and Thursdays. I wasn't going to stop if I was carrying money, which always went under my seat. There were two things under my seat: the money and my 'piss cup,' which was actually one of those things they place beside your hospital bed. Any trip involving money was planned so that I wouldn't have to stop, and that included having food, snacks, soda, and water in the car. If you stopped, you were taking too much of a chance in my eyes, leaving that kind of money in the car. Also, you didn't want to put yourself in a position to get robbed. Keep in mind that most of those trips were at night because I was working during the day. I always used my beat-up old minivan, and if I had the money with me I never sped.

"If I went somewhere and was bringing back two hundred and fifty thousand dollars or more, I always had somebody along for protection. I used the guy Mike Rinnier hired years prior to run security for his supermarkets, and I would pay him depending on where I was going and how long it was. On the rare occasions we were really concerned about safety picking up money, especially down in Atlantic City if we thought some mobsters might be looking to rob us, two of us would meet in a casino bathroom where the person who picked up the money would pass it under the stall to me, and we'd go our separate ways. That way, if my partner was being set up, I'd be long gone with the money.

"The biggest thing about big-time sports betting is being able to hide the money being moved around. There are certain offshore sportsbooks that have their own banking systems. One of them was Paramount, down in Curacao. They were interconnected with banking that was done offshore. So, you could have millions in your accounts, and do transfers from client to client. Paramount had such a stronghold on the U.S. sports gambling market. They had to control at least sixty percent of it. They started in the late 1990s and were The Godfather of the sports gambling industry. They took action online or on the phone, and they took the biggest bets. For every big-time bettor, there had to be an agent. An agent would put a customer [the bettor] into Paramount, and stand for the money. As long as you were on the 'ins' with these guys, you could move money anywhere you wanted.

"Harry was the main guy at Paramount, and was one of five partners who owned it. Well, Harry was good friends with Joe Vito, and Joe was Paramount's agent on the East Coast, for Philly and New York. They also had guys down South, in Florida, and out West, in Nevada, which we always called 'the desert.' Their network was so good that you could move money anywhere in the U.S., and to Asia, Taiwan, Europe, anywhere you wanted. The agents would get paid a percentage of the money they were being asked to move. The guy out West got busted for being an agent a month before I was arrested, and the authorities took in more than a hundred and twenty-five million dollars between a bunch of places in Arizona.

"In the late 1990s, an associate of mine needed to move a million-and-a-half back home from the desert. He rented a car in Vegas, and was driving on I-70 in Kansas when he was stopped doing ninety miles an hour listening to Bon Jovi's 'Livin' on a Prayer'! Well, he forgot his license in Las Vegas, and they found five hundred thousand in the car. They told him if he could provide the winning bet tickets for all the cash, he could get the money back. They offered him a third of it back if he couldn't, and that's all he could do. Just moving money on the streets, getting a percentage of what needs to be moved, guys were making one to two million a year.

"If you had the right clout and you had been around long enough, you had your own banking system and could transfer all kinds of money. I am talking *zillions* of dollars were moved this way on a daily basis. New York, Vegas, and Florida were the triangle of Paramount's agent network in the States. A lot of times you'd hear there was no money in the desert or that the desert was dry. That was because it was easy to get money to New York from all over the East Coast, but getting out to Las Vegas was a pain in the ass. There was so much more action on the East Coast and it wasn't that dangerous driving cash from, say, Philly to Atlantic City or to New York. There were plenty of bettors who didn't like dealing in Florida because there was so much drug and crime stuff going on down there, and people didn't want to take the risk of picking up a load of money there.

"If a big-time bettor had a rare bad week, and, for example, lost a million-three to an offshore sportsbook like Paramount, here is how that might have been handled. The bettor would tell the sportsbook he had three hundred grand in cash in New York, and a mover would be sent to get the money and hold it on behalf of the sportsbook. The same thing would happen, say, in Vegas or California, where movers would be holding another five hundred thousand total out there for the sportsbook. Then, the bettor may have a mover do a client transfer of the remaining half-million from the bettor's account to the sportsbook. The sportsbook wouldn't get their hands on all the money right away, or at the same time.

"Once the money was in one of the offshore books, they had their own internal banking systems where they could transfer money between accounts, between clients, and between other books. That's part of the reason why the U.S. government was so interested in what was going on down there because you can see how people who aren't gamblers, like drug dealers and terrorists, would want to use the sportsbooks to launder money."

On "Settling"

"Most bookmakers at 'Mom and Pop' stores made people settle every week, usually on Tuesdays," Battista says. "They might have let serious bettors settle up once a month or agree to a settlement figure. For instance, the bookmaker might have allowed someone to bet for weeks or months until he owed the bookmaker ten thousand dollars or vice-versa. Most local sportsbooks would let you bet on credit. Now, if you bet a big book out in Vegas or offshore, they usually required you to have money in an account. If you were betting in Vegas, you were actually betting in cash. If you took the Pittsburgh Steelers minus four for ten grand, you gave them eleven thousand in cash to place the bet, and they'd give you a ticket. If the Steelers won by more than four points, you gave them your ticket and they'd give you twenty-one thousand dollars.

"Back when The Animals first started betting offshore before those books really knew us, we'd have to post money into accounts. Regular customers [i.e., not pro gamblers] would have to sign up online, pick a code name and a password, and tell the sportsbook how they were going to put the start-up money in their account. Back then, they'd take money from credit cards, certified check, bank transfer, PayPal, and Neteller. For regular bettors, the offshore sportsbook would credit successful bettors' credit cards or send people checks, whatever. If you were invited to be in the 'elevator club,' so to speak, meaning if they knew you were going to be betting big money and were good for it, you were dealt with entirely differently.

"The only option of getting paid if you were betting hundreds of thousands of dollars was to work with an offshore agent. Agents would usually have settlement figures of five hundred thousand dollars, but some would settle at as little as two hundred grand. Others would settle every week, regardless of how much you made or owed. Every agent cut different deals with his clients. For instance, you might have an agent call a gambler on a Monday and say, 'Okay. I owe you seven hundred and eighty grand this week, but you had an outstanding balance of one twenty-five from last week, so your balance is six hundred and fifty-five thousand.' The gambler might then tell the agent, 'Great. Carry one-fifty-five and put the rest in my Paramount account,' or he might say, 'Carry one-fifty-five and put two hundred in Florida, put a hundred in the desert, and let me pick up two hundred in Philadelphia.'

"Typically, gamblers would leave at least twenty percent of their earnings with the sportsbook so that they wouldn't have to meet with the agents. The idea was to spread the rest around to the other parts of the country because you never knew where you'd need or want to cash out. In that club, that's how it worked. Almost all of those transactions were done in cash. You usually settled with your agents on Tuesdays, after you assessed everything from the weekend and talked to the agents on Monday."

On Paying Taxes

"Mike Rinnier was the one who taught me," Battista says, "'You never stiff Uncle Sam. You always pay your taxes.' I have a record of showing that every time I got busted, it says that I claimed being a professional gambler and that I paid taxes on my earnings. Pro gamblers usually show checks coming in from sportsbooks for winnings, and checks out to sportsbooks for losses. What people don't seem to understand is that even in good years you have stiffs and losses. When I lost money many years ago, I still claimed I won five grand just to keep the government happy."

LIFESTYLE

"I was so busy with work that I didn't go on vacation with my wife and kids unless we were going to Vegas. Anytime there were events or holidays, Denise and the kids would go without me. I'd be home on the computer betting. My life centered around that computer and those phones at the expense of my family. I'd get done betting at ten-thirty at night and then spend the rest of the time before going to bed watching games I bet. I used to justify what I was doing by saying to my wife, 'I work like this to provide for you and the kids. You can do whatever you want to do, buy whatever you want to buy.'

"Things got real stressful working seventy hours a week moving for people, making sure I destroyed the phones and stuff like that, moving from place to place so I didn't get caught, but without forgetting to do this and that. What little time there was after all of this I spent with my wife and kids. The thing was, you were always hearing about this or that guy getting picked up and you were worried about them ratting you out. I had already been arrested twice years ago and didn't want to get caught again."

None of Battista's clients worked more than one or two sports in earnest, if for no other reason than they couldn't handle the grind for longer periods of time. The Sheep was not as fortunate, however, because collectively his clients worked every sport and thus he operated year-round. "People like The Computer and Zorba have 'betting seasons' because when you're gambling around the clock you need the break," Battista says. "Gamblers that work all year round get fried. Well, I was getting fried—mentally and physically. For example, to work baseball from openers in the morning to the afternoon games to the night games and then the ten o'clock West Coast games, you were fucking spent by the end of the day. Then, you had to get up the next day and start all over again. The thing was, you *had* to be in the chair. You had to be in front of the computer because there were earners there that you didn't want to miss. It was the same thing during football season, where on a Sunday morning I was in the chair at eight and wouldn't get done until half-time of the Sunday night game at like eleven o'clock. You had to be there *all the time*. I used to actually pay people to sit in front of the computer if I had to go run an errand or pick up my kids from school or something, so that if a line changed I wouldn't miss it.

"If I had stayed with just The Chinaman, I could have handled it. I really needed an assistant to handle the other guys. No one person could have handled what I was trying to do. I had the best computers, the best setup, the best phones—everything—but it was all too much. I don't think I did what I did out of greed. I didn't seek any of those guys out. They each came to me, and I just couldn't say no. As everything got out of control, probably around fall of 2004, I started using more and more pills. Tommy introduced me to OxyContin right before the Eagles-Patriots Super Bowl, and after that I was using them all the time. Even though I was used to Percocets and Vicodin, OxyContin was so different and so much stronger than anything I had ever taken before. I was eating pills like crazy before I started using Oxys. I used to eat four or five Percocets at a time and now I could just take one OxyContin. The amount of pills I swallowed before then was unbelievable."

THE BIG PICTURE

"I dressed like a slob, always wore a baseball cap, never wore jewelry," Battista says. "I wasn't flashy. Mike Rinnier always drilled into our heads that you didn't want to draw attention to yourself. You wanted to be as far under the radar as possible. In my business, you couldn't have a personality that wanted glory. You wanted to win, of course, but you didn't want anyone to know what you were betting. If people caught wind of what I was betting, it bothered me. Sometimes you didn't want the lines to move and if people found out what I was betting, it would cause problems. People always wanted to know who the world's top guys were on, but I didn't want people to know because that meant I would make less. I wanted my hand controlling the market without anyone knowing about it. As soon as some people in the business find out what you're doing, they cut your limits back, and you can't do this and can't do that. The less people knew, the more money you made. Part of my success was because I didn't oversell myself. I wasn't anywhere near as sharp as the guys I worked with and for. But, I'd work my balls off, keep my business to myself, and make sure everybody got paid.

"Because I used runners, most casinos didn't know who I was or what I looked like. Certain casinos knew me because I had clout with them, and they'd comp me and my family with rooms, and tickets to shows and stuff. Down in Atlantic City, I'd usually stay at the Trop or at Caesar's, and they took care of me. I played some blackjack, too, but not much. They knew who I was and that I was a good customer, but still, most places wouldn't let me place big bets so I'd let suckers go in and place bets for me. Why would I go in there, have them say, 'The Sheep is here,' and be limited to a three thousand dollar bet when I could send someone in who looks like Elmer Fudd and they're gonna give him twenty thousand a game? The less seen, the better. Paying someone a hundred bucks to get ten grand more on a game was simple math and good business. Besides, if I was placing bets myself I couldn't be in front of a computer orchestrating other bets.

"There were times I saw things I wanted to bet on my own, but that was rare. I was content with what I was doing.

I enjoyed the rush of getting the best numbers, not necessarily of gambling. I didn't get into the sports betting business because I liked gambling. It was just a great opportunity for me since I never finished college. I was always a worker and I didn't care if I had to work fourteen or sixteen hours a day. I also had decent social skills that would help me get to the next step, from clerk to runner to mover. By the time I was working with the sharpest guys in the business, I was taking inside information and saturating the market to move the numbers the wrong way. Millions of squares would follow what I bet, and when it was all over I was on the opposite side.

"I didn't make numbers like the guys I worked with, and for, did. I couldn't come close to what they did if I tried. I'd lose every penny I had, these guys were that good. But, I did have good enough common sense that if I saw someone winning sixty-two percent, I was gonna get as close to them as possible. Did I consider myself a 'professional gambler? Yes, I did. I claimed it for a living. Why fuck with Uncle Sam? I paid taxes. I stated I was a professional gambler for the better part of twenty years. But, compared to The Chinaman, Zorba, The Computer, and The Englishman, I didn't even go into the same closet to get changed as they did. Of course, if you sit with them as long as I did, I got a great education. I went to the Harvard or the Penn of the sports gambling world. That's how you got sharper."

11

The Sharps

THE BIG THREE (PLUS ONE)

ACCORDING TO PRO gamblers, the triumvirate of The Chinaman, Zorba the Greek, and The Computer sat atop the
sports betting mountain. In fact, in a business which considers
a demonstrated success rate of fifty-four to fifty-six percent
impressive, Jimmy Battista estimates this heavy-hitting three-
some won between sixty-two and sixty-four percent of their
wagers. The Sheep also moved games (bets) for The Englishman,
who was widely considered the world's most consequential soccer bettor. Battista found each man impressive in
distinguishable ways, and reflects with pride on his business
relationships with them.

THE CHINAMAN

The Chinaman, who was actually Vietnamese, was the
bettor with whom Battista worked the most beginning in
2003. A medical doctor and world-class poker player, the pro
gambler was known throughout the world for his NBA and
MLB wagering prowess. According to Battista, about the
only thing his primary client couldn't bet was college sports,
because there was such a difference between handicapping
pro and college athletes.

"The Chinaman started betting when he was in med school as a way of paying his tuition," Battista says. "He made so much money that even after he started his doctor practice, he decided to just stay with gambling full-time. Besides being mathematically smarter than the other guys, he was driven. His knack for watching and evaluating talent in a game was unmatched. Game-by-game sports, he was the best handicapper in the world. He watched so much sports it was unbelievable, and had day-to-day analysis like I had never seen. He was so confident about his analysis and his bets that he wouldn't even worry about what the other bettors were doing. He knew what the number should be, and wasn't influenced by the line moves and stuff like that. He was meticulous and would work around the clock like me. Whereas The Computer had around sixteen handicappers working for him, The Chinaman was by himself. He was married, but never had time for his wife.

"The Chinaman was the best in baseball. Period. They used to talk about the Kosher Kids, the Jewish guys from New York who started back in the 1970s and 1980s. He would have ripped them a new asshole. The Koshers only worked for six or seven weeks, and then took their money and ran, whereas The Chinaman got better after the All-Star break. He got sharper and stronger. Baseball and basketball were his best two sports. When baseball ended in October, he bet pro football and even there he was no slouch. In my twenty-five years of gambling, I saw a lot of people who could analyze a game, watch it, and then bet quarters and halves. After The Chinaman watched a first half of a football game, he was *the best* second-half football gambler I've ever seen. They'd put up a number at halftime and he would just destroy it. He wasn't chasing the money, he was following the game. Whether it was him watching the line of scrimmage or whatever, he was unreal at gauging what would happen in the second half. He watched day-to-day sports like nobody did, *and* his head was like a calculator. The Computer couldn't come close to betting The Chinaman on second halves, because The Computer's handicappers couldn't process the information quickly enough. We bet twenty-seven second-half bets and lost two or three of them. I've always believed nobody else could do that. On Sundays there were several games at one o'clock and several at four, but there was only one on Sunday and Monday nights. Sunday and Monday nights he was scary. I *knew* we would be winning on Sunday and Monday nights because he could devote his time to one game halftime. Over the course of an NFL season, people like The Computer and The Chinaman would win in the high fifties to low sixties. For NFL night games, The Chinaman would win in the mid to high sixties.

"We controlled the markets and we were everywhere— Taiwan, Asia, and offshore. When I first started dealing with him, the Asian markets alone owed him between ten and fifteen balloons, and were paying him off a hundred thousand per week. He would bet them and knock the numbers into line and then the rest of the market would look over there because the Asian market comes up so much earlier than ours does. That market would be closed by eight-thirty in the morning eastern time, which is when the American markets would start to open. Originally, the Asian markets didn't think someone could go that long and keep beating them, which is how they got so in the hole to him. After a while, they realized how good he was and would let him get his numbers but then try and get those numbers for themselves when the U.S. markets opened up. They sort of became partners with him because he was essentially setting their lines and giving them the right numbers.

"What an education it was working with that guy. People used to pay him just to sit next to him and to talk to him. He didn't really have a life. He had a wife, but we would work fourteen to sixteen hours a day, every day of the week. We would do two sports at the same time and it was just incredible. You could barely keep up with everything."

ZORBA THE GREEK

"Zorba was a bookmaker based offshore, who was a 'people-person' and a great businessman," says Battista. "He was very easygoing, soft-spoken, and a hard worker who would put in seventy hours a week like it was nothing. He got busted in the U.S. years ago and moved down there and developed a great business. He got hooked up booking these big, sharp guys for hundreds of thousands a game. He could then go get the sucker money to pay the bills. As we always said, 'The suckers weren't invited to the party; they were paying for the party.'

"His Web site had such an international clientele. He put his number up first. He wasn't afraid to take a bet because he knew what he was doing. In pro football, he had The Computer in his back pocket and knew better than anybody else what the lines should have been. I developed such a good relationship with Zorba that I used to call him up and tell him what numbers to put up on the screen so we could go bet everyone else. You need to understand that people around the world were looking to him for his numbers. He ran one of the three or four most significant sportsbooks in the world. I would ask him not to move the lines so I could go around the world picking up the right numbers. He was smart. He'd leave the number up on the board as a favor to me, but wouldn't let people bet it. Meanwhile, we'd be out killing the game! He needed me and he helped me. Zorba had the world's best information, which was like what we saw when we were in Curacao. His customer base wasn't anywhere near as big as Paramount's, which was the world's biggest by far, but it was significant.

"Zorba and I got along really well. The first time I met him was in Boston, back when The Animals used to bet him. Whereas The Chinaman dressed nicely and didn't look like most gamblers, Zorba—this multimillionaire—showed up in sweatpants to the meeting. He was like most gamblers when it came down to how he dressed. He might be carrying big money in that suitcase, but he'd be dressed in shorts or sweatpants. Unlike a lot of people, he wasn't afraid to take bets from us. Originally, I'd send checks down to his offshore sportsbook to open accounts. Over time, though, he realized how much we were going to bet and that we were good for the money, so he'd let us bet just like if we were betting with a local out, without the cash in the accounts beforehand. He knew we were betting multiple times a day every day. I had a great relationship with him over the years. He always paid. We didn't really know he was working with The Computer until the early 2000s.

"When I was in Curacao, Zorba was in Jamaica when I really started dealing with him a lot. At one point, Zorba sent over one of his clerks from his sportsbook down supposedly to help Ronnie run All-Star Sports. What Zorba was really doing was sending the clerk down to spy on Ronnie's operation. He was a mole in Ronnie's company, and Zorba later explained the whole thing to me after I left All-Star Sports. That was when Zorba approached me to come down to Jamaica and start working for him. I told him I appreciated the offer but that I was looking forward to getting back to my family and that I'd be working with Tiger and Bull again. He said to keep him in mind if I ever reconsidered. Even though I turned him down, he knew that if he continued to take care of The Animals by letting us bet with him that he could get into some of our outs in the Philadelphia area. He needed us and we needed him. Turning down the offer to work with

Zorba was the best thing I ever did, because it allowed me to hook up with The Chinaman."

THE COMPUTER

Of all the sharps with whom Battista has had a relationship through the years, none compared to The Computer when it came to his standing in the sports betting universe. Commonly discussed throughout the gambling and Las Vegas media, the man with a hard Southern drawl was universally regarded as the most consequential bettor in the U.S., and likely in the world. None of Battista's other former clients or partners engenders anywhere near the excitement in The Sheep. "The Computer was a fucking monster!" Battista says. "He was the greatest. From what I heard, he was dead broke at several times in his life and then got heavy into real estate, where he was successful. Well, he applied his business savvy to gambling, got hooked up with a bunch of computer guys years ago, and brought technology into betting before anybody else. All around, he was just *the best*.

"The Computer was the Keyser Söze of the sports gambling community.[1] He would do anything in his power to get what we wanted. He had some of the top handicappers in the country working for him. As good as he was as a gambler, he was a better businessman than everybody else. He was ruthless and cunning. He'd spend a lot of money just to get somebody out of the game. I was just one person who moved for him and I was probably one of twenty. He'd use thirteen on the right side and the other seven on the wrong side just to keep everybody guessing or just to fuck with them. He had the best handicappers and the best information. He had ex-FBI guys

---

[1] Keyser Söze is a character in the 1995 film *The Usual Suspects* who was a legendary figure in the underworld.

and ex-cops working security for him. The Chinaman would have beat him head-to-head betting, but The Computer's operation was *so* much bigger and influential than anybody in the world.

"He didn't have many friends in the gambling industry. He fucked over so many people to get to where he was that nobody wanted to deal with him. Part of the reason The Computer didn't have friends, too, is that when he got so big a lot of people were trying to get into him to make money. People wanted to know what he was betting all the time, and he would put people on Queer Street to try and stop people from doing that. Well, if you put that many people on Queer Street and cost them money, those people aren't going to like you—even though they're the ones trying to make money off of your work!

"I first met The Computer in the late 1990s out in Las Vegas when he wanted The Animals to move games for him and he wanted to meet us. We actually met him, this multi-multi-millionaire, in a Burger King. I was supposed to meet him again years later in Panama with Zorba, but I was too busy. The Computer used to take his jet and fly from Las Vegas to Panama or Curacao to meet with his friend and business partner, Zorba."

THE ENGLISHMAN

Unlike The Chinaman, Zorba, and The Computer, who are interrelated in various ways, The Englishman was essentially his own story and had very little to do with the other three sharp heavies. Compared to the other three bettors, Battista had relatively infrequent dealings with The Englishman, who nevertheless was a fascinating character. He was better known as a World Series of Poker player, online sportsbook owner, and soccer club owner. Battista's only concern was betting, of course, where, he says, "The Englishman just dominated international soccer."

* * *

"Years ago, before I ever got hooked up with them, Zorba and The Computer were stepping on each other's toes because Zorba had his own incredible handicappers and was fighting with The Computer for the best numbers," Battista says. "After a while they decided to work together and it was lights out! They were pro football, college football, and college basketball. Zorba was a fantastic bookmaker and was always the first person to put up his lines. He had balls, and wasn't afraid to take a bet. Of course, because of his handicappers and because of his relationship with The Computer, he knew what the right side was. So, even though he was betting, he was booking, also. He was just cashing the check. When I worked for them, my job was to get them the best numbers with my outs, and I was paid a percentage on the volume and would get a bonus at the end of the year based on their winnings. Fridays, Saturdays, and Sundays during football season, you practically didn't sleep. At eight o'clock in the morning, we started betting college totals and it went on all day long. We'd bet, maybe, thirty-five college sides, forty-seven totals, and then half-times. We were constantly moving the market and if they ever went down on a game together, it was over. The only problem was getting the money down. We'd split up the distribution as to who would get hit with the money: 'You hit the offshore markets, I'll take Asia and Taiwan, you get Vegas . . .' One of the keys was who was in the seat at the right time to go get the games.

"If you had put The Computer and The Chinaman in a room, locked them in with a million dollars and had them bet against each other, The Chinaman would have walked away twelve hours later with all the money. The Chinaman was a better gambler, and he'd have taken every penny. But, The Computer was just fucking business savvy, he was sharp, he was a control freak, and the more money and power he got the more he worked it to his advantage. He partnered, and fucked, and played, with everyone in his way. That's what it takes sometimes to be number one. In *Godfather II*, they say there should be a statue of Bugsy Siegel in Las Vegas because of his role in building the place. Well, there should be a statue of The Computer somewhere for what he did in sports betting. He brought it to another level, a level the average person can't comprehend. He had something like fifteen handicappers working for him full-time.

"The Chinaman could take any of The Computer's handicappers out, one-on-one, but he couldn't do battle with what was essentially 'The Gambling Association of America'! No one person could, no matter how sharp they were. The Computer was God." Perhaps the only opportunity to beat The Computer's apparatus was to bet hoops, which was not one of his specialties. "There was one time when The Computer was working with a guy who bet on pro basketball and," Battista says, "he wanted to go head-to-head with The Chinaman. Zorba stepped in and said, 'Don't do that. You love your money too much.'"

The world's four best bettors are cordial with each other, according to Battista, especially considering that The Englishman is essentially a stand-alone. "The Computer, The Chinaman, and Zorba get along for the most part. They argue, they fight, but that's just business. There were plenty of times where they were betting against each other and trying to play each other—to see if they could get the other to follow bad money to move the lines. They knew I was moving for the other guys, but I would still try to get them each the numbers they wanted.

I didn't care because I was just getting a percentage on the volume of money I was getting down for them. They fought because a lot of times somebody would get out of bed earlier than the others, start moving games, get the best numbers, and piss off the others. As much as I was a mover, I felt like a counselor half the time because they were bitching and moaning about each other to me! That was part of the reason I got so hooked into drugs. I was so mentally destroyed from being on the phone with these guys all the time, dealing with their problems, betting half-a-zillion dollars for them, and hoping I didn't make any mistakes.

"I think the reason The Chinaman, The Computer, Zorba, and The Englishman all trusted me was because I had worked with Tiger, one of the sharpest guys in the industry, for years. They also knew that I put my work before my family. My family was always second. Yeah, I paid the bills, but I didn't go on vacations and during the holidays dad was working. I was known as being dependable, whereas most gamblers lived by the seat of their pants. They'd get thirty thousand dollars in their pockets and they were looking to go have a good time. I wasn't like that. When I was with Tiger and Bull, The Animals were disciplined, hardworking guys. It was three fat guys sitting in an office and all we did was eat and gamble, eat and gamble. That was the nature of it. So, by the time I went out on my own, I had a reputation as a hardworking, honest guy. When I lost, I paid, and I was efficient and on top of things.

"There might have been a few dozen people in the world at my level working at, with, or just below The Chinaman, The Computer, Zorba, and The Englishman. I knew a lot of them, but you didn't want to be stepping on other people's toes. I don't think there was anyone working for *all four* sharp guys, though."

* * *

PHILLY'S BEST

Though no one in the Philadelphia market came close to rivaling the likes of the four renowned and feared bettors discussed above, Battista's long-standing ties to Joe Vito Mastronardo and Mike Rinnier contributed to his rise in the industry. As The Sheep now juggled working with and among the world's best sharps beginning in 2003, he was still somewhat involved with each of the suburban Philly gamblers, each of whom was his own legendary figure in the area.

JOE VITO MASTRONARDO

"Joe Vito was brilliant, hard-working, and very sure of himself," Battista says. "He was always in great shape and sharp dressed, would always wear shirts with collars. A lot of people couldn't stand him because he was very opinionated and outspoken, and Joe would belittle them if they did something wrong. When I worked with him, I learned so much about booking and betting. In the 80s, when I was just a kid in high school, he was betting The Computer's games and booking those guys. He was already an icon and the wiseguys in Philly were always trying to get into him, but Joe didn't take any shit because he had the best ally in his father-in-law [former Philadelphia Mayor and Police Commissioner, Frank Rizzo]. We were always told that Rizzo couldn't stand Joe Vito, and that Rizzo's family used to get on Joe Vito to be legitimate. But, with Joe, that wasn't going to happen. I met Joe back when I worked for Mike Rinnier. After we got busted in the early 1990s, Joe got busted, too, and went to prison for a year and a half. Joe Vito set up a meeting at a hotel to arrange for maintaining his clients while he was in prison. I went up with Mike and Tiger, and Joe went with his brother John and another bookmaker from New York. Joe had the biggest book in the city and ran everything out in the suburbs.

"I dealt with Joe Vito a lot, and would tell him what the sharp bets were a lot of times. He had gotten so big by the time I was working with The Chinaman and those guys. Joe pretty much controlled the lines for Philly and New York, and had books in Florida and Alabama, so it helped him to get some of the lines through me. I would tell him what the number for certain games was going to be, so that he could adjust his lines accordingly. It was great for Joe because it meant he was less likely to take a hit with his booking and it obviously helped him a lot with his betting. Joe looked at me as a cash cow. He was getting the moves from me first-hand, so he was saving a ton by having the right numbers. As an agent, he also got a percentage of all the stuff I was moving for my guys. And, as a bettor, he had the right sides on the right numbers. I needed him to help me move games and other things, but he benefitted just as much or more by dealing with me. Any time I considered cutting back on what I was doing, he was like, 'Whoa. Whoa. Let me help you find somebody to work with you to help you out,' because he didn't want to be cut off from me.

"Joe actually came over to my house to look at my setup and was begging me to computerize my records. I didn't want to do that, though, because I never wanted any record of what I was doing in case I got locked up. Even though I used computers all the time for my gambling, I never kept files or spreadsheets or stuff like that, and I would destroy the hard drives when I had to. Joe wanted to place someone in my office to monitor what I was betting so that he could bet and move his lines without having to call and bother me. The problem with that was that I worked out of my house and I didn't want other people around my wife and kids. It was one thing for me to be in the office working, but the idea of somebody else in my house all the time bothered me. In fact, I turned down other offers through the years from people who wanted to pay to sit and watch me bet so that they could take the next number."

MIKE RINNIER

"Mike Rinnier apparently kept betting and tried to re-create the betting office after The Animals left him," Battista says. "He came to me sometime in 2004 or 2005 after he heard that since I left him I was now betting for these ultra-sharp guys. He wanted me to give him their games. He proposed that I give Seal the games for him, and that they would be another one of my outs. What Mike never knew was that I paid Seal about a hundred and fifty thousand dollars over the next year or so to work for me. I needed The Seal's outs and information. Mike assumed that because Seal worked for him that Seal would do things in his best interest. Well, me and Seal were good friends, so we worried about ourselves and however that affected Mike, we didn't care. The thing Mike got out of the deal was my football picks, and I would bet five thousand a game for him. This was in the 2005 season. By October or November of that season, I had paid Mike a few hundred thousand. My guys were crushing. Well, Mike called me and asked if I could make it ten thousand bucks a game. I was like, 'You are a greedy fucking pig! Here I am handing you bags of cash and you're still not happy.' It was typical Mike Rinnier, and I was pissed, so I ended it."

12

There's Someone in Stripes on My Side

A LIFELONG PHILADELPHIA EAGLES fan, Jimmy Battista couldn't have been more amped up for a game. He was in Jacksonville to see the Birds play the heavily favored New England Patriots in Super Bowl XXXIX. Decked out in his Brian Westbrook jersey, Battista had great seats near the twenty-yard line for himself, his wife, and his stepson, and was surrounded by the families of the Eagles coaching staff. The Sheep, who was immediately behind Eagles quarterback Donovan McNabb's family and next to Eagles radio broadcaster Merrill Reese's wife and daughter, was probably the only person in the section with somewhat divided rooting interests. "The Chinaman had a million-four on the Eagles plus seven and plus seven-and-a-half," Battista says. "He also had three hundred and eighty-five thousand on the under, which was forty-seven, and we bet the first half.

"The Eagles won the first half, and we won our bet so things were looking good. In the second half, New England started taking control of the game. The Patriots were up twenty-four to fourteen late in the game and I thought we were fucked. Then the Eagles scored a touchdown with about two minutes left in the game to make it twenty-four to twenty-one. Right then, I wanted the game to go final. We'd cover the spread and we'd win the total." After New England recovered the ensuing onside kick, Battista says all he kept thinking was, "No interception, no interception. Just fall down, just fall down!" Battista was satisfied when the Patriots ran the ball three straight times, causing the Eagles to burn their time-outs. Nirvana was at hand as the Eagles got the ball back deep in their own territory with less than a minute to play, and the game ended with a Patriots interception of Eagles quarterback Donovan McNabb with nine seconds left. "I was ready to do hand stands, I was so excited," Battista says, "because I was getting a percentage of his one-point-eight million. As we left the stadium with all the Eagles fans, they were so dejected, and they couldn't figure out why I was on cloud nine, high-fiving my stepson."

* * *

A delicate situation developed in the spring of 2005, requiring Battista to schedule a meeting with The Chinaman, who was based on the West Coast. Though the two men had known each other for a few years and had developed a serious business relationship by now, they had never met.

"There were a few times where he wanted to bet on games Timmy 'Elvis' Donaghy was reffing and I knew what Donaghy's bet was, and The Chinaman wanted to take the wrong side," Battista says. "I would usually just tell him it was a bad bet, or not place the bet without telling him. He was getting pissed at me debating him over some of his NBA bets, because he was one of the world's best and who the fuck was I telling him what to bet?! I flew out to L.A. and met him in a beautiful, four-star hotel." Battista was joined on the trip by Chinese John, Ronnie Park's partner in All-Star Sports who was now a bookmaker in Long Island who controlled a good portion of the Chinatown market. He and Battista had become good friends, and he was one of The Sheep's more significant outs in New York. Battista recruited Chinese John, who like The Chinaman was actually Vietnamese and spoke the language, for the trip as a potential translator. The curiosity of why a translator would be needed at a meeting where all the participants could easily speak English was exhibited soon after the men exchanged pleasantries in the hotel lobby.

The three gamblers seated themselves in a room just off the lobby floor, and Battista got right to the point. "'I have a handicapper that goes against you a lot,'" Battista said. The Chinaman clearly took offense at the notion anyone could hang with him when it came to betting NBA games and replied with bravado, "Well, bring him on!" "You can't beat this guy," Battista responded in a serious tone, to which The Chinaman replied, "What are you talking about?" Battista pressed to make his point, saying, "You can't beat this guy. But, when you're on the same side, we're gonna push it." The Sheep, as would be the case in a similarly touchy situation a few years hence, was trying to tell The Chinaman about his incredible coup without *explicitly* telling him. The verbal dance frustrated The Chinaman who said, "Sheep, what the fuck are you talking about?!" The increasingly heated exchange prompted Battista to grab a pen and write on a piece of hotel stationery: "There's someone in stripes on my side." The Sheep handed the note to Chinese John and instructed John to tell The Chinaman—in Vietnamese—what it said. "I just couldn't bring myself to say what I knew about Donaghy and what I was doing," Battista says. When Chinese John told The Chinaman, Battista's partner looked at him and said, "I knew it! There were so many odd things going on with those games." A sick look then came over The Chinaman's face, and he uttered, "Oh my God." "I think he probably realized how much money he lost before on games Donaghy reffed," Battista says. "So, having that conversation with him saved him a lot of money, even though the basketball season was almost over."

Importantly, the men agreed that The Chinaman would continue to handicap NBA games and if he wanted to bet a game officiated by Tim "Elvis" Donaghy, it would be up to

Battista to see what Donaghy had selected prior to placing The Chinaman's wager. On plenty of occasions The Sheep's client phoned in bets that *matched* Donaghy's pick. "If The Chinaman and Elvis were on the same side, there wasn't enough money in the market for what I would try to get down on the game," Battista says. "There were a few times when The Computer, The Chinaman, *and* Elvis were on the same side. I'd be like, *'Oh . . . my . . . God.'*"

* * *

Souderton, Pennsylvania, lies in northern Montgomery County, some thirty-five miles north of Center City, Philadelphia. The borough has a population of less than seven thousand, and its police force consists of five officers and a chief. One can imagine their angst as a few beatings took place in early 2005 involving delinquent payments to what was being described as a "Vietnamese sports betting ring." The local police soon realized the ring may have been connected to a regional betting operation, and requested the assistance of the Montgomery County District Attorney's Office. The more able Montco D.A.'s Office could provide resources such as wiretaps and undercover operations. In December 2005, a county detective placed bets with the ring, but was soon cut off because he was not betting or losing enough. By this point, however, the investigation involved informants and surveillance, and disclosed a related betting Web site called betroma.com that was ostensibly based in Philadelphia but with ties to an operation in Costa Rica. Of particular importance, it was Joe Vito Mastronardo's customers who were issued passwords for the site. Armed with this information, detectives obtained court-authorized wiretaps and the investigation ultimately led to Joe and John Mastronardo. More wiretaps were procured, resulting in taped conversations including a cabinetmaker who later told authorities he was hired to build secret compartments in Joe Vito's home and furniture to hide cash. Authorities soon learned that betroma.com was about to expand to a suburban office and that another was being renovated. Joe Vito didn't know it, but he was about to make Montgomery County history.

Investigators learned that fifty-six-year-old Joe Vito was planning to bring back a large amount of cash from Florida in late April 2006. He was pulled over in his Cadillac on April 24th when he arrived in Pennsylvania, and a subsequent search of the car resulted in a seizure of five hundred thousand dollars in cash. Authorities then executed twenty-four related search warrants for various properties, including Joe Vito's home, where they found a million dollars. The searches in total netted an additional two-point-two million in cash, mostly in twenty and one hundred dollar bills. County detectives couldn't recall a seizure for their office that was larger than the two-point-seven million dollar Mastronardo haul.

During the plea proceedings, each brother described himself as a "professional gambler," and Joe Vito's attorney took the occasion to make it clear that Joe only took bets from those "who can afford to lose." He added that the consequence for not paying Joe was simply not being permitted to bet with him. As for the origins of the impressive investigation, namely the Vietnamese betting ring, authorities explained that a member of the ring was bringing bets to an associate of the Mastronardos. It was a wiretap on the associate's phone that led police to Joe Vito. With regard to the alleged beatings, the D.A. publicly stated there was no indication the Mastronardo brothers had any knowledge of the incidents. Just like his fellow suburban gambling pal and partner Jimmy Battista, violence being employed on behalf of the self-described "gentleman gambler" was simply never part of Joe Vito's business model. Authorities also announced they did not discover connections to organized crime.

Montco prosecutors could have pursued felony charges in the case, but said they opted for the less consequential misdemeanors because the brothers pleaded guilty and especially because the Mastronardos didn't contest the two-point-seven million dollar forfeiture. This state of affairs raised eyebrows among some observers, including then-imprisoned Philly mob associate Angelo "Fat Ange" Lutz. Lutz, who was serving an eight-year federal sentence for gambling and extortion, said, "They've been booking for the past twenty years . . . For me, they make gambling a federal offense. Maybe that's because I didn't have two million dollars to give up."

Though each Mastronardo brother faced up to ten years in prison, Joe Vito received six months of house arrest followed by more than six years of probation, and John was sentenced to 23 months in prison followed by probation. Given Joe's leading role in the grand scheme of things, his significantly reduced sentence deeply concerned many of his heavy-hitting suburban gambling confederates. Though the press was preoccupied with the historic asset forfeiture, Joe's betting pals universally grappled with the likelihood that he had dimed some of them out in lieu of going back to prison. None was more fearful about Joe Vito's possible negotiations with law enforcement than The Sheep, who was sparring with Joe over a bet-gone-bad just as Joe Vito was negotiating his sweetheart sentencing deal.

"Joe Vito was my money man," Battista says. "He was my agent; he settled my money. He would guarantee up to five million dollars on a weekly basis, and he got paid a percentage of the money. He would settle through bank wires and cash transfers for my money on the East Coast, and I had another guy who did this on the West Coast. The street rate for moving money, transfers and stuff, was usually one percent. If someone wanted to move a hundred grand from New York to the desert, Las Vegas, the mover would get a thousand bucks for an hour's work, tops, just to move the money. Joe was bigger than anyone else around, because he dealt with Paramount Sports and all these other places. Joe and I were partners, where I would do the work of getting all the bets down and he would settle all the money. We were getting paid each week by the sharp guys *just to bet*—win, lose, or draw. It was a cash cow for me and Joe.

"In June 2006, I bet a horse with Paramount Sports. I bet a few times in different ways on a horse for something like seventy-five hundred dollars. I also bet around five grand for myself. The horse hit and I won one hundred and twenty-seven thousand dollars total, but they weren't going to pay me. They said they had a cap of twenty-five thousand dollars at Belmont, where the race took place. They also said I was moving the bets for The Chinaman, and that he had inside horse racing information from jockeys. So, I got stuck for a hundred and two grand that I had to cover with my friends in New York that I was moving the horse for—because I always paid. I wasn't going to stiff them just because I got stiffed. Well, I was pissed with Joe Vito as my agent for not fighting with Paramount for the money. He was saying, 'You're making so much fucking money, why do you want to ruin your reputation fighting with Harry at Paramount?' Joe was Harry's right-hand man for the East Coast, and Joe didn't stick up for me, his partner! He didn't get me paid on the horse, and I was fucking pissed. So, I paid the guys and moved on, but me and Joe were kind of at odds. We were still working together at first, though, because the wheel had to keep turning to make the money. At this point, Joe was putting out the number for every bookmaker in Philadelphia and some other places, and he knew I was moving for the crème de la crème of the sports gambling industry in the world."

While Battista was seething about the horse racing bet fiasco and Joe Vito's refusal to fight on his behalf, The Sheep was still very concerned about the deal his partner was cutting with the Montco prosecutors. Battista let the Belmont-Paramount situation rest as he hoped his longtime betting associate wasn't ratting him out. Of course, Battista's business didn't allow for down time to contemplate such matters, and he was soon offered a deal with a legendary New York bookmaker that would have long-standing—and ultimately fatal—consequences.

"Joe hooked me up with this bookmaker in New York named Bluto, who could move up to two hundred and fifty thousand dollars a game for me at the right number," Battista says. "Joe Vito and Bluto were close friends. I got to hang out with Bluto a bunch of times—in Philly, in Atlantic City, in New York. Bluto was an older Jewish guy, probably in his mid-fifties, who was built like a brick shithouse and didn't drink. When I was with The Animals, we did some business with him and we would settle anywhere up to two hundred thousand dollars down in Atlantic City. He would always have an entourage with him. We'd be at the craps tables, and he could be down a million or so and he'd tell me to 'come on over and roll the bones' to change his luck. He was betting a hundred grand on every roll. This guy was an animal, and I loved him. He was also a true businessman.

"We later heard that his father and grandfather were big-time guys with one of the world's major financial firms. Bluto was loaded because of his family, but he was also a gambler and bookmaker. I also heard that at one point he was married to the daughter of the Gambino crime family's consigliere, but that he got divorced. People also said that Bluto booked John Gotti back in the early 1980s, and that Gotti supposedly only had to pay on half of his losses. I didn't know what relationship he had with anybody, including New York mob families. It's not like people in my line of work asked people for business cards and credentials! I had no idea what people did or who they worked with, and they didn't know who I worked with.

"Well, I met with Bluto at a Yankees-Phillies game at Citizens Bank Park in the summer of 2006. Joe Vito had a nice box at the park, the kind with the bar and everything, and we met there. I told Bluto I wanted him to start moving some games for me and that I needed a quarter of a million per game for football. Up until then, he'd get me forty or fifty dimes, but I knew he had access to some of the stores that were taking astronomical bets. I knew you had to get invited to that party. Well, like a lot of people, he knew the sharp guys I was moving for, and most people were leery of taking that action. The way I got him to take my football action was that I told him that I knew of a *phenomenal* NBA handicapper [without mentioning it was referee Tim Donaghy] and that I might want Bluto to move up to two hundred grand a game without affecting the market when the season started. He knew he'd be able to make good money on those games, so he decided to help me move NBA games in a few months and we agreed to work the 2006-07 football season together."

The Sheep didn't know it, but as the summer of 2006 came to an end, the clock was ticking on his impressive career. The Joe Vito-Bluto-Battista interrelationships would be revisited in the not-too-distant future, and would manifest themselves on a national stage. Until then, Battista had pressing matters at home to address.

13

Jimmy, Tommy, and Timmy

DENISE AND JIMMY Battista wed in 1994, and by the fall of 2006 the couple had a full and active household. Denise's son and daughter from her first marriage were joined by three girls she and Jimmy had together, and the kids now collectively ranged in age from five to fifteen years old. Because of Battista's unyielding work schedule, Denise was raising all five kids by herself, and was left on her own to manage the house and the bills and practically anything not gambling-related. The Sheep's rise in the betting world had coincided with the growth of his young family and, despite his hopes and wishes, the two sets of circumstances were not a comfortable fit whatsoever. The resulting strain with Denise only increased with each passing month Jimmy was a non-factor in the family's affairs, and by now the twelve-year marriage was in serious jeopardy. Predictably, Battista's profession simply wouldn't permit him to make things right at home, and another problem arose when a colleague passed along some frightening news from the street: the FBI was investigating The Sheep.

"I had the best information, and I had the biggest outs in the world," Battista says. "When I spoke, people listened, because they would do anything to get the information from these guys I was handling. I caught wind that the feds were onto me and wanted to know how I was moving millions of dollars a week for these guys without anyone really knowing about it. It suddenly just all got too much for me. I started getting deeper into OxyContin, and started losing some money because of poor decision making while I was high." The "poor decision making" referenced by The Sheep concerns the numerous and significant bets he placed *on his own*, which marked a Battista first. Up until this point, he recognized, indeed he embraced, his finite niche as a mover. He was now personally betting on sporting events and, especially problematically, on games of chance online and in Atlantic City casinos, where his unreal connections and inside information were wholly useless.

The Sheep had gone twenty-plus years without behaving like the suckers he, The Animals, and the world's biggest sharps so routinely mocked. Incredibly, for the first time in his impressive career, Jimmy "Baba" Battista was paying for the party. "I was making substantial money," Battista says, "and because I had access to the right information, I would tell myself that I could always get the money that I lost gambling back. I could bet a few hundred thousand dollars a couple of times a day and win back a few million like nothing. That's the way I thought."

The pill popping that was designed to alleviate The Sheep's myriad problems unsurprisingly made things worse, especially at home. Though Denise didn't know her husband was consuming increasing numbers of OxyContin pills and the occasional line of cocaine, nor why things had gotten to this point in their relationship, she knew enough to prefer having Jimmy around her and the kids less and less. As a result, Battista began to work, and at times stay, elsewhere. His longtime pal, Tommy Martino, was the one who assisted him most, allowing Battista essentially to come and go as he pleased.

In the midst of this chaos, an old associate was about to make things even more interesting—and complicated—for The Sheep.

* * *

After graduating from Cardinal O'Hara High School in the 1980s, Jimmy Battista and Tommy Martino had remained good friends, so much so that each man served as best man in their respective weddings. In fact, so close was Battista to the Martino family that Tommy's brother, Johnny, was the second best man in Battista's first wedding. A lot had changed for Tommy and Jimmy by the early 2000s, when Battista first contemplated recruiting his lifelong buddy as a glorified, and well-paid, gopher.

"After high school, Tommy went to a computer school to learn how to fix computers, got a legitimate job in Delaware with J.P. Morgan, and was still selling weed," Battista says.[1] "He got married, and I was in his wedding party. Tommy's buddy Timmy Donaghy was at his wedding, too. Tommy's brother, Chuck, had a hair salon, and Tommy used to work there. A party scene was tied to the salon, too. I was friends with Chuck, just like with Tommy and Johnny Martino, which was pretty cool. We met a lot of interesting people through the salon. Pat Croce, former owner of the Philadelphia 76ers, used to have Chuck cut his hair, and sometimes we'd get free tickets to the games."

Even though Battista and Martino had never gone more than a few weeks over the years without seeing or speaking with each other, their respective illicit business ventures were left aside their friendship. "Tommy and I didn't work together until we were in our late thirties when I was on my own as a gambler," Battista says. "I wanted him to help me as a runner, essentially, and I knew he had the time to work with me because he was still selling weed. Tommy was probably making more money selling drugs than he was fixing computers. I told him to stop selling the fucking drugs and just come work with me. I was paying him around fifteen hundred bucks a week

---

[1] Tommy Martino worked for J.P. Morgan Chase Corporation in Christiana, Delaware.

just to run around for me and to keep getting me my drugs. There was one time where I was yelling at him, 'Tommy, you have ten pounds of marijuana in your fucking garage! If you get caught, you're gonna go to jail for a long time!' I think for a little while he did stop dealing his pot and just kept getting me pills and cocaine."

Martino and Battista were in each other's company more frequently than in the previous several years, and yet despite Martino's close friendship with NBA referee Tim Donaghy, Battista made a conscious decision not to be in the same place as Donaghy over the years. Of course, because of their mutual friendship with Martino, he and Donaghy were always somewhat aware of each other's affairs. "I wouldn't associate myself with Timmy," Battista says. "He was an NBA referee, and I was a known gambler and former bookmaker. Timmy didn't want to be seen anywhere near me, and I didn't want to be seen anywhere near him, and Tommy would do whatever we said." Long before Donaghy ever wagered on an NBA game he was officiating, and even longer before conspiring with Battista to bet on games, Battista assumed he and Donaghy would be dealing with each other at some point. "I always knew that sooner or later Timmy was going to need me. I knew sooner or later—I didn't know when—that Timmy would have to come to me. It was just his nature. I knew that Timmy's demand for money far exceeded his ability to get it. If the NBA gave out free tampons, Timmy would take them. That's the type of guy he was. He was fucking shrewd, and believed everyone owed him the world."[2]

---

[2] Former NBA referee Robbie Robinson similarly characterized Donaghy as greedy: "Anytime there was a money-related extra assignment, like teaching a clinic or making a personal appearance, Donaghy would want to do it. If he wasn't chosen, he would be livid. He would go into an absolute tirade . . . If the league office told him to stand on his head for two minutes before every quarter, Donaghy would do it. He was obsessed with becoming a Finals referee to get the extra money." Senior referees who work through the NBA Finals can earn as much as an extra seventy-five thousand dollars.

All of this was before Battista's surreal 2003 All-Star Sports experience in Curacao, which ended the first iteration of his "partnership" with Tommy Martino. Upon his return to the U.S., The Sheep re-enlisted Martino's services, but it was Battista's marital problems, following the split with The Animals, which eventually enhanced Martino's role in Battista's betting operation. The increasingly frequent shift in "office" location from The Sheep's home, where more than a dozen computers and numerous televisions and various communication devices were available, to Martino's house in 2006 was a major hassle for Battista. In fact, he needed to borrow the use of Martino's laptop to try and keep up.[3] "I would have his laptop next to mine on his kitchen table, side by side," Battista says. "That way, I would use one to monitor the lines on Don Best and the other one to bet. It wasn't until I was operating out of his house and I got so busy that he started placing bets for me. He didn't place a lot of bets for me, but he placed some because I was so fucking busy. I'd be on the road, and my job was so demanding with moving the games and stuff like that. I kept my laptop at his house and he could go to the betting Web sites for me. I gave him my codes and all. I also stashed money at his house.

"By that point, I was on my own and wasn't working with The Animals anymore. I needed someone to work with. I realized I was fucked; I only had two hands and needed ten. Tommy would meet people for money, go get me drugs—my coke and Oxys, and drive me to places like New York and Atlantic City when I was meeting people. That way, I could sit in the car, have my laptop, and work the phones. I could talk on two phones and gamble while he was driving me around. It was great for him, too, because he still had his full-time

---

[3] Tommy Martino's various statements to the FBI support Battista's version of events *in re:* working out of Martino's home; having Martino bet on his behalf; using Martino's laptop and allowing Martino to use his; he and Donaghy obtaining drugs from Martino; and Martino's role in the local drug trade, among other related matters.

job fixing computers and he made good money working for me. His regular job had benefits and with my line of work, you never knew when you were gonna get busted or how long people would be around, so he kept it. I'd pay him anywhere from a thousand to twenty-five hundred a week, depending on what he did for me. I always had a lot of tickets to a bunch of events, and I'd set him up with all sorts of things." According to Battista, having the forty-year-old, recently divorced Martino more involved in the life of The Sheep had little impact on Tommy's day job.[4] "Even though he still had his job fixing computers at J.P. Morgan, Tommy was never at work," he says. "When I used to operate out of his house, he'd be home laying out in the sun, and was more worried about getting a tan than with being at work."

Martino's tanning exploits were legendary among his circle of friends and were part of a long-standing pattern of behavior. "Tommy was obsessed with his appearance ever since we were little," Battista says. "If you had to sum up Tommy's life, it would be called *Weed, Insecurity, and Women.* Tommy was, like, five-foot-five, and had what some people call 'Little Man's Disease.' He was always insecure about his height, and he always felt he had to prove to someone that he wasn't a little guy. He would dye his hair and his eyebrows, and make sure he was tan all the time to overcome his height. Of course, this psychobabble is coming from a bald and fat guy!"[5]

---

[4] Tommy Martino divorced in 2005.

[5] Battista's self-described "psychobabble" regarding Tommy Martino was perhaps not as flippant as he thought. A psychologist who later evaluated Martino said that he appeared "almost adolescent in his physical and social demeanor" and that he was "fastidious about his eyebrows and hair." The psychologist also noted that Martino was "somewhat immature, dependent and in need of considerable social recognition to bolster his self-image," which may have been best exhibited on Martino's MySpace page, which then listed his interests as "cars, women, working, sports and the gym." At the time, he also posted, "I dine out 3 or 4 times a week and live every day like it's my last. If I died tomorrow, I know for a fact I've done more than most 95 year-olds." Martino was ultimately diagnosed with Histrionic Personality Disorder, in which the

Working out of Tommy Martino's house was designed to help solve Battista's problems at home, and to an extent it did. Unfortunately for The Sheep and his family, being around Martino meant an increased likelihood Tim Donaghy would somehow enter the mix. At the time, Martino considered Donaghy a "good friend," and Donaghy called Martino a "true friend." "When I was working out of Tommy's house," Battista says, "Timmy was calling Tommy all the time, mostly bullshitting about women and pot. Timmy used to ask Tommy to mail him weed down in Florida, and Tommy was so fucking stupid he would do it. He mailed him pot a few times, even though I was telling him I thought he was crazy. I didn't want him getting locked up because I needed him to work for me. It was bad enough he was selling drugs around our area, but *mailing* drugs? Are you fucking kidding?!

"When I was in high school, I didn't hang out with Timmy but we knew each other. He hung more with Tommy because they both liked to smoke pot. After high school, Timmy used to always try to come across as Mr. Almighty, better than everybody else, because he was going to Villanova and his father was a collegiate referee. Tommy was more known for getting laid, having hot girls, and selling drugs. When Timmy was a senior in high school and I was about nineteen or twenty, he was in a lot of escapades down the shore. Timmy liked drinking, like a lot of us, but he was a sick pup and really liked fucking with people. One night we were partying and he got all fucked up and went from house to house stealing shit from people. He was just a strange, mean-spirited guy." Tommy Martino, of course, was also privy to Donaghy's "pranks," which Martino says included

---

afflicted person's self-esteem "depends on the approval of others and does not arise from a true feeling of self-worth." Such persons have a "desire to be noticed and often behave dramatically or inappropriately to get attention."

Donaghy: calling police to break up a party; pulling a fire alarm to break up a party; using stink bombs; and urinating in a girl's saline solution and shampoo.[6] "Timmy and Tommy partied together a bit in high school, but they were a year apart. Right after high school they became close friends; Timmy liked smoking pot, and Tommy was the one who got it for him. They kept in contact through the years mostly because of dope and pussy, and they would get together when Timmy was in town."

By the summer of 2006, Tim Donaghy was a twelve-year veteran NBA referee earning two hundred and sixty thousand dollars per year, who also happened to be betting on games he officiated for at least the previous three seasons. By this point, in fact, pro gambler Jimmy "Baba" Battista had all but ceased referring to Donaghy as "Timmy." Rather, The Sheep opted to almost exclusively call him "Elvis," the apt nickname Battista had been using ever since making the Great Discovery while in Curacao.

"Elvis knew me for years, and Tommy would tell him, 'Baba is over here working,' and stuff like that," Battista says, "so Elvis knew what my situation was from Tommy." What Donaghy didn't know, however, was that since 2003 Battista had been tracking the bets Donaghy placed with Jack Concannon. "Even though he had been betting successfully with his NBA games the past few years, Elvis was pissing away money throughout the year betting other sports. At the start of the '06-07 NFL season, he got crushed in September and October. The guys who were providing Jack Concannon with their football picks were having a bad season, which meant that Jack and Elvis were losing good money. Elvis would always ask

---

[6] Donaghy apparently continued such behavior long after high school. In the late 1990s, according to a retired dentist named John Minutella, Donaghy put a dead, maggot-infested, bird in Minutella's golf bag, which was not discovered until the following day. Minutella said of Donaghy: "Nobody wanted to play golf with him. I can't say one nice thing about him. I believe this guy was almost soulless."

Tommy, 'Who's Sheep on?' For three or four weeks starting in late October or early November, I was giving Tommy my football games to give to Elvis.[7]

"My guys were picking winners and his guys were picking losers. It was that simple. Elvis would call Tommy every week and say things like, 'Sheep's guys don't lose!' After a few weeks, he said, 'Nobody can be this good!' My guys were absolutely crushing that season, and Elvis got hooked up with me at the right time. That, really, is how the whole 'thing' between Jimmy Battista and Timmy "Elvis" Donaghy started in the fall of 2006. Elvis asked Tommy how he could thank me for giving him the winning football picks. I said that we'd talk about it when we got together when he came into town next time, but he insisted. So, I said that Elvis could get me a signed Kobe Bryant jersey for my stepson. Pretty soon, a FedEx package arrived at Tommy's house and it was Kobe's signed game jersey. The first payment in the NBA betting scandal was actually an autographed Kobe Bryant Lakers jersey from Elvis to me. He got it done, which I really appreciated."

As Battista spent more time with Tommy Martino, The Sheep could sense that the days of mimicking Jack Concannon's bets would soon be over. "I knew Jack wasn't paying Elvis because Tommy told me Elvis couldn't stop complaining about Jack owing him money. There was a night in late October or early November when Elvis called Tommy at one o'clock in the morning, complaining that Jack owed him forty thousand dollars, and that Jack lost the money in Atlantic City. Elvis was also bitching to Tommy that Concannon said people [losing bettors] weren't paying him, so he couldn't pay Elvis for the games he owed him. I never let on to Tommy that I knew for a long time that Elvis was betting with Concannon, and obviously I didn't mention anything about Elvis betting on his own games."

---

[7] Battista says he gave Donaghy six to eight football picks each week.

Weeks before hooking up with Battista for his football picks, Donaghy and his colleagues had tipped off the 2006-07 NBA season. This season would be unlike any other for the league, and for Donaghy. "By the time the NBA season started in late October, Elvis was deep in the hole from his other sports bets," Battista says, "which is probably why he bet every fucking game he reffed from the start of the season." Noting that until then, Donaghy had only bet on a few dozen games he officiated each of the past three seasons, Battista says, "His betting behavior changed in the '06-07 NBA season." Donaghy went an astounding ten-and-o to start the NBA season, according to Battista, wagering on each of the first ten games he officiated. These wagers were placed with Jack Concannon, who couldn't possibly have known how the next few weeks would alter his life—and the lives of everyone involved—forever, beginning with the now-infamous December meeting at the Philadelphia International Airport Marriott.

"I only met with Elvis after I got him off of Queer Street with his football bets," Battista says. "The meeting we wound up having at the Marriott would have occurred earlier, but Elvis wasn't going to be in town until December 12th. Starting in late October or early November, Elvis called Tommy every day because he was getting my football picks. At that point in the year, there is football to bet almost all the time. Tommy was trying to schedule a meeting between all of us since right after Thanksgiving. I finally got to thank Elvis in person for the autographed Kobe Bryant jersey when we met in the Marriott."[8]

---

[8] Battista's version of events *in re:* the meeting with Donaghy at the Marriott (discussed in the Prologue) is supported by Tommy Martino's statements to the FBI, including such details as the conversation at the restaurant table between Battista and Donaghy regarding Donaghy's pre-existing betting on his NBA games with Jack Concannon, and the side conversation soon afterward between Martino and Donaghy, during which Donaghy "admitted to betting on his own games with Concannon."

* * *

So, the men gathered on the evening of December 12th,
ultimately cutting the deal to wager on Donaghy's games
inside a pot smoke-filled car outside a convenience store, with
all three conspirators flying high. Before the night ended,
Donaghy told Battista the Boston Celtics were "going to kill"
the Philadelphia 76ers the following night, and The Sheep
placed his bets throughout the next day accordingly. Indeed,
the Celtics destroyed the Sixers, winning by twenty points,
resulting in the conspiracy's first successful wagers. The next
night, on December 14th, the three men convened again. This
time they met at Tommy Martino's house, where Battista had
been spending so much time since summer, and where Tim
"Elvis" Donaghy often made it a point to stop when he was in
town. The purpose of the meeting was to iron out the specifics of the newly consummated deal to bet on games Donaghy
would be officiating.

"At the meeting at Tommy's house the night after Elvis reffed the Celtics at the Sixers," Battista says, "I put five thousand
dollars wrapped in a rubber band on the edge of Tommy's
couch and told Elvis, 'This is for our new partnership.' I didn't
want to put it in his hand. I paid him two thousand for that
game, but the five grand was just a 'Welcome to the party'
kind of thing; like a signing bonus.

"I didn't want to talk to Elvis on the phone, so I told him
that he needed to call Tommy in the morning of a game—at
the latest—with his pick so that I could get the best numbers.
I told Elvis that if we were going to bet the favorite and some-

---

Donaghy, according to Martino, complained that Concannon was not paying him what
he was owed, and thus Donaghy "wanted to start giving picks to Baba." Martino says
that after the meeting, Battista acted "like a savior who was there to help Donaghy,"
and the FBI sums up the situation thusly: "Martino had the impression that Donaghy
wanted to provide picks to Baba for Donaghy's own financial gain." Of minor note,
Martino told the FBI it was Battista's idea to schedule the meeting, whereas Battista
claims that Donaghy requested the conference.

body else liked that side, the line might move a point-and-a-half or two points, which was a *huge* move for an NBA game. We didn't want to miss getting the number before other people started betting, so he had to call Tommy early in the morning or the night before. I also told him that whatever the line was in the paper, I would get us a better number. So, if we were picking an underdog that was listed in the morning paper as getting eight points, he knew I'd be getting us *at least* nine points. I explained to him how I would finagle to get us the best numbers because I was controlling the market."

As they concluded the meeting, two days into what would later become known as the NBA betting scandal, Battista left Martino's house with supreme confidence the scheme would produce significant and immediate results. The Sheep had parroted Jack Concannon's bets on Tim Donaghy's games for the previous three NBA seasons, and would now get Donaghy's picks directly. The new arrangement would permit Battista to manipulate the world's betting lines much more in his favor now, because he would be getting the picks on Donaghy's games much earlier. Of course, the scheme ultimately depended upon Donaghy's picks, and with respect to that component of the conspiracy, Battista had no doubts. "I knew he was going to do whatever it took to win," Battista says. "Elvis could set the tempo of a game, and affect the outcome of the game. To me, Timmy was 'Elvis' aka 'The King' because I had been winning so much on his games, and because I didn't want to be on the phone using his name."

The first few weeks of the arrangement were successful, and minor adjustments were made to the scheme's logistics. "The set up was working good," Battista says. "The first three games we crushed, and I said to Tommy, 'Tell Elvis I'll move him to five thousand a game.'"[9] Battista's and Donaghy's mutual

---

[9] In various court filings, the federal government stated that the arrangement did, in fact, change from $2,000 to $5,000 per winning bet. Tommy Martino told the

friend was not left out of the illicit and profitable deal. "Tommy got twenty-five hundred bucks a game," Battista says, "and just like Elvis' deal, he didn't have to pay if we lost. This was in addition to whatever I paid Tommy to run around for me." Right around this time, Battista told Donaghy that in the event of a "stone-cold lock"—as sure a winner as Donaghy believed there could be—the code for such a pick would be "schmaga." "The term 'schmaga' came from when me and Tommy were growing up," Battista says. "Tommy had a neighbor who was a mentally handicapped boy whose nickname was Schmaga. We got real close to him because he used to come to all of our sporting events; Holy Cross football, CYO basketball. We became pretty close with him and treated him like a little brother. Elvis knew who Schmaga was, too, just like most of the people we went to high school with." The payment for a winning schmaga pick would be ten thousand dollars, resulting from Battista's more consequential wagering on such incredible Donaghy "handicapping."

Because the plan was to bet exclusively on Donaghy's games, the conspirators could more easily use coded language to conceal the true intent of their conversations. "Elvis would call Tommy as early as possible to tell us who he liked," Battista says, "and to find out what the number was at that point. We would never say the teams. At first we said that 'Chuck' was the home team and 'Johnny' was the away team.[10] So, if I called Tommy, I'd say something like, 'I'm going over to Chuck's house for dinner tonight and I'll be there by six.' That was my way of telling Tommy the home team was favored by six. If I said 'seven-thirty,' it meant the line was seven-and-a-half. Whatever the line was, I spoke like that to Tommy. We later changed it to 'Mom' for home and 'Dad' for away.

FBI that Donaghy's payment was increased from $2,000 to $5,000 per win after approximately ten games.

[10] These were inspired by Tommy Martino's brothers. Chuck ("home") lived closer than Johnny ("away").

"Once I knew what side Elvis liked, I'd get to work. I'd bet, like, a hundred and twenty thousand in Europe, then maybe thirty to fifty thousand at a few outs in Asia, all of it before people were gonna start betting in the U.S. The hope was that I could get some money accumulated over there without affecting the offshore and U.S. markets." Of course, there were also plenty of times Battista wanted to fool the market, and get others to follow the wrong sides of his bets, allowing him to get the betting lines he actually wanted from the start. "I had the most sophisticated computer setup moving these games, and I was trying to filter the games through Europe, Taiwan, Vegas, and the rest of the U.S. I would use money from the sharp guys to bet around fifty thousand dollars and invest it betting on the games the wrong way. I was just sabotaging the market. So, if I wanted to take seven on a game and the game was four-and-a-half and five, I'd lay the four-and-a-half and five. The followers would lay the five-and-a-half and six, and force the bookmakers to go to seven. Now, it was sitting around seven, and I'd be taking back the seven. I'd be sending people offshore, 'Go get me a *half a million* plus seven.' Bookmakers were in a frenzy because the lines were moving so much, and they were getting opened up to being middled. The lines would move from three, to four, to five, to six, to seven. They were fucked. If I laid four and four-and-a-half and the game went to seven and I take seven, and the game lands on five or six, the bookmakers were getting destroyed. I had people in England betting for me, people in Taiwan, and the money would filter back into the United States. No one had any idea where the action was coming from.

"Elvis would call us back in the afternoon or early evening on game days to see what numbers I got, and to let me know if there were any lineup changes or if someone was sick or injured. Sometimes, he would actually call Tommy from the locker room right before his game to see what numbers I got on the game. He wouldn't start a game until he knew what the number was."

Because Battista was still betting for his heavy-hitting clients, including wagers on NBA games, there were some awkward moments when bets would be phoned in on games Donaghy was officiating. Most often, the bettors would call in with their picks early in the morning, and Battista would tell them he wanted to hold off and see how the betting lines were going to change—without explaining that he was behind whatever line changes were in the offing. The Chinaman, of course, had known for a while what was going on and commonly benefitted from Battista's "handicapper" picks. Some challenges remained for The Sheep, however. "There were times that it was a pain in the ass if my bettors wanted the same side of a Donaghy game," Battista says, "because there wasn't enough money in the market, and I wanted to get my bets down at the right number. I would never fuck them over, though, and put them on the wrong side. I would usually tell them I could get them 'X' number, which was close to what I was going to take but wouldn't affect my bets."

14

Trouble Shooting

THE NEW YEAR hadn't even begun, and already there was a sense of trepidation filtering in among the exuberance felt by the scandal's beneficiaries. Battista's role in the scheme, and more importantly the outrageous amounts of money he was now placing for himself and his clients on Donaghy's games, was unnerving even to seasoned, big-time sports bettors.

"After the first five games with Elvis, we were five-and-o," Battista says, "and Bluto was freaked out by what was going on. He was one of my bigger outs in the U.S., and wanted to know if they were The Chinaman's games, The Computer's games, or if they were my 'handicapper's' games. The thing was, if my guys wanted the same side as Elvis did, there wasn't enough money in America. If the world's two sharpest handicappers liked the same side *and* Elvis was reffing the game, there weren't enough banks in the country. The information was just too strong. We were laying two and three on a game, and bookmakers were coming in and laying four and five. That's why bookmakers knew something was going on. These were the most respected bookmakers in the world. They didn't cheat on the numbers, and they were very good at what they did. The lines were moving so much, and it wasn't like there were injuries or anything else that could account for the big line moves. People couldn't do anything about what I was doing, and the best they could do was take the next number. Sometimes you'd see a line go from two or two-and-a-half all the way up to eight, and that started happening a lot."

An example of line moves repeatedly referenced by Battista can be found by looking at those from one of the scandal's first games. Tim Donaghy was going to be officiating the game between Team A and Team B, an eight-and-a-half point favorite and Donaghy's pick. As was typical of his betting pattern throughout the NBA scandal (and, indeed, for many of his bets generally), Battista got to work by giving what pro gamblers call a "head fake," placing bets on the wrong side in the hopes of getting the sucker money to follow. This action ultimately forces sportsbooks to alter lines accordingly, and results in the progenitor of the action getting a more advantageous line on the side he wanted all along, which he now bets in sums that dwarf those placed earlier on the wrong side. That is precisely what happened in this instance, when Battista placed forty thousand and five hundred dollars on the underdog Team A plus eight-and-a-half points, after which the line moved down to eight by the next minute. Battista bet twice more within two minutes, bringing the total investment in reducing the point spread to ninety-five thousand dollars placed in a span of less than three minutes.

Now, Battista simply waited for the suckers to do their part, and watched the spread drop to where he wanted it from the start. Within an hour's time, the line had incredibly, and yet predictably, moved three full points, and Battista had a line he liked (Team B minus five). He started firing away, and his first two bets on the favorite, totaling sixty-six thousand and five hundred dollars, moved the line a minute later to Team B minus six. The new spread was still fine by The Sheep, who proceeded to bet an additional three hundred and forty thousand dollars over twelve bets in various ways on Team B within the next six minutes. Altogether, Battista bet over four hundred and seven thousand dollars on Team B. For this particular game, Battista also wagered a total of more than fifty-two thousand dollars on the "over." The tally for Battista's bets on this game—in this single offshore account—was: five hundred and fifty-five thousand and two hundred and fifty dollars over twenty-one bets within sixty-three minutes. This tidy example illustrates how fast the market almost always adapts to the sharp money, and why pro gamblers need to bet discreetly or quickly lose the wanted betting line. In the specific case of Battista's bets on games Donaghy was officiating, obvious bets like those above were sure to arouse the curiosity of all sorts of parties, none of whom had The Sheep's best interests in mind.

* * *

Jimmy Battista didn't have a particularly high regard for Tim Donaghy, dating back to high school. Now a partner with him in an illicit betting scheme, the longtime gambler with a penchant for controlling outcomes was constantly worried the referee would seek out additional opportunities to profit from games he was officiating. Such Battista concerns were only aggravated when the betting lines of Donaghy's games either moved early or in a direction that didn't follow the expected pattern. Still worse, The Sheep discovered within weeks of cutting his deal with Donaghy that he, just as he feared, couldn't trust the referee or the scandal's intermediary, mutual friend Tommy Martino.

"There was one time when Elvis called in his pick like always," Battista says, "but when I tuned in to watch the game that night, Elvis wasn't on the court during the pregame. He wasn't reffing the game he picked! I was like, 'Fuck!' Tommy didn't tell me Elvis was betting someone else's game that night. By that point, I had already moved close to a million dollars on the game, a lot of it with Bluto up in New York. I immediately called him and said, 'We gotta get off this game,' and he screamed, 'What are you talking about?! I can't get off the game.' We tried to buy the game back, but there was no way Bluto could go back to these guys who took all the action because they would be opened up for a middle. We put so much money on the game that the line moved three to four points, and if the stores now took our money on the other side, they'd be fucked. I didn't know how much he bet for himself, but there was no way he wasn't piggybacking what I was doing. He'd bet a million dollars on a game like it was nothing.

"Bluto was really pissed at what had happened, and it cost him a lot of money. He called me and said, 'That's it. I'm paying you your money and you're never going to stick it up my ass again.' I found out a week later that he had bet heavy on the game and lost two to three million. He paid my agent in Vegas the six hundred and seventy thousand he owed me, but was still furious over getting fucked, and stopped doing business with me entirely.

"That game was one of [NBA referee and then close Donaghy friend] Scott Foster's games, and it was a loss. I told Tommy to tell Elvis right after that game that I wanted to see his referee schedule, because I couldn't trust him or Tommy. Once I had his schedule, and Elvis would tell me ahead of time who he liked, I could manipulate the lines and it was fat city." Beyond the issue of trust, there was also discord between Donaghy and his co-conspirators over his payments. "For what we were doing," Battista says, "Elvis wanted to be paid, like, the next moment. I kept telling him that because of who he was and because we were dealing in cash, that I would pay him in segments, like forty-five or fifty grand each time. He also drove Tommy crazy because he was always calling and asking, 'How many apples are in my basket? How many apples are in my basket?!'"[1]

By early January, Battista suspected that his runners were selling his picks on Donaghy's games, which adversely

---

[1] "Apples" was the (easily decipherable) code the men used for dollars. Thus, "five thousand apples" meant $5,000.

impacted much of what The Sheep was trying to do. As a result, in addition to betting the wrong side simply to move the line in his favor, Battista would often bet the wrong side to harm those who were trying to copy his bets. "I was so mad," he says, "because I would tell the runners, 'Go get me X amount of dollars per game,' and the market would move in ways it shouldn't have, and I'd say to them when they got back to me, 'What the fuck did you do? You know what? You either do what I tell you to do or you're gonna get it in the ass, and it's gonna come hard. You won't know what the right side is, and you won't know where the real money is coming from.' The beauty of the gambling market was that you could move the money in from Europe, from Asia, from offshore, to Vegas in all sorts of ways."

Within weeks, Battista encountered more problems when the betting lines on Donaghy's games started moving prematurely. "Some of the games started to scoot out early," Battista says, "and I was screaming, 'Why are these fucking games moving?! I'm trying to get X number of dollars on the game and it's already starting to trickle.' The days I was working, I was glued to the computer all day watching the lines move, and I knew where the money was being moved and who was moving the games. People who bet where I did weren't betting just for the fun of it. If a line moved, it was because of solid information. The Englishman, the Chinaman, and Zorba were using me to move their games, so I knew what their NBA picks were. If one of Elvis' games moved, I knew it wasn't because of them.

"I don't know if Elvis was bragging to people or betting with Jack Concannon or other people or what. Even though I told him from the beginning not to deal with Concannon anymore or any other guys because I didn't want it to get out, I think his greed factor got to him and that he was giving the games out.[2] Elvis had his little entourage of bookmakers and other people that were betting the games. At that point, Concannon wasn't using Pete Ruggieri to get down on the games. Whoever Elvis or Concannon wound up using had to know what was going on, or whoever that person was placing bets with did, because otherwise the bets they placed wouldn't have been enough to move the lines. Even though I was betting good money for Tommy already, I found out later he was betting the games with a friend of his. Tommy was only betting three hundred bucks a game, and meanwhile his guy was betting thousands offshore.[3] Greed became a big factor for everybody.

"Who knows how many people were piggybacking games Elvis was reffing when you think about everybody telling their friends about these sure winners? I was such a control freak that it was driving me fucking crazy to see the lines move when they weren't supposed to. My guys—The Chinaman, The Computer, Zorba, and The Englishman—were consistently picking fifty-six to sixty percent, and people were dying to know these picks. Well, *Elvis was picking seventy-eight percent*, so you can imagine how much people wanted to jump on games he was reffing. There's that scene in the movie *Wall Street* where Charlie Sheen [playing the role of insider stock broker Bud Fox] says, 'Blue Horseshoe loves Anacott Steel' and that sets off all this activity—phone calls, stock trades.

---

[2] According to the FBI, Battista's intuition regarding Donaghy betting with Jack Concannon on games Donaghy officiated after December 12, 2006, was well founded. There is disagreement on precisely when Donaghy reunited with Concannon, however, because the FBI says that Donaghy didn't resume betting on his games with Concannon until February. Importantly, Donaghy admitted to betting with Concannon from February to April 2007, which had ramifications for the Battista-Donaghy-Martino conspiracy.

[3] Martino discussed this situation with the FBI, though he apparently did not discuss how much money was being wagered. The FBI summary states, "a friend of Martino's whom Martino knew from Costa Rica . . . liked sports gambling so Martino provided [him] with some of the picks made by Donaghy." The FBI added that the friend "was aware that these picks were coming from Donaghy."

Well, that's what it was like when I was betting anything, and when I was betting Elvis' games. It was like, 'Whoosh!' The lines were flying, and all you'd hear people saying was, 'Sheep's on this game! Sheep's on this game!' By January, people knew I was betting on sure winners."

No one can know just how widespread the knowledge of The Sheep's stone-cold NBA locks was, but there is little dispute among the world's big-time betting community that by early 2007, word within that crowd was that Tim Donaghy was fixing games and only a fool would have ignored Battista's ridiculously obvious wagering success. Because the world's sharps had access to at least the same resources (i.e., runners, insiders, outs) and technology (i.e., sophisticated computer models, Don Best subscriptions) as Battista, his moves on the referee's games were being mimicked around the globe almost from the time Battista cut his deal with Donaghy. Indeed, so significant was the buzz within betting circles surrounding Tim Donaghy's games that the FBI soon caught wind of the situation during a routine investigation into an organized crime family in New York.[4] Agents working for the FBI's "Gambino Squad" stumbled upon the Battista-Donaghy betting scandal on a wiretap, and it wouldn't be too long before agents paid The Sheep a visit. Of course, Battista had heard the rumor that he was being eyed by the feds a few months prior. The borderline paranoid pro gambler was always secretive about his actions anyway, and thus didn't much alter his behavior or his business. As such, Battista was still hyperactive moving games for the world's sharpest bettors all the while he was

---

[4] As of May 2010, the origin of the FBI's investigation into the NBA betting scandal remains one of the areas authorities with intimate knowledge of the probe are unwilling to discuss. In court filings, the federal government has stated: "In early 2007, the Federal Bureau of Investigation . . . received information that James Battista, a professional gambler, was engaged in betting large amounts of money on NBA basketball games and was receiving assistance from Timothy Donaghy, an NBA referee since 1994, in determining his bets."

conspiring with an NBA referee, which left him—at some level—vulnerable to an *actual* federal investigation.

As the FBI out of New York began working behind the scenes generating intelligence on the alleged NBA plot, the conspirators pressed on. Times were good, at least as far as Battista et al. knew, and they were soon looking to expand their criminal enterprise.

* * *

Tim Donaghy was in Phoenix to referee the January 5th game between the host Suns and the Miami Heat. The game was just part of the Arizona jaunt for Donaghy, because Tommy Martino was traveling out to meet him and drop off ten thousand dollars from Battista—and more. "When Tommy went out to see Elvis in Phoenix for one of the payments, I gave Tommy a thousand dollars to take Elvis out and show him a good time. They wound up staying in the same hotel, went to a strip club, and Tommy ordered a couple of girls from some service. They were like two teenagers with money out there doing stupid shit. Tommy was laying out by the pool with one of the hookers, and Elvis was upstairs in one of the hotel rooms throwing full cans of soda down at him. One of the cans just missed hitting one of the girls, and another whizzed by Tommy's head. Tommy called me on his cell phone and said, 'You wouldn't believe what this fucking nut is doing.' Elvis was forty going on fourteen; he didn't want to grow up, and he was just a different cat."

Martino and Donaghy also met with a female acquaintance of Donaghy's named Cheryl during the Arizona trip, and the salacious circumstances later became tabloid fodder. Though Martino referred to Cheryl as Donaghy's "girlfriend," Battista only knew that *something* was going on between the ref and his Phoenix-based female friend. "Elvis was unhappy in his marriage and couldn't stand his wife," Battista says. "He always made it clear that he loved his kids, but couldn't stand his wife. He used to say how much he'd love to kill her, he hated her so much. He'd talk about his pre-nup and brag that she 'wasn't going to get a fucking penny' if they ever got divorced. Well, supposedly Elvis was cheating on his wife with this girl named Cheryl out there who owned a bar, and Tommy hung out with them during the trip. I never met Cheryl, and I never talked to her on the phone. She sent me an Arizona State baseball hat and a T-shirt from a strip club after that trip, because I had treated them all. At that point everyone was happy, we were making money on games we were betting, and life was good." Indeed, things were going so well that Martino and Donaghy used the occasions of two other betting payment meetings, respectively, in Toronto and Washington, D.C., to obtain prostitutes from an online service.[5]

* * *

The night after Tim Donaghy refereed the Suns-Heat matchup, he was in Denver working the Nuggets-Utah Jazz game. After the Jazz beat the host Nuggets, the ref had a rare break ahead of him. Donaghy's next game wasn't for another nine days, an eternity during the grind of an NBA official's schedule. Another meeting with Battista and Martino was in the offing as Donaghy returned to the Philadelphia area to meet with family in advance of his January 15th assignment in Philly, where the Sixers would host the Toronto Raptors.

Battista and Donaghy had not been in each other's presence since the December 14th meeting that followed their first

---

[5] Tommy Martino detailed many of these events for the FBI, including: the circumstances of the Phoenix trip, such as the $10,000 payment, Donaghy's "girlfriend," and smoking pot with Donaghy; the payments in D.C. and Toronto; and the name of the online service he used to obtain the services of prostitutes for himself and Donaghy. The *New York Post* later identified Donaghy's acquaintance in Phoenix as Cheryl Wolfe-Ruiz, a "divorcee . . . mother of two who owns a sports bar in Phoenix." Her lawyer said Wolfe-Ruiz "did not have a sexual relationship" with Donaghy.

successful bet together. On the docket for this meeting, at least as far as Battista knew, was a major Donaghy payment. Such payments were a hassle to arrange, given Battista's paranoia about moving hot money. "Elvis had to go by train, bus, or car," Battista says, "because I didn't want him to have to explain why an NBA referee had forty or fifty thousand dollars in cash on him if he flew and his bags got searched." Given these concerns, Donaghy's trip to the area was convenient for all involved. "When Elvis came into town to work the Sixers-Toronto game," Battista says, "we met at Tommy's house in the afternoon for his first big payment. I think it was forty or forty-five thousand dollars. I gave Elvis some Percocets because he was complaining his back was sore, and I did some blow." What happened next became the subject of numerous conspiracy theories over time. "While we were there," Battista says, "Elvis had his laptop and he showed me the master referee schedule. He pointed at the computer and showed me the four guys whose games he was going to bet. He'd say, 'This is a good guy, this is a good guy,' and stuff like that. He didn't say anything to me about why he wanted to bet their games, and I didn't ask."[6] Needless to say, when presented with the prospects of growing the market, so to speak, Battista was ecstatic. "When he told me about those other refs, I was so fucking excited! All I could think about was how we were going to get more inside information and more sure winners."

It was also during this fairly momentous meeting that Battista, who was never close with Donaghy despite knowing him for years, got an up close view of the person so reviled by many who knew him. Whereas Gerry Donaghy was universally revered among his referee peers and embraced by those who

---

[6] As of May 2010, no other NBA officials have been charged with criminal wrongdoing, and none other than Tim Donaghy has been found to have wagered on NBA games. Of note, the four referees Jimmy Battista says Donaghy identified during the January 2007 meeting are not precisely those who have been publicly discussed by Donaghy.

were fortunate enough to come in contact with him, his son Tim had a markedly different disposition and reputation.[7] In fact, Tim Donaghy's temper and off-the-court behavior almost cost him his job with the NBA, not long before hooking up with Jimmy Battista. When asked to describe his close friend Tim "Elvis" Donaghy, Tommy Martino simply calls him "greedy and cheap." Battista's assessment, based in part on the January 2007 meeting, is a bit more biting. "Elvis was the greediest motherfucker I ever met in my life. He was only worried about getting paid. He was also a racist, and was resentful toward the NBA. Elvis would bad mouth them to death, and say things like, 'These niggers are overpaid.' He took it personal that these guys were making so much money more than he was. I didn't really give a shit about his views. I just wanted to make money, and just wanted to hear who he liked."

* * *

A few weeks later, The Sheep was tending to other, more significant matters involving his role as one of the world's most consequential sports betting movers. The Super Bowl each February was always one of the primary events at which pro gamblers settled with agents, movers, and bookmakers. For Battista, one of this year's settling figures was in dispute, since he was still livid over the horse racing bet fiasco with Paramount Sports and Joe Vito. Battista felt Joe Vito should have fought harder with Paramount on The Sheep's behalf, and that he was owed one hundred and two thousand dollars. Battista, who was willing to round the total figure owed him down to a neat hundred grand, saw an opportunity to settle the score with Joe Vito at the Super Bowl.

---

[7] Before retiring in 1997, Gerry Donaghy officiated for forty years. A highly regarded referee, he worked nineteen consecutive NCAA Tournaments, four Final Fours, and the 1992 National Championship.

"When it was time for me and two of my partners to settle up money at the Super Bowl," Battista says, "we owed Joe fifty-two thousand dollars. I told my partners that I would take care of the situation, and that we wouldn't be dealing with Joe anymore; we'd be taking our customers elsewhere. When I spoke with Joe I told him, 'You know what? I am settling for these guys and you can take the fifty-two grand off of what you owe me. Now you can just owe me forty-eight thousand.' My sense of everything was that he still owed me for the horse, so I would take their money and not pass it along to Joe. Well, we had a 'phone war' over this, and he wound up sending his assistant over to my house asking me to straighten everything out. Joe's guy used to be over my house a lot, and was friendly with my kids, but I was like, 'Get the fuck out of here! He fucked me, so here's the Vaseline.'" And so, the roughly twenty prosperous years of working with Joe Vito were over, and Battista felt a degree of vindication. There was, however, the underlying concern that Joe had ratted him out within the past year during Joe Vito's plea negotiations with the Montgomery County District Attorney's Office. Indeed, Battista would revisit his fears in this regard within months, and the question of who had won this battle would be revisited as well.

* * *

Now more than a month into the Battista-driven scheme, his bungling co-conspirators were creating problems for The Sheep again. Though none necessarily proved fatal, the difficulties demonstrated that the sure thing of earnings on Donaghy's games was still, at its core, reliant upon Donaghy and Martino. "There was one time where Tommy tried to give his own selection on a game. Elvis said to Tommy, 'You choose the game.' I got into an argument with Tommy after we lost that bet. I said, 'You don't fucking choose the game. Elvis is the one who is working the game. How can *you* choose the game?' Tommy said, 'But why can't I pick a game?' and I yelled back at him, 'Because Elvis is gonna control the game, you idiot!' I just think it was a situation where the two of them would get together, smoke a few bones, get stoned off their asses, and Elvis probably said something like, 'If you think you can pick a game, pick a game.'"[8] The dynamic duo of Martino and Donaghy also caused Battista grief when it came to speaking on phones registered in their names—a no-no if there ever was one in Battista's betting operations over the years. In fact, The Sheep's phone concerns would be validated in the near future, causing considerable problems for all three men. For now, the lack of adherence to protocol simply added to Battista's anxiety. "I didn't want them using their regular cell phones for our calls," Battista says, "especially because they talked so much. I was paranoid about their phones being tapped. I got Elvis and Tommy their own dummy phones—phones that were not in any of our names—for calls about the bets and stuff like that. But, they were too fucking stupid to use them. One time, Tommy called me using the proper phone, the dummy phone, but then called me minutes later from his regular phone! It was so stupid, but there was nothing I could do about those two."[9]

By the time February came to an end, Tim Donaghy had refereed thirty-two games since the December Marriott meeting, and the scheme was as fruitful as the co-conspirators had envisioned. Unfortunately for Jimmy Battista, the easy and considerable profits brought him little joy and certainly no peace, because the Donaghy situation was just a blip on The

---

[8] Tommy Martino told the FBI that he picked one game during the months-long scheme.

[9] The FBI wrote the following of the situation, based on interviews with Tommy Martino: "Early on in the scheme, Baba and Martino got new cell phones to use just for the scheme. Because of problems with those phones, Martino just went back to using his regular cell phone."

Sheep's busy radar screen. Battista still had the onerous job of betting games for the world's sharps and concealing all he did, while incessantly worrying about the FBI whispers and Joe Vito's rumored actions. Battista's addiction to OxyContin, which was greatly influenced by his over-active career and related lifestyle to begin with, worsened, and was finally affecting his business. Jimmy's relationship with his wife and kids was also never this bad, and Battista found himself at the lowest point in his life, even as he was in the midst of one of the biggest scandals in U.S. sports history.

Jimmy Battista (Class of 1983), Tommy Martino ('84), and Tim Donaghy ('85) each graduated from Cardinal O'Hara High School in Springfield, PA. Interestingly, current NBA referees Joey Crawford, Ed Malloy, and Mike Callahan also attended O'Hara.

James Battista

Beyond his sports activities, Battista, in the fourth row and second from the left, exploited his "people-person" persona to earn a spot on O'Hara's Student Council.

. . . Tomorrow's Leaders

Underclassman Donaghy in Battista's senior class yearbook. Donaghy, the future NBA ref, and Battista, the future pro gambler, were nothing more than acquaintances in high school.

The Sheep during his rise from small-time hustler to big-time sports bettor.

Martino (right) was best man for Battista's first marriage in 1989. Battista (left) was later in Martino's wedding party, and they were joined at the reception by Martino's pal Tim Donaghy.

The Animals worked for Mike Rinnier in his large Delaware County bookmaking and betting operation out of this office building on West Springfield Road, just down the street from Cardinal O'Hara High School. Rinnier rented out the entire second floor of apartments in the early 1990s and created a massive betting office staffed with dozens of employees.

The Lamb Tavern, a popular Springfield, PA establishment, was frequented by Mike Rinnier and The Animals after long, stressful days of bookin' and bettin'. The Lamb was conveniently located directly across from the betting office on West Springfield Road. Numerous consequential meetings were convened here, and the business decisions emanating from them often affected sportsbooks around the country.

For a time in the early 2000s, Battista ran Marina's Sports Bar in Havertown, PA. Notwithstanding his "day job," he was still hyperactive in the sports gambling world.

As a result of winning an on-air bet with Philadelphia Sports Radio 610 WIP personalities Howard Eskin (middle) and Mike Missanelli (left), Battista (right) hosted them at Marina's where they served as celebrity bartenders for a charity event benefitting the family of a Battista friend who was killed in the September 11, 2001, World Trade Center terrorist attacks. The WIP hosts likely had no idea the role Battista was playing in the sports gambling world by February 2002, when the event took place.

As technology affecting the sports gambling world evolved, Battista was always on the cutting edge. The remnants of the desk in his diminished home betting office were photographed in the spring of 2008, a year after the Sheep's last betting action. For years up through the spring of 2007 this office housed a blizzard of desktop and laptop computers, computer screens, and televisions (each connected to satellites), all geared around the quickest possible processing and transmission of worldwide sports gambling information.

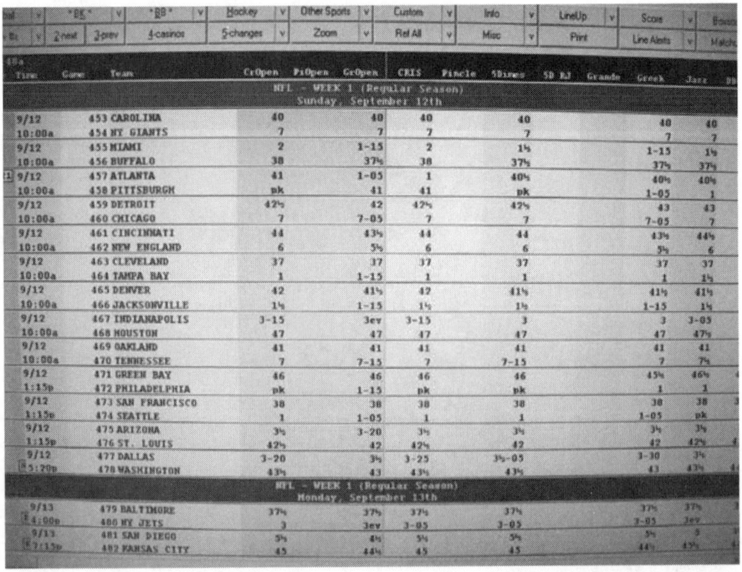

Time	Game	Team	CrOpen	PiOpen	GrOpen	CRIS	Pincle	5Dimes	SB BJ	Grande	Greek	Jazz
		NFL - WEEK 1 (Regular Season) Sunday, September 12th										
9/12	453	CAROLINA	40		40	40		40			40	40
10:00a	454	NY GIANTS	7		7	7		7			7	7
9/12	455	MIAMI	2		1-15	2		1½			1-15	1½
10:00a	456	BUFFALO	38		37½	38		37½			37½	37½
9/12	457	ATLANTA	41		1-05	1		40½			40½	40½
10:00a	458	PITTSBURGH	pk		41	41		pk			1-05	1
9/12	459	DETROIT	42½		42	42½		42½			43	43
10:00a	460	CHICAGO	7		7-05	7		7			7-05	7
9/12	461	CINCINNATI	44		43½	44		44			43½	44½
10:00a	462	NEW ENGLAND	6		5½	6		6			5½	6
9/12	463	CLEVELAND	37		37	37		37			37	37
10:00a	464	TAMPA BAY	1		1-15	1		1			1	1½
9/12	465	DENVER	42		41½	42		41½			41½	41½
10:00a	466	JACKSONVILLE	1½		1-15	1½		1½			1-15	1½
9/12	467	INDIANAPOLIS	3-15		3ev	3-15		3			3	3-05
10:00a	468	HOUSTON	47		47	47		47			47	47½
9/12	469	OAKLAND	41		41	41		41			41	41
10:00a	470	TENNESSEE	7		7-15	7		7-15			7	7½
9/12	471	GREEN BAY	46		46	46		46			45½	46½
1:15p	472	PHILADELPHIA	pk		1-15	pk		pk			1	1
9/12	473	SAN FRANCISCO	38		38	38		38			38	38
1:15p	474	SEATTLE	1		1-05	1		1			1-05	pk
9/12	475	ARIZONA	3½		3-20	3½		3½			3½	3½
1:15p	476	ST. LOUIS	42½		42	42½		42			42	42½
9/12	477	DALLAS	3-20		3½	3-25		3½-05			3-30	3½
5:20p	478	WASHINGTON	43½		43	43½		43½			43	43½
		NFL - WEEK 1 (Regular Season) Monday, September 13th										
9/13	479	BALTIMORE	37½		37½	37½		37½			37½	37½
4:00p	480	NY JETS	3		3ev	3-05		3-05			3-05	3ev
9/13	481	SAN DIEGO	5½		4½	5½		5½			5½	5
7:15p	482	KANSAS CITY	45		44½	45		45			44½	45½

Pictured is the Don Best screen for the opening week of the 2010-11 NFL season. A subscription to the Don Best Web site has long been a must for professional gamblers like Battista, who treasure the one-screen snapshot of consequential betting line information that is constantly being updated with real-time odds and line moves from sportsbooks around the world.

The exterior of the Philadelphia International Airport Marriott, where Battista and Martino met with Donaghy late in the evening of December 12, 2006.

The Marriott lobby, where Battista and Martino greeted Donaghy before entering the hotel's brassy Riverbend Bar and Grill (at right). The three men seated themselves in the establishment's empty restaurant area, away from the busy bar, so that their incriminating conversation would not be overheard.

From left to right, defense attorney Vicki Herr, Martino, Battista, and defense attorney Jack McMahon enter the federal court house in Brooklyn, New York on August 15, 2007. Unbeknownst to Jimmy Battista, Tommy Martino had already met with the FBI three times by then and had cooperated against his lifelong friend. Their relationship would never be the same once Battista heard the shocking news months later. (AP Photo/Louis Lanzano)

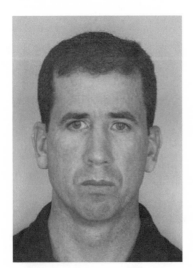

Tim Donaghy following his 2007 arrest.

Battista in 2010, following his stint in federal prison for his role as architect of the NBA betting scandal.

15

The Harder They Fall

BACK IN 1996, The Sheep was traveling up the New Jersey Turnpike to pick up a hundred and fifty thousand dollars in New York. The meeting would have to be postponed, however, because, as Battista says, "The idiot who was driving me was really hung over and driving like an asshole, moving back and forth between the lanes. The next thing I know, we got hit, the car spun three times, flipped, and caught fire. We both survived, but I broke a few ribs and pinched a couple of nerves in my neck." The crash had a lasting effect on Battista because it introduced him to prescription pills. "After surgery," he says, "I started using Percocets, and they were like candy. I was like, 'Ooh! One pill and I'm happy.' I tried to get off them a bunch of times over the next several years, but I would use them and Vicodins. I really only used cocaine after that for special functions like weddings and stuff like that. I was so stressed out with my lifestyle, I ate pills. I loved them. I could have one or two drinks, be relaxed, and still be stoned. I thought I was living the American dream; I gambled, I made good money, and nobody knew about it."

Battista's clandestine pill use continued for the next decade without any noticeable adverse effect on his personal or professional circumstances. By the end of February 2007, with Battista now hooked on OxyContin and overwhelmed with his work, the same could not be said. The first hints of trouble came the previous spring. "Every May I would throw a party at the Radnor Hunt," Battista says, "which was a steeplechase event that draws around thirty thousand people each year. I can distinctly remember being in my car at the races in 2006 betting baseball on my laptop and wanting the drugs more than I wanted to gamble or hang out with everybody. I didn't care about the gambling. I didn't care about what was going on at my party or at the races. I just wanted to get high." His physical condition soon began deteriorating, and within months he knew his addiction had become a serious problem.

"I started throwing up blood," Battista says, "because I was eating so many pills and flushing them down every once in a while with some fast food. I was just tearing up my stomach. I tried stopping 'cold turkey' a few times, but I couldn't. I was so hooked; it was like heroin in my system. I'd go three days without the pills and get the shakes. I'd give up and take a few Percocets or Vicodins just to stop shaking. I kept trying to stop because the Oxys were hurting my gambling career and my marriage. I was never thinking straight, and at the same time it was killing me that something I had worked so hard and so long to achieve was being affected. Those fucking pills were taking everything away. As hard as I worked and all the hours I put into my work, everything I had worked for was going away.

"Denise didn't know how significant my drug use had become, and that that was why I was such a fucking mess and not acting like myself. She just thought I was power hungry with my gambling, and would tell me over and over that I didn't have to work for all those guys. She was right, because my mind was overwhelmed with, 'Oh my God, I have to deal with The Chinaman, and The Computer, and Zorba, and The Englishman, and this guy, and this guy. And, I have to get this done, and get that done, and I can't let anyone know what I am doing.' On top of all that, I had a wife and five kids I knew I wasn't being fair to. The pills became my way of dealing with all of that stress, and I tried really hard to keep them a secret. My wife knew something was going on starting in early 2007, but even then she didn't really know how much I was using. There was a time that January when I went to Las Vegas with Denise. We went out to dinner at seven o'clock at night, and I had one drink and passed out at the table because I had so many pills in my system. I used to have drugs shipped out to me; they'd be left at the front desk of whatever hotel I was staying at. The next night we went to a Prince concert and were supposed to go to an after-concert event with him, but I just wanted to get back to the hotel and do more drugs. My wife knew at that point I was gone. Gambling was always first, before family, and now it was the drugs that were first and then gambling and then family. By March, Denise was at her wits' end with me and knew there was something wrong because by then I wasn't really functioning. I was still trying to work the best I could when I wasn't passing out from the drugs and the stress."

On Thursday, March 15th, basketball fans were—as usual around this time each year—consumed with March Madness. The NCAA basketball tournament's first round of games were being played, and the sports betting world was its usual mania when the field of sixty-four tipped off. For the first time in decades, such was not the case for Jimmy Battista. His mind was focused elsewhere, namely on his drug problem and related woes. For whatever reason, Battista finally decided to confront Denise with some stark news that day. "I let her know that I was a few dollars in debt—a few million," Battista says, "and she was obviously very upset. Up until then, she had no idea what I was doing because I kept everything on a 'need-to-know' basis so that nothing ever happened to her. Because of everything that was going on, I was staying over Tommy's house as much as possible. The next day, one of my brothers-in-law called my cell phone in the afternoon and told me to come outside of Tommy's house. He and other family members knew Tommy was the one who got me the drugs, and knew I was there. When I got outside, four of my brothers-in-law were in a car and told me I had to go get help. I said, 'I know I do, but I have to clean up some business first. I can't just walk away from my responsibilities.' I called the people I worked with to let them know I was going away to get help, and my sister arranged for me to go to a place in Lancaster called White Deer Run. I would have gone into rehab the next day, but I had to wait for a bed to open up, which didn't happen until Sunday, the 18th. I knew I had a problem, and I wanted and needed help. I was out of shape, crazy, throwing up, sick as can be, everything. I could always stop the coke and the drinking, but I couldn't stop the pills. I could control everything else in my life, but I couldn't get off the shit.

"When I went into rehab, they put me on Soboxone for three days.[1] I was used to having a bunch of Percocets or Vicodins a day going back to my car accident in the mid-90s, but once I got OxyContin, it was euphoria. I used to take the OxyContins from the moment I woke up. I had a ton of pills, so much so that I used to have a pill bag, but no one knew until the last few months before rehab. I stayed in White Deer Run for twenty-eight days, until the third week of April. It was run like a military base, and we did everything there but cook. I loved it. It was exactly what I needed at that low point in my life. I just knew I needed to change my life and get it together, especially because my marriage was almost out the door."

Though Battista's foremost concerns were his family and his health, there remained numerous outstanding issues with

---

[1] Like methadone, soboxone is used as treatment in cases of opioid dependence.

his betting partners and clients. Importantly, he owed several people, including The Chinaman and Zorba, significant amounts of money that he squandered in his Oxy-influenced online poker sessions and the like. "When I got hooked on OxyContin and owed Zorba a lot of money," Battista says, "he didn't even worry about the money. He was more concerned with my health. He told me to get my health and family straightened out, and wished me luck. The Chinaman said pretty much the same thing, and I owed him money, too. I spoke with both of them after I got out of rehab, and they understood why I was leaving the business for good. They each forgave my debt, and were as good to me or better when I left them as they were when I worked for them; real professionals, and all class."

* * *

The Sheep's remarkable run as a big-time mover was over, and the four weeks of rehab afforded Battista time to reflect on the unreal Donaghy scheme, which had only recently come to a halt. Battista says his involvement ended shortly after entering rehab, and that he bet on three or four Donaghy games after March 18th. "Before I went into rehab," he says, "I had it set up that Tommy could still get the calls from Elvis and place them through Pete Ruggieri. Well, there was a group of guys who I had been using in Asia. They were still getting the bets and were moving the lines on Elvis games and crushing over there, and bookmakers were getting pissed. By then, *everybody* was jumping on Donaghy's games. I was in rehab but people were still saying, 'Sheep's on this game!' and things like that. Talk on the street was nuts, and everybody in the gambling industry knew what was going on. I found out from Tommy one day when I called him from rehab that Pete was shutting everything down because he said the games were moving too many points, and we were attracting too much attention.[2] I only got paid on Donaghy's games through March 26th, but from what I understand, it may have gone on a few more games just because there was so much easy money out there. It was like stealing, and Elvis didn't want to stop." In fact, according to an FBI memo summarizing Tommy Martino's interviews: "After Ruggieri decided to shut the scheme down, Donaghy pushed Martino to take one more game. Donaghy said it was a schmaga game." There was apparently no bet on that game, and Martino claims the scheme lasted at most until March 28th, by which point Donaghy had officiated forty-three games dating back to December 12, 2006.

For most gamblers, sure things like Donaghy's games would have been all but impossible to give up. To the beaten down and recovering Sheep, though, the conspiracy's demise didn't merit much more than his disappointment. "I was hoping it would go on as long as possible," Battista says, "but I wasn't really upset when Pete ended it. I knew it had gotten out of hand, and I was more focused on getting my life together, anyway.

"From the time we hooked up on December 12th until I went in rehab, we bet every one of his games, and then three or four more when I was in White Deer Run. We went something like thirty-seven and ten in games Elvis reffed.[3] I never asked

---

[2] Tommy Martino's version of these events in FBI memos regarding Ruggieri's involvement and decision to end the betting scandal almost perfectly mirrors Battista's.

[3] When Battista says he went "something like 37 and 10" with his bets on Tim Donaghy's games, this is either very loosely stated, inaccurate, or he can't be referring explicitly to games Donaghy officiated between December 12, 2006, and March 26, 2007. When pressed on the issue of his betting record on Donaghy's games in consideration of the fact that Donaghy only officiated 42 games total between 12/12/06 and 3/26/07, Battista says, "On the Elvis games I bet, we went 37 and 10, or something really close to that. The whole time we were betting on games he reffed, we were winning in the mid- to high 70s [percents]." A record of 37 and 10 equates to a winning percentage of 79%. As the only person who was responsible for millions of dollars among his co-conspirators (who had no money at stake if a pick resulted in a loss), Battista's insistence regarding his recollection of the 37–10 record can't be discounted out of hand. Furthermore, Battista's decades-long history of processing betting stats, win rates, and payout matters must be considered. Although it is certainly possible

him to fix a game or anything like that at all, I just wanted to know who he liked but, in my mind, Elvis knew he was only getting paid if he won.[4] I made him a good deal: 'You get paid for your wins; your losses you don't have to pay.' I knew he was picking great already, long before I ever hooked up with him. A referee can control the flow of a game, and one call can affect the outcome of a game. I never let myself get on the phone with Elvis, and I only met with him on three or four occasions, always at Tommy's house when Elvis was in town."

As much as Battista benefitted from Donaghy's picks on games the referee officiated, he was frustrated by the losses he took on Donaghy's pick for other referees' games, following the "laptop meeting" in January 2007. "We started betting those games," Battista says, "but after a while I was like, 'These fucking games suck! Why are we betting these games? I don't want to bet these games! Elvis, when you're reffing the games, I know we're winning seventy-two to seventy-eight percent.' The other refs' games went one-and-six; we weren't covering the number. I don't know if Elvis was getting bad information from the other refs, or if they were the ones placing the bets, or whatever. I never knew what actually transpired with him

---

Battista's recollection could simply be inaccurate, there are alternative explanations that are at least as likely. First among them is the likelihood that Battista is cognizant of his plea allocution statement, which includes his comments regarding his criminal conduct as follows (*emphasis* added): "from December of 2006 to *March 2007*, I was engaged in the business of sports betting, and I agreed with Tom Martino and Tim Donaghy to use the telephone across state lines to obtain information to assist me in wagering on sporting events, on NBA basketball games." Thus, if the scandal went into April as some informed people believe, Battista likely can't admit to participating in and/or profiting from them. Simply stated, it is possible Battista was a party to bets beyond March but can't admit to this activity because of his plea agreement. [From 12/12/06, Donaghy officiated: 44 games through March; 52 regular season games total (including playoffs) through April; and 57 total (including playoffs) through May.]

[4] Battista says he does not recall a discernible pattern in Donaghy's picks vis-à-vis home/away, favorite/underdog. An independent review of bets placed by Battista in an unrepresentative sample of Donaghy games during the scandal suggests he was more likely to bet favorites.

and the other referees. I just know that Elvis couldn't control those games, and I was losing money. It got to a point where I stopped taking the bets, because it was throwing the good money away from when he was reffing the games.[5]

"Inside information like injuries and stuff like that might have accounted for a small part of Elvis' ability to pick winners, but being able to control the outcomes was the big reason he won his games. That was why he couldn't pick those other games."

In addition to the seven non-Donaghy games Battista references, there was one other game bet that Donaghy didn't officiate. The 2007 NBA All-Star game was played on February 18th in Las Vegas, of all places, and Battista says, "Elvis told Tommy that he wanted to bet on the All-Star game. I said, 'But, he's not working it,' and Elvis told Tommy a friend of his was. Elvis called us, like, four hours prior to the All-Star game and said the West was going to crush the East. We laid two or three with whatever inside information he had, and the West destroyed the East."[6]

Jimmy Battista, who will not—or cannot—discuss his own profiteering from the scandal, claims he paid Donaghy more than two hundred thousand dollars by the time the scheme had ended.[7] More specifically, Battista says he gave Tommy

---

[5] The FBI's summary of Tommy Martino's version of these events similarly states: "Occasionally, in the beginning, Donaghy provided picks for some games he was not refereeing. After a few losses, though, Baba did not want any more of those games." Martino estimated that they bet a total of 37 games, which included the few non-Donaghy games, and that their record was 27-and-10.

[6] It was the first time Sin City hosted the game, and Las Vegas sportsbooks agreed not to take action on the game as part of the city's agreement with the NBA. The West squad beat the East 153-132, and the officials were Monty McCutchen, Mike Callahan, and Sean Corbin.

[7] Battista's calculations are as follows: <u>high estimate</u> = \$5,000 (start up) + \$4,000 (first 2 games @ \$2,000) + \$30,000 (3 schmagas @ \$10,000) + \$160,000 (32 games @ \$5,000) + \$5,000 (2007 All-Star Game) + \$5,000 (non-Donaghy game) = **\$209,000**; <u>low estimate</u> = \$5,000 (start up) + \$6,000 (first 3 games @ \$2,000) + \$20,000 (2 schmagas @ \$10,000) + \$160,000 (32 games @ \$5,000) + \$5,000 (2007 All-Star Game) + \$5,000 (non-Donaghy game) = **\$201,000**. While Battista recalls "two or three" schmaga games, Tommy Martino told the FBI there was perhaps only one schmaga.

Martino approximately two hundred and twenty-eight thousand dollars over three months, and that Martino kept the difference after paying Donaghy his earnings.[8] As was true with other illicit, profitable, and oft-scintillating moments in his career, Battista says he was never afforded the chance to grasp what he was doing. "I didn't feel any different when I watched Elvis' games than I did on other games I bet," Battista says. "To me, it was just money, just business. It's not like I was laughing at his calls if they helped us, or pissed at his calls if they hurt us. The 'Timmy "Elvis" Donaghy thing' was only a small part of everything I had going on, and I didn't want anyone to find out. So, I didn't really have time to focus on it, let alone enjoy it."

* * *

As Battista settled into his new reality, he had mixed emotions. He was sober and getting healthy for the first time in years, and was very much enjoying the company of his wife and kids. Most of his debts were forgiven, and the stress he had weathered for many years was gone, and yet, with each day he spent at home—within paces of his once formidable betting lair—he couldn't believe all he had worked and sacrificed for was over. There was also the issue of what he would do now; how to make a living. Cognizant that his betting life could not be revisited for the sake of his family, and fearful of the drug temptations that were omnipresent in the restaurant business, Battista was forced to consider options outside of the areas for which he had experience and a record of success. He had little time to focus on his career options, it turned out, because within days of his return home from rehab he was visited by the FBI.

---

[8] Tommy Martino told the FBI that he gave Tim Donaghy between $115,000 and $120,000 over six payments between mid-January and early April 2007.

16

The Dance

ABOUT A WEEK after Jimmy Battista got out of rehab, he took his kids and his younger sister to nearby Valley Forge Park. They left the vast historic park at about three o'clock in the afternoon, and as they drove up Battista's street, they passed a white minivan parked a few doors down from his home. As his kids and sister hopped out of his car, Battista watched the minivan, which had New Jersey tags, park right in front of his house. "Two white guys in suits got out and started walking towards me," Battista says, "and before they ever introduced themselves, I knew who they were. I asked my sister to take the kids inside, because I knew these weren't Avon salesmen. I didn't know why they wanted to talk to me, and didn't really think about the NBA thing, but I knew I owed people a lot of money and that anything was possible. After they introduced themselves, they said they needed to talk to me. I asked them, 'Can we please meet somewhere else because my kids are here.' They were polite and asked where would be a good place, and I said there was a Dunkin Donuts nearby. I got in my minivan, went to the Dunkin Donuts, and sat down."

FBI Special Agents Paul N. Harris and Gerard "Gerry" Conrad operated out of New York, and were part of the Bureau's Gambino squad, charged with investigating the legendary "crime family." Harris, the case (lead) agent for the burgeoning NBA betting probe, and Conrad were a considerable distance from their squad's office (and its mission, as they later discovered) when they met with Jimmy Battista in April 2007.

"When they arrived at the Dunkin Donuts," Battista says, "they offered to buy me a cup of coffee, but I said I would pay for me and for them. I didn't let them pay for the coffee not because they were FBI agents, but because I never wanted to owe anybody anything. Denise always said I had a problem with that, and it's true. When I went to pay for the coffees, I reached into my pocket and pulled out my 'wallet.' I had a rubber band that wrapped around my driver's license, room keys for Vegas hotels, my social security card, and whatever cash I had on me. I never carried credit cards, and always used cash. Back when I was in my early twenties when I was working at September's Place on a Sunday morning, I got a call that my dad was jumped—robbed—and was in the hospital. He was at a train station reaching into his back pocket to pull out his wallet to get his train pass, and these guys beat the shit out of him and took his wallet. They put him in the hospital for eleven fucking dollars. I never carried a wallet since, and always kept my money and everything else in my front pocket. Well, both agents' eyes stared at my 'wallet,' checking to see how much money I was holding, even though I only had like twenty-six bucks on me.

"After they reintroduced themselves as part of a crime unit up in New York, their approach to me was really sharp. They said, 'We know you lost a lot of money and we'll protect you in case someone comes after you.' My response was, 'Protect me? Who do you think I owe money to?!' They said the word on the street was that I owed money to The Chinaman, Zorba, and some other guys. 'That you didn't pay them and you just drifted away.' They knew their real names, their nicknames, their professions, and pretty much had the dollar figure I owed correct. It was unbelievable. I told them that I really had nothing to say, and that I would like to have a lawyer present if I was going to speak with them. They said, 'Well, come with us and we'll work that out, and there's another matter we'd like to talk to you about. We know you move games, and we know you're a bettor. Were you working with anyone on NBA or NFL games?' I told them, 'I bet a lot of sports, and I deal with a lot of handicappers. They give me the information and I go bet them.' They said, 'Are you sure you didn't have any particular customers or people that you dealt with on a daily basis?' I said, 'Well, there's a lot of people I dealt with on a daily basis. I dealt with a lot of handicappers. You obviously know some of them, because you just told me I owed them millions of dollars.' They said, 'We think you are involved in a scandal and that you were behind it. You should be talking to us.'

"I didn't know what they were getting at. Besides Elvis and the NBA, I had a lot of good inside information on the NFL; not as good as Elvis, but some incredible information on injuries and stuff like that I used to get before anybody else. People in my line of work knew I was involved in that aspect of everything. I told the agents I needed to obtain the services of a lawyer before saying anything else to them, and they handed me papers and told me I'd be going before a grand jury. The whole thing was very cordial, and they gave me their business cards before we all left. I always thought before I went into rehab that I was being followed, and now I knew I was."

On the short drive home, Battista was more focused on how to handle the situation than he was nervous. Before phoning anyone, he simply waited for Denise to get home from cosmetology school so he could tell her first. "She was understandably upset," Battista says, "and our marriage was already on the rocks because I was more concerned about gambling and drugs the past few years than I was about my family. Now she knew I blew all of our savings and more; *all of our money was gone.* I told her that I had to alert certain people about the feds visiting me."

After putting the kids to bed that night, Battista drove to use a pay phone and call various people who would need to know what was happening. At a minimum, he wanted to alert people that his phones were probably tapped. Up next was obtaining the services of a lawyer. "The guy I used before was also Joe Vito's lawyer," Battista says, "so I couldn't use him because I assumed this had something to do with Joe, going back to his arrest and the money seizure." The following morning, Battista drove into Center City, Philadelphia, to see a friend of his named Lucky, who was a ticket broker. "He was a great guy and a good friend whose brother-in-law was a chef who used to work with me and Louie the Lump," Battista says. "I'd use Lucky to get tickets when I would wine and dine people or take my wife and kids to games and concerts. I'd spend thousands of dollars a year just in getting good tickets. Lucky was a well-respected guy who knew a lot of the right people, and he would always tell me that if I ever got jammed up to come and see him. So, I paid him a visit and he told me to go see a well-known defense lawyer named Jack McMahon. Of course, before I left he gave me tickets to a Phillies game because he felt bad for me and thought it would be good to take the kids to a ball game!"

When Battista got back home that afternoon, he arrived to find FBI agents Harris and Conrad waiting for him. "They pretty much said the same thing as the day before," Battista says. "They said, 'We want to give you another opportunity to work with us,' and I said, 'Well, that ain't gonna happen.' They told me they understood and that they'd be in touch. They were very cordial and asked about how my sobriety was going. They drove all the way down from Brooklyn for a five-minute conversation. Before they left, Paul Harris said, 'James, I think you have a lot to tell, but you're not telling anybody.'"

After the FBI left this time, Jimmy asked Denise to join him out in the backyard so that he could more openly discuss everything. "I assumed my house was bugged and didn't want to discuss anything inside," Battista says. "I finally told her what was going on, which made her even more upset than she already was; she had every right to be. She just couldn't believe what I had done." Despite her growing disdain for Jimmy, Denise understood his refusal to work with the authorities. "I never considered cooperating for a second," Battista says. "My wife never asked me to consider it, either, because she knew me. I am not a rat. I told Denise, 'Look, I fucked up. Drugs are one thing, and I fucked up our marriage, but I am not going to fuck anyone else because of the mistakes I made.'"

At that point, Battista, who assumed he was under constant surveillance and that his phone was tapped, still had all of his computers and his sixteen cell phones. He immediately got rid of fifteen phones, saving only what he called the "Tommy-to-Elvis" phone. All of the other phones had the contact information for all of his clients, and thus had to be destroyed and discarded. The all-knowing computers each met the same fate as the fifteen phones. Battista called Lucky's lawyer friend Jack McMahon that night, who told Battista to come into his office the next day.

Jack McMahon Jr. was a fiery and well-known Philadelphia defense attorney who had served as a prosecutor with the District Attorney's Office. A trial lawyer who worked on several high-profile cases, McMahon was perhaps best known for representing alleged mob soldier Martin "Marty" Angelina in a much-publicized Philly-organized crime racketeering case in 2001.[1] Battista knew none of this when he reached out to McMahon, and he certainly wasn't aware of the attorney's personal background, which was too ironic to be believed,

---

[1] In that case, Angelina, who was a codefendant with six others including reputed mob boss Joseph "Skinny Joey" Merlino, was charged with attempted murder, extortion, illegal bookmaking, and receipt of a stolen Lamborghini.

given his prospective representation of a client targeted in a betting scandal involving the NBA.

"My dad was drafted in 1952 by the Rochester Royals [who are now the Sacramento Kings] out of St. John's, where he was an All-American guard," McMahon says of his father, Jack McMahon Sr.[2] He played two or three seasons with the Royals and got traded to the St. Louis Hawks, and he played for them for about five seasons. He was on the 1958 NBA championship team that beat Bill Russell and the Celtics. Right after retiring, he started coaching in the ABL [American Basketball League], where he coached the Kansas City Steers. He coached them for a year before the league went under, and then got hired as the head coach of the expansion Chicago Zephyrs, where he coached Don Nelson. He next got hired to coach the Cincinnati Royals in 1963, and he coached them for four years. In Cincinnati, he coached great players like Oscar Robertson, Jerry Lucas, and Wayne Embry.[3] I was a ball boy for the Royals; I did the jackets, the coats, wiped up the sweat, all that stuff. Anybody that tells me that Oscar Robertson wasn't the best, I tell them they're full of shit. Oscar was just an unbelievable basketball player. The NBA expanded in 1967, and my dad was hired away from Cincinnati to coach the San Diego Rockets [who are now the Houston Rockets]. He coached them for two-and-a-half seasons before getting fired. He didn't get along with the team's superstar, Elvin Hayes, and as the old saying goes, 'It's easier to get rid of the coach . . .'

"Next, he coached in the ABA [American Basketball Association] with the Pittsburgh Condors for two seasons. Then, in 1972, the year the Sixers were nine-and-seventy-three—that debacle of a year—Kevin Loughery became the

---

[2] In his senior season at St. John's, McMahon was team captain of the squad that made it all the way to the NCAA Championship game, where they lost to Kansas.

[3] In the 1963-64 season, alone, Oscar Robertson was NBA Most Valuable Player, Jerry Lucas was NBA Rookie of the Year, and Wayne Embry was an All-Star.

coach when they fired Roy Rubin in the middle of the season. Kevin Loughery and my dad were very good friends; both were Brooklyn guys and both went to St. John's. My dad became an assistant coach and became their director of player personnel, where he was essentially their chief scout around the country. When the Sixers won the NBA Championship in 1983, they had the families of the coaches on the floats in the parade in front of two million people. I was about thirty-one years old, and it was one of the most memorable moments of my life. My father left Philadelphia in 1986 to join his good friend Don Nelson, who had gotten the job as the Golden State Warriors coach. He coached there and was their director of player personnel for three seasons until he died of a heart attack in a Chicago hotel as they were doing a pre-draft camp for rookies in 1989."[4] Years later, when Don Nelson tied legendary Boston Celtics coach Red Auerbach with nine-hundred thirty-eight wins, Nelson called Auerbach and Jack McMahon Sr. his two mentors.

When Jimmy Battista first met Jack McMahon, he was still in his 'need-to-know' mind-set, which may have been okay in other circumstances, but wasn't suitable for a meeting with a criminal defense lawyer. "When I met with Jack," Battista says, "he started by saying, 'Okay, what's going on?' Before I had a chance to respond, he said, 'Tell me *the truth*. If you lie to me, I can't make rational decisions; the more that you tell me, the more I can help you.'" Unfortunately for McMahon, Battista's initial replies were less than candid. "I gave him the same spiel I give every client when they come in for their first interview," McMahons says. "'You never lie to your lawyer.

---

[4] Jack McMahon says that his ties to the NBA were of no consequence to him once Battista explained the context of his actions. "When Jimmy first came to me," McMahon says, "the issue of my dad's background with the NBA didn't enter into my decision as to whether to take the case. A guy comes to me with a problem and this is what I do, I am a defense attorney. The fact that there was some tangential relationship with the NBA made no difference to me whatsoever."

Your doctor and your lawyer are two people you never lie to because they can't help you unless they know the facts.' I told him, 'Everything you say to me is confidential . . .' and he started talking. He was talking in, like, cryptic sentences. He was really nervous, and paranoid, and kept looking out my window like there was someone out there. He kept giving me these cryptic answers and finally I said, 'Look, man. This is just bullshit. This is wasting your time and it's wasting my time, because *you're not even close* to telling me the truth. You're telling the doctor the pain is in the right leg and it's in the left leg.' That first meeting ended with me telling him to leave." Having made no real progress in this initial attorney-client meeting, other efforts were needed before any decisions could be made before moving forward, but even these weren't productive initially.

"It was like we were doing a dance in those early days," McMahon says, "and I kept telling him how frustrating and stupid it was. The conversations required me to figure out what he was saying, and I would tell him, 'This isn't a quiz game. I'm not here to try and solve your cryptic messages.' Most clients come in and tell you one of two versions of what they did. Some guys will tell you the truth, straight out, and some guys will flat out lie to you. Jimmy was different. He didn't tell me *anything*. He would give me a little bit of information, and I'd have to figure out what he was trying to say. Then he'd give a little more, and on it went. It was like he didn't want to tell me things, and felt better about talking to me if I somehow came to my own conclusions."

During one of the first meetings Battista had with McMahon, the full story finally began to emerge. Battista started talking about his gambling career, about moving games for the world's sharpest and most consequential bettors, and about being in the hole for millions of dollars. McMahon then pointedly asked, "What did the FBI agents ask you?"

Battista explained that he was asked about inside information and a scandal in the NBA or in the NFL. McMahon, his curiosity piqued, followed up, "Why would they ask you that?" Battista, as was his standard, held back the whole story and simply told his new lawyer that he had a lot of handicappers who obtained and disseminated inside information. The back-and-forth continued, frustrating McMahon, who could sense Battista was holding something back. The lawyer said, "Listen, I want to help you, but I don't need your case. Now, what's your involvement? Who were your handicappers?" Battista replied that he had "a few guys on the inside" who gave him information, to which McMahon countered, "How 'inside' were they?" Battista, *still* holding back, said, "They were right there on the firing line." McMahon couldn't take Battista's act a second more, and shouted, "JUST FUCKING TELL ME!' The rattled Battista finally said, 'One of my handicappers was an NBA referee," causing McMahon to pause as he processed what he had just heard. "I was surprised," McMahon says, "but I wasn't shocked. I guess I have always felt that area was fertile for corruption in any sport. In any group of human beings, there are going to be some who succumb to temptation. I was a little upset it was the NBA because I had grown up with the league. I wish it had been another sport, but that didn't affect anything I did." Importantly, the dam had broken, and the working relationship between client Battista and attorney McMahon was healthy from that point forward. "He knew he could trust me," McMahon says, "and everything went fine from there."

With that unnecessary fiasco resolved, Battista was left to deal with his other problems, which at the time were dominated by his quest to stay drug-free. Even that, however, now incorporated his fears about the ongoing federal investigation. "I went to Morning Miracles for my addiction meeting at the start of the day," Battista says. "You needed a sponsor in the program, and this guy offered to be mine. I was convinced he was an FBI agent. So, I made a few phone calls and gave somebody his license plate number, and made sure he was who he said he was. That is how scared I was about everything that was going on." At the time, Battista was trying to get back in shape, and his daily regimen included walking five miles in Valley Forge Park. He thought a white Ford Explorer was following him during the walks, and was fighting his paranoia each time he thought he saw the SUV. Times were tough for Battista, and would be getting more challenging in the coming days and weeks as he learned what loomed for the recently neutered Sheep.

Gambling Investigation Rocks NBA

JIMMY BATTISTA'S UNYIELDING paranoia was aggravated sometime around the first week of May, when FBI agents Harris and Conrad visited his home a third time. "The agents and I spoke in front of the house on my sidewalk," Battista says, "and they asked me for the first time about Tommy. I said, 'He is one of my friends.' They wanted to know if I used to work out of his house, and I explained that I did. I didn't want to get into anything further, and handed them Jack's card and said, 'You really need to talk to my lawyer about all of this.' They asked again, 'Are you sure you don't want to come work with us?' and I told them that I wouldn't do something like that. Each time I spoke with them it was very professional, not like some people would expect.

"As I walked back to the house, I was thinking, 'Fuck, I gotta call Tommy.' Now I was really nervous because Tommy was a weak seed who would sell his mom out for two joints. I went to a pay phone and called him, and said I needed to meet with him right away. I told him about the FBI coming down two weeks before, and that they asked about him that day.[1] He acted all tough and strong and said, 'I won't say anything to them or to the grand jury.' The FBI showed up at Tommy's work pretty soon after that, and he called me right afterward so that we could meet in the parking lot of a steakhouse at the

---

[1] Martino told the FBI that he first learned of the investigation from Battista.

King of Prussia Mall.[2] We used to meet there all the time to discuss business, and I didn't care if people were watching me or taking pictures, whatever. After talking about the FBI, I told Tommy I needed some of my money back from the last payment he made for me. There was a mix-up and he wound up with ten thousand dollars he shouldn't have; Tommy thought it must have been a gift. Well, he said he didn't have any money left, that he had put new rugs in his basement. I was pissed because I essentially furnished his entire fucking house, and there was no way rugs for his basement cost him ten grand. He always took money that wasn't his, anyway, so I just let it go. He gave me about five hundred bucks, and we made an appointment to go down to see Jack McMahon the next day. Tommy and I went to Jack's office together so that we could fight this together."[3] "I first met with Tommy Martino when he was subpoenaed to appear before the grand jury and needed a lawyer," McMahon says. "I spoke with him and his father a number of times. I recommended a good friend of mine, Jake Griffin, who is a criminal defense attorney."

Martino soon complained to Battista that the FBI had visited him a few more times, pressuring him with all the information they were picking up off the street. "Like Jack did with me," Battista says, "Jake had been telling Tommy not to talk to the feds and that he was going to 'take the fifth' in front of the grand jury. When the FBI visited him, though, Tommy tried to tell them stuff so they'd think he was being cooperative, things like what he and Elvis did, how long they were friends, how long he knew me, that I worked out of his house, that I was a gambler, and that I owed a lot of money

---

[2] An FBI summary of Martino's interview about this states, "After Martino was interviewed by the FBI and received a subpoena, he called Baba and met him at the King of Prussia Mall."

[3] Tommy Martino characterized the payment in question for the FBI as an "additional $10,000 for [his] work on the scheme." Of minor note, Martino told authorities he gave Battista $400.

to people, and stuff like that. Just from what he told me he discussed with them, I was getting more nervous."[4]

There was no chance Battista was going to adopt Martino's "tell them something" strategy before the grand jury that was convening in New York to hear the early stages of the NBA betting scandal case. "I was supposed to go up right around the time Tommy was," Battista says. "The feds came back to my house again about a week before I was supposed to appear. By this point, Jack had already notified Tom Siegel, the U.S. Attorney in Brooklyn at the time, that I was going to invoke my Fifth Amendment right before the grand jury.[5] [FBI Agent] Paul Harris said, 'We'd really like you to re-think your decision not to speak with us. You can either hop on the train now, or it's gonna run you over.' My heart sank when he said that because I immediately assumed Tommy spoke with them; he was a two-to-one favorite to fold! But, I told them, 'I'm not going to "get on the train," I'm just going to "roll the dice."' Paul said, 'Okay, but you're going to regret this.' It was another brief exchange. I was assuming by now they weren't traveling all the way down from Brooklyn just to see me for five minutes. They were probably making the rounds interviewing people in the area, because me and Tommy didn't live too far from each other. They also might have been staying in a hotel or something, because otherwise it didn't make sense to me."[6]

Tommy Martino was slated to appear before the grand jury on May 30th, and as the date approached Battista grew

---

[4] An FBI memo summarizing one of Martino's early interviews in mid-May (i.e., before agreeing to cooperate with the federal government, after which he was more forthcoming) discloses a mix of fact and fiction, the latter best embodied by his comments regarding Tim Donaghy and Jimmy Battista: "Martino describes Donaghy as straight-laced . . . Donaghy, as a referee, knew that he could not be associated with gambling. Martino stated that Donaghy would never provide inside information to Battista."

[5] Tom Siegel was chief of the Organized Crime and Racketeering Section (OCRS) of the U.S. Attorney's Office for the Eastern District of New York, housed in Brooklyn.

[6] It was later rumored the FBI had either purchased or rented a home across the street and three houses down from Battista's Phoenixville, PA, home.

increasingly worried over what his pal might do before the panel. It was clear to him that, just as with Martino's on-the-street FBI interviews, his co-conspirator wasn't going to follow his lead and simply refuse to answer any of the panel's questions beyond those required by law. "Before Tommy went up to go before the grand jury, he told me that his father and some other people told him that he should answer some questions. Well, his lawyer, Jake, wrote down on a piece of paper what things Tommy was not to discuss whatsoever. He told Tommy, 'Anytime the names "James Battista," "Sheep," "Baba," "Elvis," or "Timothy Donaghy" come up, you take the Fifth.'"

When speaking to the grand jury, Tommy Martino was asked two questions that would cause him, and ultimately his co-conspirators, problems in the very near future. First, he was asked, "Can you give an explanation of why you so frequently have conversations with Mr. Donaghy followed by calls with Mr. Battista?" Martino incredibly replied to the grand jury, "He always called me at inopportune times. I talk to everybody. It is coincidental." The other, more direct, query was, "Have you ever communicated any information from Mr. Donaghy about a game to Mr. Battista?" Martino responded with a simple, and blatantly false, "No." These circumstances helped get the ball rolling for authorities, who suspected Martino had just perjured himself, which would likely assist them in efforts to flip Martino into a cooperating witness. That would have to wait, however, and for now Battista was getting bad news about Martino's performance. "Tommy's lawyer, Jake, called my lawyer, Jack, to tell him what a fucking idiot Tommy was. Jake, of course, wasn't allowed in the room during the questioning, and couldn't believe that Tommy kept stopping the questioning to leave the room and ask Jake what he should answer. All the stuff Jake had written on the paper went out the door when Tommy started answering questions. Jake told Jack that Tommy was the dumbest person he had ever defended."

Tommy Martino would probably have been surprised to hear such a critical assessment of his grand jury appearance, because, Battista says, "Tommy came back and told me, 'I didn't tell them anything. If anything, I helped you.' He told me what he remembered about the questions, and the way he was describing everything made me nervous. 'If anything, *I helped you*'? How the fuck could he help me if he wasn't supposed to say anything?! To make this more ridiculous, Tommy went to the grand jury high. He told me he got high beforehand to relax him. None of this affected what I was going to do when I went up, but I knew right then that things weren't looking good. I said, 'Tommy, you better get in touch with Elvis so that he knows they're gonna get in touch with him.' The FBI was going to 'put two and two together' if they hadn't already.

"Tommy told me that he called Elvis the next day, and that Elvis was freaking out on the phone. All this shit with the FBI and the grand jury had been going on for a while, and Elvis didn't know anything about it. I was telling Tommy to tell Elvis to keep quiet, 'We don't know what evidence the government has, whether they have wiretaps or anything. You gotta first know what's going on before you do anything.' We had a code, 'cranberries,' which meant you didn't talk to anyone. We'd say, 'Everything is cranberries,' or 'Is everything still cranberries?'[7] The FBI knew I wasn't going to talk, and it was obvious to me that they were going to reach out to Elvis after Tommy. Jack McMahon called Elvis to try and get him to come to Philadelphia for a meeting, but Elvis didn't want to do that." "I wanted to know if Donaghy had a lawyer," McMahon says. "At that point in time I was thinking, 'If Jimmy is telling me the truth, there are only three players

---

[7] According to Tommy Martino's FBI interviews, the code word "cranberries" was suggested by Tim Donaghy and meant "keep your mouth shut." The FBI wrote of this situation, "Baba told Martino to keep everything between himself, Martino and Donaghy."

in this that know anything: Donaghy, Tommy, and Jimmy. That's it.' Absent any of the three talking, the government had no case. I called Donaghy's representation a few times, left messages, but no one ever got back to me. I just assumed at that point Donaghy was cooperating, or was planning to cooperate. Anytime you get involved in a federal case, the two questions you ask yourself are: 'Are there wiretaps?' and 'Who is cooperating?'"

Notwithstanding McMahon's troubles contacting whoever was representing Tim Donaghy in early June 2007, Tommy Martino was initially still speaking with Donaghy. "Elvis and Tommy kept asking if I was 'cranberries,'" Battista says. "Well, to me, I was cranberries and there was nothing to it; we didn't know what they had against us. I was always so careful with the phones that I couldn't imagine they had phone conversations, but with those two fucking idiots you never knew." As the three conspirators fretted constantly about the federal investigation, Battista learned he would not have to appear before the grand jury. "[Assistant United States Attorney] Tom Siegel called Jack about a week after Tommy spoke to the grand jury," Battista says, "and said, 'Let your client know we don't need him before the grand jury. He's going down.'

"The whole time all of this was going on, I kept waiting for this to break in the news. I couldn't believe no one knew about the investigation. The NBA playoffs were going on at the time, and the championship was coming up.[8] I just assumed the league had somehow pressured everyone to keep quiet. Meanwhile, Tommy kept updating Elvis with stuff that was going on until about seven to ten days after Elvis found out about everything. Elvis stopped taking Tommy's calls, and we knew what that meant."

---

[8] The 2007 NBA Championship series between the Cleveland Cavaliers and the San Antonio Spurs took place between June 7 and June 14, 2007.

On June 15, 2007, Tim Donaghy traveled to Brooklyn with his attorney, Tampa-based John F. Lauro, and met with the FBI for his first proffer session with federal law enforcement officials.[9] The referee had last worked a game back on May 12th, during the NBA playoffs, and had to know his career—and much of his life—was over as he spoke with authorities. Unlike his co-conspirators, Donaghy opted to cooperate from the jump. The move was savvy, and would manifest itself in ways benefitting Donaghy that he couldn't have imagined when he decided to work with the feds. When Donaghy first met with authorities, they saw someone who was contrite and broken. They also saw someone who had, by his own admission, destroyed something he loved—his career as an NBA referee. In large part because he approached them proactively and because of his self-criticism, authorities found his version of events compelling and credible.[10] It also didn't hurt that Battista wasn't cooperative whatsoever, and that authorities strongly believed Martino had perjured himself before the grand jury. Donaghy had played his cards brilliantly, and his version of events would dominate the investigation and its media coverage for the foreseeable future.

Though not one of the agents working the case, FBI Supervisory Special Agent (SSA) Phil Scala headed the Gambino

---

[9] These conferences essentially consist of subjects and targets of investigations offering information to authorities in the hopes of obtaining beneficial plea agreements, immunity against prosecution, etc. According to the U.S. Attorney's Office for the Eastern District of New York, before pleading guilty, Donaghy met with federal law enforcement officials on June 15th, June 27th, July 6th, and August 8th.

[10] As the U.S. Attorney's Office for the Eastern District of New York wrote much later in support of a downward departure from the sentencing guidelines in consideration of Donaghy's cooperation, "In early 2007, the government began investigating illegal gambling activity involving the NBA. By May 2007, the investigation had identified Donaghy as the referee, and had uncovered the basic roles played in the scheme by Donaghy, Battista, and Martino. On May 30, 2007, Martino appeared before a grand jury, and committed perjury. Several days after Martino's grand jury testimony, the government was contacted by an attorney [not John Lauro] representing Donaghy. Prior to that point, the government had not approached Donaghy, nor had the government publicly disclosed that it was investigating him."

Squad (which housed the investigation) and was privy to many aspects of the NBA betting scandal probe.[11] Scala's comments accurately reflect the sentiments of others privy to the Donaghy proffer sessions when he says of the three-person conspiracy, "You always try to corroborate, but there are other things you can't corroborate that are 'he said-she said.' When you sign someone up, until something's proven to be a lie, you gotta go with the person who signs the agreement. You gotta go with the cooperator's sincerity in things that are painful to him, and there were a lot of things Donaghy told us that we felt he was being honest about." Such sentiments had implications for Donaghy, Battista, and Martino, not to mention for anyone who would later try to understand the NBA betting scheme. Days after Donaghy's New York trip, on June 20th, the FBI notified the NBA's Senior Vice President of Security (and former FBI agent) Bernie Tolbert of its investigation. The following day, NBA Commissioner David Stern and other league executives met with the FBI, and were told that thirteen-year veteran referee Tim Donaghy had bet on NBA games, including games he officiated. None of this was made public, and Donaghy's former partners were still nervously pondering what he was telling the feds.

"In early July," Battista says, "I met with Tommy and he told me that Elvis had called to say that Tommy and I were fucked. He said, 'Sheep did this and Sheep did that, and he's going away for a long time.' He also told Tommy that I threatened him, and Tommy didn't understand what the fuck he was talking about. That was the first time I got a sense of what was going to happen. I didn't *know* that Elvis was cooperating, but I suspected he was because he essentially cut off contact with Tommy. Tommy was really worried about everything.

---

[11] FBI SSA Phil Scala has since retired, and is the lone agent who can speak publicly about the case.

"[FBI agents] Paul Harris and Gerry Conrad came down one last time to talk to me. Paul said, 'This is your last chance. We'd really like you to come work with us.' I said 'No' again, and just asked that they consider my kids. I said, 'Let me turn myself in or meet me around the corner.' I had been busted before with a dozen cop cars and state police. I didn't want a scene in front of my house. Paul was pretty cool about everything, and said he would pass my concerns along to Tom Siegel, the U.S. Attorney, who had the final say. By now, the feds probably knew that I wasn't up to anything, that I had gotten clean, and that I wasn't back to work betting. I'm sure they were waiting for me to start calling Zorba, The Chinaman, and everybody, but I stayed clear of all of that. By then, my life was nothing but sobriety meetings and trying to take care of my family." Soon afterward, Battista soon got the expected news. "Tom Siegel called Jack to let him know they were going to arrest me," Battista says, "and Jack just asked that they let me turn myself in instead of making a big show of everything. They agreed, but in a few days the story broke in the *New York Post*."

"NBA in a 'Fix'" screamed the newspaper's headline on July 20th, grabbing the attention of those who followed sports and beyond. The tabloid article began, "The FBI is investigating an NBA referee who allegedly was betting on basketball games—including ones he was officiating the past two seasons—as part of an organized-crime probe in the Big Apple." Though the piece made no mention of the co-conspirators, the wall of secrecy surrounding the scheme was about to collapse, and Battista immediately made plans. "I told Denise, who was done with cosmetology school," Battista says, "that she should go down the Jersey shore with the kids for the rest of the summer and stay with a family member because I didn't want them around for what was probably going to happen. I could tell by her reaction that our marriage was really on the rocks." The national hype that followed the seminal article was followed four days later by a lengthy news conference held by NBA Commissioner Stern, who said, "I have been involved . . . with the NBA for forty years in some shape or form. I can tell you that this is the most serious situation and worst situation that I have ever experienced."

Stern defended the league against suggestions they could or should have known about Donaghy's illicit activities in part by stating, "we have for many years retained a consultant in Las Vegas whose job it is to inform us whether there are any movements or unusual movements in betting on the NBA about which we should be concerned, and we're also in contact with the Nevada Gaming Board who monitors that for their own purposes to determine whether there has been anything that we should be concerned about or particularly aware of." Stern also noted that since the 2003-04 season, the NBA has employed thirty observers to capture and critique every call a referee makes in every game. These observers then review a tape of each game, and many game tapes are reviewed by group supervisors. These assessments offered no evidence Donaghy's on-court behavior was problematic. In fact, Stern made a point to say that Donaghy, who formally resigned on July 9th, was "in the top tier of accuracy" among referees.

The criminal justice process was moving forward in late July, essentially unaffected by the circus that was now taking place in the media, in the blogosphere, and especially on chat boards, where conspiracy theories were running wild. Jimmy Battista and Tommy Martino were still on the outside of the federal investigation looking in until July 26th, when Martino made the fateful decision to cooperate with authorities against his lifelong friend.

18

The Dog Days of Summer

TOMMY MARTINO MADE the trek up to Brooklyn in the hopes of somehow backtracking his earlier false statements to the FBI and, more importantly, to the grand jury. The late July meeting was the first of three such conferences that would take place within two weeks for Martino, who was now represented by Delaware County attorney Vicki Herr.[1] The proffer session was attended by all relevant federal officials: FBI Special Agents Conrad and Harris, their squad supervisor Phil Scala, and Assistant U.S. Attorneys Tom Siegel, Jeff Goldberg, and Jack Smith. Martino offered the authorities insights into all sorts of consequential matters, ranging from his background with Battista and Donaghy to Martino's role in the local drug trade to exquisite details of the NBA betting scandal that only he and Battista would know. Just as was the case with much of what Donaghy told authorities, there were no records to buttress Martino's claims on a host of important matters, including and especially Donaghy's bets and Battista's financial transactions orchestrated throughout the scheme. Even if the feds had come to accept Martino's latest version of events as a fair and truthful assessment, there was no way to support or refute his many statements without access to Battista or his records. After all, The Sheep was the lone conspirator with a mind for numbers and a pedigree for

---

[1] Tommy Martino attended three proffer sessions in the U.S. Attorney's Office for the Eastern District of New York: July 26th, August 6th, and August 9th.

record keeping—and for whom keeping track of everything was a necessity. Just as Martino began working behind the scenes against his childhood buddy—literally, on the same blistering summer day—Battista was dealing with a more overt and pressing problem a hundred and sixteen miles southwest of Brooklyn in Phoenixville, Pennsylvania.

"The first time I noticed the press," Battista says, "was one day when I was going out to walk Fluffy, my dog, and there was this guy parked right in front of my house. He said he was so-and-so, and I told him I couldn't talk to him and that I didn't want him on my property. Meanwhile, it was so hot and humid—it was a million fucking degrees—and I noticed this guy had his dog in the car. I said, 'You're gonna kill that poor thing.' I came out later and gave him a bowl and a bottle of water and told him, 'This is for the dog, not you.' That guy camped out front, and stayed overnight.[2] A lot of reporters were on my block, waiting to get pictures of me, usually walking the dog, and they would go door-to-door asking my neighbors about me. Luckily, my wife and kids were down the shore because I didn't want them to have to deal with that." It was also fortunate for Battista that he and his family were so open about his chosen profession since, when the nation's media outlets pressed friends and neighbors for a "gotcha" story or a sensational revelation, virtually all knew Jimmy Battista was a gambler.

"I always told people I was a professional gambler," Battista says, "going back at least to the early 2000s. I never introduced myself that way, necessarily, and I was always as evasive as

---

[2] The situation was chronicled in the *Daily News* (NY) on July 27, 2007, by Mike Jaccarino, who wrote: "Here's the first look at the reputed small-time bookie behind disgraced referee Tim Donaghy and the NBA scandal. James Battista, who attended the same Pennsylvania high school as Donaghy in the early 1980s, is in the eye of the illegal gambling storm that has rocked pro basketball, but he was calmly walking his Shih Tzu when the *Daily News* tracked him down in an affluent Philadelphia suburb. 'No comment,' Battista said gruffly. 'Stay off my property.' Later, Battista softened somewhat and emerged from his brick Colonial with a bowl of cold water for the reporter's dog, who was along for the stakeout."

possible, but if people actually asked me, that's what I would tell them. I never made anything up or lied to people. When we went to parties in our development, it was hard to explain to our friends and neighbors what I did. I'd tell them I was a gambler, but they couldn't grasp I was doing that *full-time*. I'm sure some people thought it was a shady line of work, but they didn't know what kind of people I was working with. They probably couldn't imagine people like medical doctors, hedge fund traders, real estate moguls, and sports team owners betting on sports as a major part of their business lives." Part of the reason so many people knew about Battista's profession was because of his large and active family. Having five children who were involved in school and with sports meant that the kids were constantly among their friends, classmates, and teammates, and conversations would often give others a glimpse of The Sheep's career and lifestyle.

"Everyone knew I was a gambler," Battista says. "A couple of years I went out to Vegas for a few weeks and invited my entire family to come visit. We'd have like fourteen kids out there with us, and we'd vacation together. I'd stay at the South Coast Casino, and get some work done while we were there. I had a friend there, Larry, who had a relationship with one of the sportsbook managers. Larry was a mover and he had outs; I would give him the games, and he would let me bet big dollars. Larry introduced me to the manager of one of the bigger sportsbooks, this guy named Ernie, who allowed me to place big bets. We would open him up early in the morning, before anyone else and before the market got saturated. He'd let me bet five games at a hundred thousand apiece before anyone else saw the lines. In the four or five years I bet with them, I never worked with them myself. I always had people working for me deal with them. Larry and Ernie got a percentage of the earnings, and we'd settle at the end of the year. That is why I was treated like royalty when I'd visit Vegas.

"I'd stay for ten days, three weeks, whatever, and they'd put me up in a suite. The rooms we used to stay in were incredible, and everything was comped. We'd have five or six bathrooms in our room. Each of my kids would have their own bathroom. We'd eat great, and my kids would eat everything under the sun, from chicken tenders to lobster tail. Over the years, my wife and I got to see so many great shows, always had incredible seats, and we never had to pay. They wanted to take care of me out there, and I didn't ask for as much as a lot of people. We lived simple lives, we liked having nice meals, and seeing some shows. We did a lot of things with our kids out there, too. Of course, I worked a lot when I was out there, too. We'd get out there at least once or twice a year, and we did that for years. We always went as a family. My wife and I only went out there once without the kids, for a weekend, because there was so much for the kids to do. We stayed at the Coast Casinos, at Caesar's, Bellagio; it varied. The thing is, though, that all of our neighbors and our kids' friends knew we used to vacation out there and why."

Events surrounding the betting scandal investigation were now fast and furious, with many playing out in the public sphere. One of the more curious, and yet key, moments took place on July 30th when Pete Ruggieri's attorney, prominent Philly defense lawyer Christopher Warren, held court with the press to discuss his client's cooperation with the FBI. Ruggieri had met with agents eight days earlier in Warren's Center City office, where the pro gambler explained why and how long he and others knew to bet on games Tim Donaghy officiated, and also his understanding of why Donaghy switched from betting with Jack Concannon to Jimmy Battista. Ruggieri, of course, had known Concannon and Battista for years, and knew them extremely well. He explained that Concannon, whose last name and involvement were not publicly discussed yet, had approached him years prior seeking advice on where he could place bets, at which point Ruggieri referred him to offshore betting operations.[3] Ruggieri tracked Concannon's bets and, as Warren explained, "Ruggieri noticed that Jack kept winning bets on NBA games," Warren said. "Ruggieri looked harder and noticed that Jack bet on games officiated by Tim Donaghy." As the *Philadelphia Daily News* put it, "Pete Ruggieri thought he had it all, the inside track to winning the majority of bets he would place on the NBA. The method was simple: bet games that Tim Donaghy officiated."

Ruggieri told authorities that he estimated bets on games Donaghy officiated won between sixty and seventy percent of the time, and that the same was true later when Donaghy switched from betting with Jack Concannon to Jimmy Battista. Warren's discussion of what Ruggieri told authorities was succinctly recounted in the New York *Daily News* on July 31st: "Donaghy first partnered with a fellow professional gambler named "Jack" . . . [and] grew dissatisfied with the money Jack funneled back to him as part of the betting scheme . . . Donaghy then turned to high school chums Jimmy Battista and Tommy Martino . . . Soon, a word or bet from Battista would send the point spread on a given NBA game flying. Eventually others realized the common denominator that Ruggieri had already discovered: ex-NBA ref Tim Donaghy."

Ruggieri's version of events regarding Donaghy's dissatisfaction with Concannon and subsequent move to Battista perfectly mirrored what Tommy Martino was telling federal

---

[3] It goes without saying that by cooperating with federal authorities, Ruggieri was, like Martino, essentially cooperating against Battista, if only because Battista had opted to keep quiet. Importantly, Ruggieri's version of events is almost precisely the same as Battista's regarding numerous consequential matters, such as: Concannon seeking Ruggieri out; mimicking Concannon's bets on games Donaghy was officiating (without any explicit discussion between Concannon and Ruggieri in this regard [i.e., Ruggieri and Battista simply put 'two-and-two together']); Donaghy's switch from Concannon to Battista, and the reason for it; and mimicking Battista's bets on games Donaghy was officiating.

authorities at the time. Ruggieri's comments regarding what he
was betting and why were also important to the understanding of Donaghy's actions. Just as Martino was depicting for
authorities, pro gambler Ruggieri told the FBI he was mimicking bets first placed by Concannon and then by Battista *only
for games Donaghy was officiating.* These were the bets winning
at a ridiculous clip and thus sending bookmakers and sportsbooks into a frenzy with wild line swings and producing huge
earners. Somehow, this key point would wind up getting lost
amid all sorts of conspiracy theories within a year's time, and
it thus bears repeating: those with 'skin in the game,' namely
the sportsbooks and the big-time bettors (and their hangers-
on) with millions of dollars at stake, were only concerned with
NBA games that Tim Donaghy was officiating.

History's take on the scandal would have to wait, however,
and the other cooperating witnesses were in the midst of
completing their respective proffer sessions. Tim Donaghy
met with authorities for a fourth time on August 8th, and was
on the verge of accepting a guilty plea. Tommy Martino, on
the other hand, met with officials for the third time on the
following day, and yet was nowhere close to a deal despite
his newfound appreciation for the truth. By this point in the
investigation, case agent Paul Harris and his colleagues knew
Battista was not going to cooperate and were confident they
generally understood the scheme and felt comfortable with
Donaghy's story at its most basic level. The now-former NBA
referee bet on his own games with Jack Concannon dating
back to the end of the 2002-03 season, and on thirty to forty
games he officiated during each of the '03-04, '04-05, and '05-
06 seasons. In the particular matter involving Jimmy Battista
and Tommy Martino, Donaghy admitted to participating in
a scheme with his co-conspirators during the 2006-07 season
whereby he would be paid for winning picks (to Battista, via
Martino) but not have to pay for losing wagers.

The only real matters left for debate were the possible fixing of games to advance Donaghy's betting propositions, and the nuances of the scheme (e.g., duration, bets, results). Concerning the former, Donaghy insisted he did not fix games and that his betting success was instead due exclusively to his access as an NBA referee to "inside information," including things like the officiating crews for upcoming games (which were not publicly disclosed in advance at the time) and the relationships between players, coaches, referees, etcetera. Regarding the scheme's logistics, Donaghy claimed: the scheme ended on March 18, 2007, when Battista went into rehab; he bet on thirty games total, including sixteen he officiated, and his betting success was the same regardless of whether he worked the games or not; and he received less than thirty thousand dollars total for his role.

Much of this flew in the face of what authorities heard from Pete Ruggieri and Tommy Martino, who, for example, had each independently explained to the FBI that it was only wagers on games Donaghy officiated which produced such out-of-this-world results. Ruggieri told the FBI that he copied Donaghy's bets on games Donaghy was officiating, and Martino told the FBI that Donaghy bet thirty-seven games, including "some" that Donaghy didn't officiate, implying that the vast majority of the bets were on Donaghy's games. The clear inference of Martino's and Ruggieri's claims was that Donaghy's version of events was not accurate, to say the least, regarding his betting record, and his assertions that access to "so-called" inside information alone accounted for his betting success.[4] Martino also told authorities the scheme continued

---

[4] I say "so-called" inside information because many of the trends Donaghy described for authorities are precisely the sorts of things to which the world's sharps are also privy (based on analyses from their research teams, computer models, and informants within various relevant spheres). For example, referee-player, referee-team, referee-coach relationships and the like are quite seriously analyzed qualitatively and quantitatively by those who bet for a living, and who are placing big money on games. That such

for three or four Donaghy games after Battista entered rehab, and that Donaghy pushed Martino to take one more game after hearing that Ruggieri was shutting the scheme down. Lastly, Martino had informed the FBI that he paid Donaghy at least one hundred and fifteen thousand dollars total over three months or so.

Federal authorities, for whom a white-collar gambling probe based in Phoenixville, PA, was a far cry from their traditional Brooklyn-grounded mob cases, concluded that trying to resolve these discrepancies was not worth their time and use of resources. This was in large part because of a lack of supporting evidence, most of which resided with Jimmy Battista and his files and which was therefore out of the FBI's reach. In addition to that significant void in the probe, there were no court-authorized wiretapped conversations of the parties during the conspiracy. The Bureau did what little it could to vet Donaghy's claim he didn't influence or manipulate games, including having a team of agents review approximately fourteen of Donaghy's 2006-07 games, and saw nothing overtly dubious in Donaghy's actions. Agents also interviewed various people in the sports betting world (some of whom no doubt who had interests to protect) regarding things like whether they had heard of anything odd involving NBA games, especially those officiated by Tim Donaghy.[5]

---

persons may not be privy to the nuances of *why*, say, referee A has a demonstrated history of calling B fouls, especially against player C or team D, is irrelevant for the purposes of wagering. All that matters to the bettor is that such causal relationships are factored into the betting analysis for that particular game and wager. The general public, including Donaghy, would likely be awestruck to witness how much time, energy, and research goes into the assessments conducted by, or at the behest of, the world's heavyweight bettors.

[5] Individuals in the sports betting world, especially sportsbook managers, were in a tight spot when it came to the NBA betting scandal. If they admitted to having heard about the scheme and/or witnessing odd line movements, etc., during the scandal, they would have had to explain their lack of inaction. Indeed, their possible culpability could have been revisited if it was suspected they not only knew of the scheme, but profited from it. On the other hand, if these individuals claimed they did not notice

These inquiries again, in the parlance of law enforcement, produced negative results.

Incredibly, federal officials never researched one wholly objective set of data which doesn't need a witness to vouch for its validity and which was available to them—betting line move analyses for NBA games, including those just for games Donaghy officiated. Unlike the statements of cooperating witnesses, which are always viewed with a critical eye, especially when the witness has interests to protect, the historical and unassailable betting line data has no motivations. Such an analysis could have disclosed, for instance, whether the line movement in Donaghy games was constant during the years he was betting, if it changed in any particular year (i.e., 2006-07) or in any specific time period (i.e., December 12, 2006–March 26, 2007), and so on. No one set of data or analyses in a circumstantial case like the NBA betting scandal is likely sufficient to conclude or prove anything. Rather, when hard, objective data exists, it can at least form the foundation for lines of inquiry, and assist in supporting or refuting the many subjective areas of a case.

In addition to more important aspects of the case, investigators also briefly humored two claims Tim Donaghy made during his proffer sessions, including one that would become legend when it became public. During his interviews, Donaghy told authorities that the origin of the scheme was Jimmy Battista threatening Donaghy twice on December 12, 2006, to give him his NBA picks. Specifically, Donaghy claimed Battista said that unless Donaghy gave him the picks Battista would "out" Donaghy to the NBA regarding his betting on games he was officiating, and that Battista told Donaghy, "you don't want anyone from New York visiting your wife and kids." Donaghy further explained to authorities that he assumed

---

the wild betting line swings that took place for Donaghy's games during the 2006-07 NBA season, their reputation and credibility would be jeopardized.

"New York" meant "the Mafia" because Tommy Martino had mentioned at some point that Battista knew someone who was connected to organized crime.

Donaghy's accusations were put directly to his close friend and fellow cooperating government witness, Tommy Martino, as can be gleaned by an FBI memo summarizing the exchange: "After the meeting [in the Marriott], all three got into a car. Baba acted like he was a savior who was there to help Donaghy [who had complained of Jack Concannon's delinquent payments to Martino during the meeting in a side conversation]. Martino never heard Baba threaten Donaghy in any way. Martino had the impression that Donaghy wanted to provide the picks to Baba for Donaghy's own financial gain. Martino was not aware of Baba ever threatening Donaghy that he was going to hurt Donaghy or tell the NBA about the betting." By the first week of August, authorities had vetted Donaghy's various claims and perhaps sensed where he was going with these assertions. In the ensuing weeks and months, the federal government incorporated explicit statements into court filings making it plain that Donaghy was always a willing participant—and that all three men were equally culpable actors—in the scheme.

Though the various threat allegations made by Donaghy carried little sway with the authorities as they prepared to charge the former ref and his co-conspirators, Jimmy Battista would have to deal with them later when they entered the public arena, if only in his personal life. For now, Battista was simply waiting—and hoping—for the call to let him know he was finally going to be arrested.

19

Former N.B.A. Referee Pleads Guilty

THE ANXIETY CAUSED by not knowing when he'd be arrested was driving Jimmy Battista crazy as August entered its second week. He was also hoping he'd get arrested while his family was still down the Jersey shore, and greatly feared the prospect of having his kids watch their father hauled out of their home, possibly with reporters and cameras all around as he got whisked away. "I got a call on August 14th," Battista says, "to be in Brooklyn the next morning by eight to turn myself in. I was ecstatic; my kids wouldn't have to see me being locked up!"

August 15, 2007, would turn out to be a landmark day in the history of U.S. sport, but for Battista the appearance before a federal judge regarding a criminal conspiracy didn't have quite the sobering effect his attorney, Jack McMahon, expected it would. When McMahon met with his client to take the trip to the U.S. Courthouse in Brooklyn, he was shocked and furious to find Battista wearing khaki shorts, a golf shirt, and sneakers.[1] McMahon yelled at him, "You are going before a federal fucking judge!" Battista didn't understand McMahon's outrage and, to the contrary, thought it was absurd to get dressed up to be arrested as if it were a wedding or other event to be celebrated. There was no time for Battista to get changed into something more proper for

---

[1] Battista's wardrobe was so curious it earned a mention in the *New York Post* the following day.

the court appearance, anyway, and the men ventured up the New Jersey Turnpike in McMahon's sparkling foreign SUV. When they arrived, it soon became clear the day would hold some surprises.

"Me and Tommy and our lawyers met outside the courthouse with [FBI agents] Gerry Conrad and Philip Scala," Battista says, "and they took us to Starbucks because the system wasn't ready for us. [FBI case agent] Paul Harris was with Elvis over in court. They already had his deal all worked out, which we knew nothing about." Indeed, as Battista and Martino waited to be arraigned, Tim Donaghy was in Judge Carol Bagley Amon's 10th-floor courtroom pleading guilty to two felonies: conspiring to commit wire fraud, and conspiring to transmit gambling information across state lines.[2] The deal also required Donaghy to forfeit thirty thousand dollars as proceeds obtained from the betting scheme. The former referee faced a combined maximum of twenty-five years in prison and five hundred thousand dollars in fines. The Donaghy cooperation agreement was drafted by Assistant U.S. Attorneys Thomas Siegel and Jeffrey Goldberg, the latter of whom would take over the case when Siegel left the Justice Department days after Donaghy's guilty plea. Siegel would miss out on quite a bit of drama by leaving in advance of the sentencing phase of Donaghy's process, which would play out over the next eleven months. Before his departure, Siegel had been privy to at least

---

[2] In summarizing the conspiracy to commit wire fraud, the government in part wrote, "On or about and between December 1, 2006, and April 30, 2007, both dates being approximate and inclusive, within the Eastern District and elsewhere, the defendant Timothy Donaghy, together with others, did knowingly and intentionally conspire to devise a scheme and artifice to defraud the NBA by depriving the NBA of the intangible right of honest services, and for the purpose of executing such scheme and artifice, transmitted and cause to be transmitted writings, signals and sounds by means of wire communication in interstate and foreign commerce, in violation of Title 18, United States Code, Sections 1343 and 1346."

one considerable area of dissension between Donaghy and his federal handlers.

Included within the charging document was a line which read, "Donaghy also compromised his objectivity as a referee because of his personal financial interest in the outcome of NBA games." Donaghy had insisted to authorities that he knew so much "inside information" that he didn't' have to throw or manipulate games. Phil Scala says he and his colleagues told Donaghy that even if this was true, "Once you bet on a game you're officiating, your judgment is impaired. When your judgment is impaired, your decision making is damaged." Donaghy did not want to concede this line of reasoning, says Scala. "We went back and forth with that a hundred times. He didn't want to make that admission. He would say, "You don't understand how easy it was, blah, blah, blah."

After the Donaghy proceedings were sufficiently through, Battista and Martino were brought into the system. "Eventually," Battista says, "we went over to the federal building, got strip searched, and had our pictures taken and everything. They had Tommy in one room with four agents, and three agents with me in another. The guys with me were all young, in their thirties or early forties, and all we talked about was sports and gambling. It was August 15th and there was a month-and-a-half left in baseball, so we were talking about the Phillies and the Mets a little bit. We had a good time going back and forth about gambling, the right numbers, and who I liked for certain things. Then, one of them asked me about his fantasy football team for the upcoming season. He had a sheet of paper and I wrote down the guys I thought would produce the best numbers that year, and I wished him luck. Finally, we got the call to come down to the courthouse. We had ankle bracelets on us and everybody in the media was waiting for us; it was a show. They told us we'd be in another holding cell for an hour.

They put me and Tommy in a cell together in the courthouse. Tommy was breaking down crying after Gerry Conrad told us that we'd be going to jail for a long time. I asked Gerry to leave it alone, because Tommy was a mess. When we were left alone in the cell, Tommy told me, 'I know Elvis told them everything,' and I said, 'Well, we'll find out.'"

Jack McMahon was killing time waiting for Battista and Martino to be brought into court, and took the occasion to satisfy his curiosity regarding one salacious aspect of the case. "Right in the beginning when I first met Jimmy," McMahon says, "I was saying to myself, 'Is there anything to this "mob" stuff?' I didn't think so, but I didn't know. I happened to be with the FBI guys in the courthouse as we were waiting for Jimmy to come up, and I asked them, 'Is there anything to this stuff about the Gambino crime family?' and they said, 'Absolutely not.' I mean, they were adamant that there was no organized crime connection. They told me the only reason the name 'Gambino' was ever brought up was because the scheme came up on a Gambino wiretap." Indeed, federal authorities would never reference organized crime throughout the numerous proceedings and filings that ultimately spanned more than a year.[3]

Eventually, Martino and Battista went separately before Judge Amon to be arraigned on wire fraud charges, were released on

---

[3] Technically speaking, Donaghy's unsupported and self-serving claim re: Battista supposedly threatening Donaghy, which included one sentence re: Donaghy's supposed perception of Battista vis-à-vis organized crime, was quoted in the government's "5K1" letter in consideration of Donaghy's sentencing. Importantly, though, this appeared without comment by federal authorities regarding Donaghy's allegation against Battista, and instead included an explicit comment by authorities re: Donaghy being a willing participant in the scheme (i.e., not an extortion victim of some supposed "mafia" plot). For its part, the federal government never described this as an organized crime conspiracy, and thus never promoted it as such, despite the fact the investigation was conducted by FBI agents in an organized crime unit and prosecuted by Assistant U.S. Attorneys in the Department of Justice's Organized Crime and Racketeering Section.

two hundred and fifty thousand dollars bond, and told they would likely be indicted within thirty days. "We left the courtroom," Battista says, "and then I had to do a piss test. When we were done with everything and were about to come out, there was this older Irish guy working in front of the courthouse who said, 'Listen, fellas. We're going to take you to your car. But, you're going to see something that you've never seen before in your life. There are about a hundred and fifty news reporters and TV crew people waiting for you to come outside. You don't have to smile; just maintain your composure and walk straight to your car.' I was thinking to myself, 'It can't be that bad.' Well, there was probably a hundred and fifty-one! You couldn't move, and getting through there was like parting the Red Sea. They had to walk us about a hundred yards to our car, and the whole time I was thanking God Denise didn't come."

That Denise had not seen him arrested, and didn't witness the mayhem outside the U.S. Courthouse in Brooklyn, wound up being only temporary "wins" for Battista. Within weeks of his arraignment, Denise again revisited how to handle the seemingly constant problems Jimmy was causing for her and the kids. "By now," Battista says, "my name and picture were everywhere, and I was constantly in the news. She asked me to leave the house, so I rented an apartment really close by. In fact, it was right down the street from the Dunkin Donuts where I spoke to the FBI agents the first time. I'd still come home every morning at seven and get the kids ready for school, pack their lunches and everything. Denise would go off to work every day, and I would do stuff around the house until the kids came home. I was Mr. Mom. I'd do the laundry, make dinner, and all that stuff; I just wouldn't sleep in the house."

Battista was very much looking forward to getting the criminal justice process moving so that he could at least get on with his life. "I was supposed to be indicted by September

15th," Battista says, "but they called on September 8th and said they wanted a ninety-day extension to December 8th.[4] I was frustrated, but at least I wasn't in jail. I was going stir crazy and just wanted to get out of the house, but I filled out over forty job applications and no employer would hire me. The thing I had built my whole life around—the thing I knew best—was gambling, and that was out. The other thing I was trained to do was work in the restaurant business, but I didn't want to get back into that environment fresh off of giving up drugs and alcohol."

Ever since the seminal *New York Post* article back in July, Battista paid close attention to news regarding the probe, and got into a daily routine of searching certain Web sites to keep abreast of any developments. He was particularly interested in the August 21st announcement by the NBA that the league was initiating an "independent review" of various league policies relating to gambling and officiating. The review was to be led by Lawrence B. Pedowitz, a lawyer who was formerly Chief of the Criminal Division in the U.S. Attorney's Office for the Southern District of New York. Battista, though, wanted no part of assisting that effort because he didn't believe for a moment that the NBA wanted to hear the true extent and duration of the scandal, particularly since so many other people in his line of work had caught on over the prior four years. The former pro gambler was of the opinion that if vast segments of the gambling underworld knew about the can't-

---

[4] Regarding the process of authorities "requesting" extensions for indictments, Jack McMahon says, "They have thirty days to indict from the time of the complaint and warrant. Many times a prosecutor will ask for more time to take it before a grand jury simply because of time management issues. It isn't unusual, and there's nothing nefarious about it. Defense attorneys usually agree to it because it's not going to get you anything to say, 'No.' If they don't get it done, they just dismiss it, and refile the charges. They can come at you again. It's not like its double jeopardy and the case is going to go away. Asking for an extension is simply a procedural thing and a professional thing. You don't want to break balls with a prosecutor that I am going to have to work with as a case moves forward. I have never objected to a prosecutor's request for an extension."

miss bets on Donaghy's games, *somebody* in the league had to have known—or at least must have heard the buzz—about wagering activity on games Donaghy was officiating. Battista had witnessed sportsbook officials, some of whom he was certain had known about—and profited from—the scheme, feign ignorance about the ridiculous betting line movements on Donaghy's 2006-07 games when the scandal's basic framework became public knowledge. He thus did not envision the NBA's "investigation" getting any closer to the truth, since Battista could only imagine what implications there would be for the league if it concluded (let alone announced) that one or more referees were either active in, or privy to and/or profited from, the influencing of games by one or more referees. "You're talking player's contracts and clauses being affected, teams not making the playoffs and losing revenues, fans pissed at the league for not preventing a rigged product from being put out there. How could you even start to calculate the losses to all sorts of people who could sue? In my eyes, there was no fucking way the NBA was ever going to document Elvis or anybody else fixing games."

Now with the NBA ostensibly poking around for information about the scandal in addition to the FBI, Battista continued to speak with Tommy Martino to see if he was still "cranberries." Martino unsurprisingly kept lying to Battista, insisting he had not spoken to authorities, leading Battista to maintain hope he could somehow beat whatever case was compiled against him. As fall 2007 started in earnest, the gambling world kicked into high gear as always; it was the prime betting season. College and pro football were in full swing, the NBA season was set to kick off in late October, and for pro gamblers there was essentially no down time ahead until the Super Bowl. It would have been understandable if Battista pined for a return to the action, the profits, and the acclaim to which he was accustomed all those years, but times had changed for good. The Sheep—the onetime hustler, book-maker, gambler, and mover—was no more. All that remained for Jimmy Battista was finding resolution with the looming criminal case against him, and working on returning to the person he was before his life spiraled out of control.

"The NBA season was just about to start up," Battista says, "and the news about the scandal was still going on. People were speculating about how many referees were involved, and whether Elvis fixed games. In September, a representative from the NBA contacted Jack McMahon to see if we were going to fight whatever charges were brought against me, and if they should prepare to look at other referees. Jack told him he didn't know what we were going to do yet because I hadn't been indicted. The fall was good for my family life. Sobriety was good; everything with me and my kids was great, and my wife and I started working things out. After a month or two with me living outside the house, Denise said it was silly to be paying rent, and that I should just sleep in the basement at home as we worked things out. I hoped to change her opinion of me, and wanted to be around my kids.

"Throughout October, November, and December 2007, I had no idea what was going on. I was supposed to be indicted this time by December 8th, but the U.S. Attorney's office called during the first week of December and asked for another exten-sion. They said I'd be indicted within sixty days, by February 8th. I just wanted it to happen. All this time, I couldn't travel anywhere, I had to go into downtown Philly once a week to take a urine test, and an FBI agent was assigned to follow me." Battista noticed the FBI agent was tailing him starting back in the spring, but didn't approach the man until just after his August 15th arrest. "After my arrest," Battista says, "I approached the driver who had been following me since April the next time I saw him, and he said he was with the federal government and that they just wanted to know where

I was at all times. I used to see him every morning at Valley Forge Park, where I'd walk for exercise. He'd usually keep his distance, but we'd wave to each other. We'd be the only two people in the park at five-thirty in the morning in the rain! It got to the point where if I slept in, he would ask me why I was late for my morning walk.

"He was a good guy, and we obviously got to know each other. In fact, he was a recovering alcoholic, and we'd talk about the program, and about football and other stuff. He actually told me they were going to use trainees to follow me, and they did. They would take field agents and do field training, surveillance training, with me as the mark; they were assigned to follow me. At some point they assigned another agent to work with him, and when I'd do my walks in the park one would be at one end of the trail and another would be at the other end. I am guessing they wanted to make sure I wasn't meeting anybody from my former business in the park. He eventually got pulled off the detail and was replaced by another agent, but I didn't talk to either of the other agents, who were both females."

Getting used to constant FBI surveillance, urine tests, and travel restrictions was easy for Battista compared to adjusting to the subtleties of life that were now problematic. Being seen in public, regardless of why, was often a cause for media attention and thus an avoided hassle if at all possible. For the father of five active kids, this was not much of an option many times, and one particular example offers insights into Battista's mind-set as 2008 began. "My kids were playing on their basketball teams in the YMCA league," Battista says. "Well, normally I'd be like other parents and volunteer to keep score and ref games, but I didn't because I could just see how some people might view me reffing with all that was going on. I could just see the pictures everywhere of me with a whistle in my mouth reffing a basketball game."

The anxieties and hassles besetting Battista since his August 2007 arrest finally came to a halt when he was indicted on February 8, 2008, alongside his co-conspirator and longtime friend Tommy Martino. "When I got arrested in August 2007," Battista says, "I was told I would be indicted in thirty days. But then they filed an extension for ninety days, and then another extension. It was like a toothache that wouldn't go away, and our lives had been on hold that entire time." Battista, who had gotten the message and wore appropriate attire to court this time, and Martino were each charged with conspiracy to commit wire fraud and conspiracy to transmit wagering information across state lines. Martino was also hit with two counts of perjury for his false statements before the grand jury. Each man was facing up to twenty years in prison on the gambling charges, with Martino facing an additional ten years total for the perjury counts against him. With those formalities aside, Battista and his lawyer, Jack McMahon, moved on to the next key piece of business.

"We went up, got indicted, and asked for the evidence against us," Battista says. Jack McMahon took a shot at getting some advance notice regarding his main concern. "We were discussing discovery," McMahon says, "and I was evaluating the strength of the government's case. I just threw out there to see if they had wiretaps, 'My understanding is that there are no tapes in this case,' to see what their response was. They said there were not, which was a good thing." "When I heard that they didn't have any wiretapped conversations," Battista says, "I was relieved, and it validated all the stuff I had done with the phones." McMahon also broached the idea of a plea agreement with Assistant U.S. Attorney Jeff Goldberg, Battista says. "Jack reached out to Jeff Goldberg about a deal and said, 'Listen. We'll take illegal gambling right now, but we're not going to take wire fraud,' and Goldberg turned us down.

"I think they thought the scandal was bigger, and wanted to see if I was involved with any other referees, any other sports. By then, they knew I moved for other sports and probably knew how much money I was moving on games, and assumed something was going on. I think they figured I couldn't just be gambling if that much money was involved." There was at least one moment of levity among the other, more serious, moments. Battista had a brief exchange with an FBI agent to whom he had earlier offered advice. "One of the FBI agents I helped with his fantasy football team when I was arrested back in August winked at me and thanked me for the picks," Battista says. "Apparently, he did well with them."

The media awaited Battista, McMahon, Martino, and Herr as they left the courtroom, and McMahon, never one to shy away from the cameras, explained that he expected to put Tim Donaghy on the stand, at which point "a lot of things may come out through cross-examination . . . There's a lot of things that everybody doesn't know about." McMahon added that if Donaghy was to testify, "There's more to come, that's all I can tell you. I think it could get messy." When McMahon made his comment regarding things possibly getting "messy," he had no idea how prophetic this would be, though in different circumstances than he was envisioning, and for wholly different reasons. McMahon, like his client, Jimmy Battista, had no idea that Tommy Martino—whom McMahon had assisted for months, even though Martino wasn't his client— had cooperated with authorities. Furthermore, no one knew of the impending battle that was soon to be fought between Tim Donaghy and the federal government, whom Donaghy wrongly assumed was unconditionally by his side. The spring of 2008 was about to bloom with more high drama for the three NBA betting scandal conspirators.

20

What Characters

SOON AFTER BEING indicted, Jimmy Battista and Tommy Martino each pleaded not guilty, and they at last knew what it was they'd be fighting together as a team. That, at least, is what Battista and his attorney, Jack McMahon, thought. McMahon, though never Martino's counsel, had worked with Tommy and his father from the start, including recommending McMahon's friend Jake Griffin as Martino's lawyer. Griffin represented Martino shortly after Martino realized he was the target of a federal investigation, including accompanying Martino during his trip to appear before the grand jury, but was later replaced. "I don't recall why he got rid of Jake Griffin," McMahon says, "but Tommy wound up getting Vicki Herr to defend him. She was from Delaware County and I didn't know her that well. I called her up and told her that since she was now on the case we should communicate and all that, to which she agreed. I drove her up to do the first appearance, the bail appearance. When we had lunch together that day, she expressed to me that she didn't know much about federal procedure and that she hadn't really done any federal cases. I explained what she needed to know, and told her it was no big deal.

"After the first appearance, she and I corresponded frequently about everything. I was also talking a lot to Tommy and to Tommy's dad. Jimmy would call me up and tell me that Tommy's dad was real nervous, and that he was such a nice man, and would ask if I could meet with him. Well,

Tommy's father didn't trust Vicki Herr to give him the right information, so I would talk to him and meet with him. I spent a good bit of time trying to give him the best insights I could." Though McMahon humored Battista's repeated requests to assist Tommy's father, he never knew why Jimmy was so concerned about Mr. Martino. The reason was simple: Battista had not forgotten Martino's father offering various forms of assistance over the years, including and especially bailing Battista out of jail many years before when Battista feared contacting his own parents. Given these circumstances, one can only imagine what Battista and McMahon thought when they made an alternately unbelievable yet believable— and heartbreaking and infuriating—discovery in early April 2008 as Assistant U.S. Attorney Jeff Goldberg, on behalf of the federal government, was attempting to negotiate a plea deal with Battista and Martino.

"Goldberg came in with an offer," Battista says. "Tommy's lawyer, Vicki Herr, said the deal was based on the amount of money I supposedly paid Elvis. She kept referencing an amount of money, which was one hundred and twenty thousand dollars. Jack kept saying to Vicki, 'What are you talking about?' The whole time I couldn't figure out what the fuck was going on, because we had never talked about money. Meanwhile, Vicki kept telling me I should take the government's deal. It was April, and the government had come in with a deal where I would be facing three years, which was down from four to six years. They then brought that down to twenty-one to twenty-four months, but I didn't think the government was giving me all the evidence I was entitled to.[1] I said, 'Fuck it.

---

[1] Though Jimmy Battista was not satisfied with the pace or contents of evidence discovery, his attorney, Jack McMahon, had no problems with the process or actions of the government in this regard. The "dribs and drabs" of evidence that so troubled Battista, were of little concern to McMahon, who says, "Discovery in a federal case often comes in piecemeal fashion, so that wasn't that unusual." Records indicate the first discovery letter from authorities to McMahon was sent on March 13, 2008, fol-

Let's go to trial. You're not giving me enough evidence, and I don't care which statements you have.' Vicki called me in early April saying, 'They've got a deal. We'll get twenty-one to twenty-four months, and you'll probably have to do eighteen to twenty-one months.' I told Jack, 'I'm not going to jail for two years when they haven't even given all the evidence against me.' Vicki said the U.S. Attorney's office told her, 'If Battista takes the deal, we'll wipe away Martino's perjury,' and we'd each do eighteen to twenty-one months. I was like, 'How can I take the deal when I don't know what they have to incriminate me?' At that point, it was their third or fourth offer, and I was getting pressure from Vicki saying 'Take the deal, take the deal.'"

The tension was building between the Battista/McMahon and Martino/Herr camps, even though they had ostensibly been fighting the case together as one until this point. "I got a call late one night from Vicki, and she was just drilling me," Battista says. "She was saying, 'You don't understand. You're going to save Tommy from the perjury. He's your buddy. This was your idea. You got him hooked into this. If you don't do this, you're not a good friend!' I was also getting pressure from Tommy's father, and I kept saying the same thing back about the lack of evidence. It got to about midnight, and I turned the deal down and went to sleep. Vicki called me the next morning and said, 'Goldberg won't give you another chance.' I was like, 'Are you fucking kidding me?' I was thinking to myself, 'Something's up. Why is she so persistent about this?' It was ten o'clock in the morning, and I turned the deal down *again*. I wanted to go to trial; I thought we had a good shot. They were asking too many times if I was going to take the deal. I didn't know if somehow the NBA was trying to avoid embarrassment, or if the government didn't want to get ready

---

lowed by 2,541 pages of material made available on March 17th, another 355 pages of material on March 31st, and an undisclosed amount of material on April 3rd.

for a trial. Two o'clock in the afternoon came around, and I was sitting in my kitchen with a few relatives and Jack called. He said, 'I need you to get to a fax machine,' and I asked, 'Why?' Jack said, 'You wanna know why they want you to take the deal? Because Tommy went behind your back, went up there on three different occasions, and told the feds everything except who kidnapped the Lindbergh baby!'"

Among the thousands of pages of discovery materials sent by the U.S. Attorney's Office to Battista via McMahon were memos documenting Tommy Martino's proffer sessions with the FBI, which McMahon had just come across. "Jack and I, of course," Battista says, "didn't know that Tommy went up to New York to meet with the government on July 27th, August 6th, and August 9th of 2007, met with the FBI and the U.S. Attorney, and told them everything. Here, Tommy was the one that told the feds about the money I gave Elvis. Of course, Tommy lied about the money, because it was much more than a hundred and twenty thousand dollars that I paid Elvis. Anyway, that's why Vicki and Tommy wanted me to take the deal; they knew Tommy had proffered, and had been denied a '5K1' letter.[2]

"If I had taken the deal, I never would have known that Tommy cooperated against me. I couldn't believe it; I was mad, disgusted, you name it. Here, the whole fucking time Jack and I had been working with Vicki and Tommy the past few months, they had already worked with the government against me. Jack helped Vicki because Tommy and his dad thought she was a bumbling idiot, and because I felt bad for

---

[2] Section 5K1.1 of the 2001 Federal Sentencing Guideline Manual, "Substantial Assistance to Authorities," states in part: "Upon motion of the government stating that the defendant has provided substantial assistance in the investigation or prosecution of another person who has committed an offense, the court may depart from the guidelines." Such motions, which are essentially requests for reductions in sentences, are commonly referred to as 5K motions, and the submissions are often referred to as 5K letters.

Tommy. I called Tommy up, furious, and told him I knew he cooperated against me, and he denied it. I was looking at his fucking proffers while I was on the phone with him, and he was still denying ever talking to the FBI about everything." The April 2008 conversation marked the last time the two men, who had been pals since grade school, spoke at any length with each other. Jack McMahon, though certainly not a stranger to legal soap operas, says the ordeal represented a career first.

"We were working on a plea negotiation," McMahon says. "The government's position was that Jimmy and Tommy both had to take the plea or both had to go to trial. They offered Tommy a plea within certain guidelines and it was up to Jimmy to accept a plea for Tommy's deal to be accepted. Vicki Herr called me up to discuss it, and when I told her that Jimmy wasn't going to take the plea deal that was offered to him, she got into this hysterical rant: 'Jimmy owes it to Tommy! He should do it for him. What about loyalty?!' She basically said Jimmy was a piece of shit if he didn't take the deal and help out Tommy because he got Tommy into this. During that phone call, she also started throwing around dollar figures regarding how much money Jimmy and Tommy paid Donaghy. As she was talking, I was thinking, 'Where is she getting these figures? Something's not right,' because we had never talked about them before. Meanwhile, she was begging me about this plea.

"During all of those months prior, Vicki Herr knew she had taken Tommy Martino in and that he talked to the feds, never letting on to me at all. She totally misled me; just a rotten thing to do. What should have happened is that Vicki should have come to me and said, 'Look, we probably shouldn't be talking anymore about the case. It's not proper we discuss strategy right now.' That would've told me what I needed to know going forward, without ever saying he had cooperated. That's what a lawyer would say to another lawyer, and you would know exactly what that means. She wouldn't have violated her attorney-client privilege, but it would have been a professional way to say to me, 'You shouldn't, for your own client's sake, be talking to me right now and giving me ideas about what your defense is, because my client is cooperating.'

"Remember, Jimmy had asked me numerous times to talk to Tommy and to Tommy's dad. His dad thanked me I don't know how many times, because he knew I didn't have to talk to him or meet with him. I helped him because I'm a father, too, and I can imagine what he was going through, and because it mattered to Jimmy, who clearly felt bad for Mr. Martino. The whole time I was talking to them and giving them information, at least Vicki and Tommy, if not Mr. Martino, knew Tommy went behind Jimmy's back and talked to the feds. Unbelievable. Just unbelievable! It has never happened to me before. Look, Tommy had every right to cooperate, and every lawyer has to do the best they can for their client. But, don't lead the other party along for months and months trying to get them to help you after you've cooperated against them! It was the most underhanded, sneaky, rotten thing I have seen in the legal profession in a long, long time." Meanwhile, Battista was faced with yet another of his friends and business associates cooperating with authorities against him. The latest revelation had no impact on his beliefs or actions going forward. "I never even thought about being a rat," Battista says. "I wasn't going to harm somebody else for the choices I made. The feds came to me several times with different offers to help me help myself, as they looked at it. My view is that you have to take ownership of what you did. If you're gonna gamble, if you want to get in the game, you gotta pay the price. It sucks, but you knew what you were doing. I know a lot of people who have gotten caught over the years who informed on others to save their own asses. I could never do that."

Following the discovery that Martino had met with federal authorities, Battista and McMahon predictably parted ways with Martino and Herr, and soon witnessed Martino accept a plea deal on April 16, 2008.[3] Martino pleaded guilty to wire fraud, with authorities dropping the remaining charges (two for perjury, and one for transmitting wagering information), and agreeing to seek a prison sentence of between twelve and eighteen months. Martino's deal was predicated on Battisa accepting his plea deal soon thereafter because if federal authorities were going to have to prepare for a trial, anyway, they reasoned there was little sense in accepting Martino's deal by itself. For Martino, matters essentially remained unresolved, because it was not a given Battista would plead guilty. The former pro gambler was in a fighting mood throughout the entire process when it came to defending himself and, perhaps more importantly to him, to addressing Donaghy's version of events. "They next offered me twelve to eighteen months for the conspiracy and wire fraud," Battista says, "and I said, 'Nope. We're going to trial.' They said, 'This is the best you're going to get. Take it.' I wasn't taking wire fraud because I didn't bribe anybody. I was just a gambler. I wasn't in a conspiracy to defraud the NBA like they were saying."

It would have been understandable for the general public to question Battista's defiant stance immediately following Tommy Martino's guilty plea. After all, two of the three conspirators had reached deals with the government and Donaghy, if not Martino, would be a witness against Battista at trial. What many outsiders never knew was that Jack McMahon and Jimmy Battista firmly believed from the outset that the government had little chance of victory in court if the case was based largely on the words of Tim Donaghy. "Jimmy and

---

[3] Vicki Herr decribed Tommy Martino as a "minimal participant" in the conspiracy, and said that Martino "allowed himself to be used by two people he considered to be very good friends."

I never took the position we weren't going to try this case," McMahon says. "Tim Donaghy would have had to testify, 'a corrupt and polluted source,' as the law says; a guy who was jammed up and who had to bring other people down to help himself. And, they had no corroboration from tapes. They had phone records, but they didn't have any phone calls from Jimmy Battista. There were all kinds of theories we could have thrown out there as a defense. Some cases you evaluate and tell your client he has no shot. I never felt that way in this case, and Jimmy wanted to fight. Anytime I mentioned the possibility of going to trial, he was ready to rumble."

Jack McMahon's likely defense plan was essentially two-fold: cut the legs out from under the government's case by attacking the character and credibility of its lead witness, Tim Donaghy; and cause prosecutors considerable grief by changing the venue of the case, most likely to Philadelphia from Brooklyn, where *everyone* from the federal government working on the case was based.

The assault on Donaghy's character and credibility was likely to go all the way back to high school, when Donaghy admitted getting into Villanova University in part by having someone take his SAT exam for him. Donaghy's SAT scam was a hot topic among the Delco crowd from that era, and Tommy Martino had discussed his knowledge of the situation with the FBI, including the name of the person Donaghy supposedly paid to take the test in Donaghy's stead after performing poorly on the exam himself. Martino added that it was his understanding that Donaghy also cheated on tests while at Villanova. Though Martino's comments were never made public, a former Cardinal O'Hara teacher was quoted in the news after the scandal broke in 2007 saying things of a similar nature. "I taught him for a year," the anonymous teacher said, "and I think every homework assignment he turned in to me was copied," before adding that he heard Donaghy years later boasting to pals that he cheated his way through Villanova. One of Donaghy's high school classmates was quoted in the same story as saying, "Timmy had a bad temper. He was the troublemaker of the Donaghys. Timmy had a fuse, and that fuse was short." Such accounts of Donaghy's alleged misdeeds were sure to be part of McMahon's presentation before the jury, and they were numerous, compelling, and spanned his adult life. Even a sampling of these, perhaps chronologically spelled out, would provide a damning critique for jurors to process as they weighed Donaghy's testimony.

One incident for which details emerged in news accounts involved Donaghy allegedly threatening a mail carrier in 2002 after the mailman had accidentally knocked over Donaghy's recycling bin. According to coverage of the incident in the New York *Daily News*, "Mail carrier Charles Brogan, 48, said he was making a delivery at Donaghy's home when his car knocked over a container containing bottles and cans . . . 'He just freaked out,' Brogan said. 'He came out screaming and hollering.'" Brogan said he drove down the street thinking, "No way I'm going back there," and simply attempted to continue with his route. Brogan said that Donaghy then got into his car and sped after Brogan's postal truck, cutting Brogan off and almost ramming into his truck. "He wouldn't let me deliver the mail. At one point he got out of his car and started threatening me face-to-face," Brogan said. "He was yelling, 'I'll have your job. I know so and so.'" Donaghy allegedly attempted to intimidate Brogan by saying he played golf with famous players like Charles Barkley. "He tried to belittle me like I'm just a public servant and he's the big NBA ref. I guess he wanted me to fight him," Brogan said, "but I would have lost my job." Donaghy was arrested and charged with disorderly conduct, harassment and stalking."[4]

---

[4] According to the *Philadelphia Inquirer*, the charges against Tim Donaghy were dropped when Charles Brogan did not show up for a hearing. That this matter and

Chronologically speaking, the next news item for McMahon's consideration was the widely-publicized Donaghy imbroglio with his next-door neighbors, Pete and Lisa Mansueto. The matter generated media attention in January 2005, dead smack in the middle of Donaghy's four-year run of betting on his own NBA games, and two years before the FBI stumbled upon the ref's scheme with Jimmy Battista. As the *Associated Press* summarized the situation, the Mansuetos "sued Donaghy for harassment and invasion of privacy, and accused him of vandalizing their property and stalking Lisa Mansueto. In their lawsuit, the Mansuetos also alleged that Donaghy set fire to a tractor they owned and crashed their golf cart from Radley Run Country Club into a ravine." According to the *Philadelphia Inquirer*'s coverage of the suit, "In the summer of 2003. . . Donaghy initiated 'a pattern of public harassment' that included yelling obscenities at the Mansuetos." The paper added, "The suit also states that Donaghy was charged by West Goshen Township Police with disorderly conduct and harassment in June 2000" and that "similar charges were lodged against Donaghy in 1995." The suit noted that Radley Run conducted an internal investigation of the Mansueto-Donaghy matter, resulting in Donaghy's suspension from the club for the summer and early fall of 2004. Lisa Mansueto said of the situation, "We were terrorized by him," and her husband Pete added, "We were under attack . . . He set my house on fire," in reference to Donaghy allegedly igniting a fire on their deck. The Mansueto lawsuit also alleged that Donaghy demanded police arrest the Mansueto's five-year-old son for throwing mud balls onto Donaghy's property.[5]

---

others were later dropped, of course, would likely have had little impact on Jack McMahon's use of the seminal court filings for the purpose of examining Tim Donaghy's character and credibility.

[5] According to the *Philadelphia Daily News*, the Mansueto lawsuit was eventually dropped. The paper offered no further insights regarding when or why this was so.

The Mansueto matter could have been reasoned away as a simple neighbor dispute, with no clear wrongdoer, if not for others who stepped forward to offer their insights on the matter. Another Donaghy neighbor, Kit Anstey, a West Chester real estate agent who had played golf with Donaghy at Radley Run, said of the former ref, "He was so bad, you can't imagine . . . The guy had a personality problem from Day One, with ninety-nine percent of the people" with whom Donaghy came in contact. Anstey added, "Unless everything went exactly his way . . . he just became a flaming maniac." Incredibly, even West Chester's mayor was personally aware of Donaghy's behavior. As the *Philadelphia Daily News* reported, Mayor Richard Yoder "said Donaghy used to pester him with calls and visits to his office, demanding that he intervene in petty disputes with his neighbors. 'He just had a very dictatorial personality, a very aggressive personality.'" The paper added that "Donaghy tied up West Chester police with at least eight calls between May and December 2004 . . . In most of those instances, Donaghy was the complainant."

By 2005, Donaghy's various extra-business antics so troubled the NBA that the league prohibited Donaghy from working the second round of that year's playoffs. According to Commissioner David Stern, they sanctioned Donaghy "as a consequence of making us unhappy with his [off-the-court] behavior," including Donaghy's ongoing dispute with his neighbors. Stern added that "the sheer volume" of reports involving what a reporter termed "anger management situations" made the NBA "call [Donaghy] in and say if it happened again, anything like it, he was going to be terminated, and to show that we meant it he was being pulled off a round of playoffs."

Compounding these considerable issues, there were more recent problems with Donaghy's character and credibility to be exploited by McMahon. For starters, Donaghy had just admitted lying to his employer for years, allegedly cheated on his wife (during the betting scandal, no less), and had ratted on his good friend Tommy Martino at the first mention of a criminal investigation into Donaghy's activities. Then there were the serious differences between Donaghy's version of events and those offered by two other cooperating witnesses, Tommy Martino and Pete Ruggieri. Martino's and Ruggieri's stories mirrored each other, and seriously undercut some of Donaghy's main arguments, most especially his claim that he wasn't influencing the outcomes of games. Donaghy had also seriously understated his profits from the scheme, according to Martino. Of course, beyond Martino's statements regarding the logistics of the scandal, there were also Martino's details of drug use and prostitution solicitation with Donaghy when the two men met during the scandal.

Most recently, as McMahon was prepping for trial, Donaghy's wife was in the news alleging behaviors that fit the pattern McMahon was sure to hammer at trial. Kim Donaghy, who had filed for divorce in September 2007, requested a restraining order against Donaghy in March 2008. In court filings, she claimed that after a March 14th incident, Donaghy threatened to "knock my . . . head off my body." She added that Donaghy "was enraged, out of control, cursing at me in front of our four children and making threats," and that he broke into her E-mail account.[6] Incredibly, this list of matters that were sure to be picked apart on a witness stand *was only of those that had already entered the public arena.* The government's prosecutors knew there was more to come, and must have assumed there was another area in particular that was going to be vetted in court.

---

[6] The matter was later dropped when Kim Donaghy failed to show for a court appearance.

As Jack McMahon and the U.S. Attorney's Office were prepping for trial, Jimmy Battista was using some of his unwanted free time to analyze what he considered a key part of the discovery evidence, namely Tim Donaghy's phone records. "It was late March," Battista says, "and Jack was on a murder trial in Florida. I was at home in Pennsylvania getting ready to go to war. I put together a spreadsheet of Elvis' calls to other referees and to other bookmakers. I then made another chart of his phone calls taking into account his referee schedule, looking at how many were gambling-related and how many weren't. Looking at those specific days of phone calls was like, 'This is a bookmaker, this is a referee, this is a bookmaker, this is Tommy, this is Jack Concannon, this is a bookmaker, this is a referee, this is a friend Elvis bets with'—all these people he was dealing with on a continual basis. It painted a picture that this fucking guy was steaming—betting his balls off with a bunch of people.[7] Jack and I agreed that we would wait everything out when we were being offered different deals, then go to trial, put Elvis on the stand, and put the other referees and a few of his close friends on the stand. They were gonna have to come out, and the phone records weren't going to lie if we were going to be able to question Elvis. Jack was going to fucking destroy him."

Despite the defense team's preoccupation with attacking the character and credibility of Tim Donaghy, McMahon says there was no real effort put into digging up dirt on the prospective lead witness. "I never thought of hiring a private investigator to get anything on Donaghy as we were preparing

---

[7] In betting circles, the term "steam" typically refers to the movement of betting lines caused by significant action by the likes of Jimmy Battista. Many a bettor simply follows "the steam" when placing a wager. That is, they monitor betting line moves and bet with the movement, assuming a sharp is placing bets on that side. As evidenced by Battista's career, following the steam can be a big mistake if the steam is actually a concerted effort to move a line for the purpose of taking the other side of the proposition when the line has been sufficiently manipulated.

for trial. There was no need to. I had so many things already, especially from Tommy. Pretty much all the way through, Tommy was telling me everything about him and Timmy. Tommy was a good source because he and Timmy were good friends. My God, we had so much information against Donaghy. A 'P.I.' could never have gotten the stuff Tommy had! When this got to trial, I had so much information on Donaghy, it was going to be a massacre. Bear in mind, I am not even referring to the things the public has seen about arguments with his neighbors and stuff like that." These legal and ethical matters were in addition to the litany of mean-spirited pranks for which Donaghy was reviled in certain quarters, and offered a defense attorney with a wealth of ammunition to use in court against a key witness.

Jack McMahon, for instance, may have pointed out that in many cases, including those involving far more serious crimes than gambling, it is common to find scores of people who know a defendant who express shock and dismay at the defendant's alleged actions because they are counter to their personal experiences. And yet, such persons were hard to find when it came to the allegations against Tim Donaghy. It was easy to envision McMahon asking a jury, "Where are the neighbors, and classmates, and colleagues who are stepping forward to say, 'This doesn't sound like the Tim Donaghy I knew'?"[8] The pattern of Donaghy's behavior from high school straight through his NBA career could fairly have been characterized to a jury by McMahon as that of a spoiled brat who threw temper tantrums when he didn't get his way. Oftentimes, it could have been argued, this meant Donaghy threatening those with whom he disagreed, and blaming others for his own

---

[8] In this regard, the *Delaware County Daily* (Delco) *Times* later wrote, "Aside from former O'Hara coach Buddy Gardler, every former teammate, classmate, or associate contacted . . . by the *Daily Times* either chose not to comment on Donaghy or didn't return phone calls. . . While there are those empathetic to Donaghy and his gambling-related plight, many others consider his a karmic downfall."

actions. In sum, the decades-long collection of consequential Donaghy personality flaws would greatly assist McMahon in discrediting Donaghy as a witness.

Tim Donaghy's character and credibility were certain to be a liability for the government's case, and authorities knew as much when they debated moving to trial against Battista. The U.S. Attorney's Office, as was its protocol, had already conducted its own assessment of how Donaghy would fair on the stand, and was well aware the case rested largely on someone with plenty of baggage. Prosecutors also knew that Jack McMahon was a skilled cross-examiner and a feisty trial lawyer, who could make considerable hay with a cooperating witness like Tim Donaghy on the stand.[9] There was also the more basic issue of taking a case based primarily on a cooperating witness to trial. As one experienced prosecutor says in this regard, "Who knows what you're gonna get with a cooperating witness at trial? Any cooperating witness case is a tough one at trial because there's always a chance the jury is going to reject the credibility of the cooperator or just not be happy that there's a rat on the stand."

In addition to these assessments, the U.S. Attorney's Office was also addressing the issue of venue, which McMahon had raised long before. "The first time I was driving back from the courtroom in Brooklyn in August [2007]," McMahon says, "I said to myself, 'Why were we just in Brooklyn? Why is the

---

[9] Jack McMahon was going to be pitted against a worthy adversary in AUSA Jeffrey Goldberg, who was accustomed to high-profile cases, including those involving cooperating witnesses with checkered backgrounds. In fact, just as he was overseeing cases against the NBA betting scandal's three co-conspirators, AUSA Goldberg was successfully prosecuting another important and much-publicized case before a jury—one which relied heavily upon cooperators with checkered pasts. On December 28, 2007, Goldberg, along with two of his USAO colleagues, obtained guilty verdicts against Colombo crime family acting boss Alphonse "Allie Boy" Persico and high-ranking member John "Jackie" DeRoss. Following eight weeks of trial, Persico and DeRoss were found guilty of orchestrating the 1999 murder of Colombo family underboss William "Wild Bill" Cutolo, and later received life sentences for their roles in the slaying.

venue Brooklyn?' I called the Assistant U.S. Attorney soon after that and asked him, and his answer was unconvincing. There was a reason for that—there was no venue in Brooklyn! Their main argument as to why the venue was the Eastern District of New York was that this guy from the NBA would go back and look at game tapes every night, and he lived somewhere in the Eastern District so that somehow gave Brooklyn venue. When I heard that, I laughed and thought, 'You've got to be kidding.'"[10] In the "motion to dismiss due to proper venue" filing with the court, McMahon noted among other things that the government admitted that none of the scheme's bets, meetings, or officiated games took place in the Eastern District of New York.[11]

"We had filed a change-of-venue motion with the Court," McMahon says, "and there was a scheduled hearing about the issue. About two days before the hearing, the government approached us about a plea deal that would be just for illegal gambling, meaning they would drop the wire fraud. That was the first time they offered that to us. Until then, there was no chance we were going to accept a plea. We were going to have our day in court and go to trial."

---

[10] Specifically, the U.S. Attorney's Office for the Eastern District of New York wrote that the "primary basis for venue" was "Matthew Winick's review of game reports in Nassau County, Long Island." The Eastern District consists of Brooklyn, Queens, Long Island, and Staten Island. As of March 2010, Matt Winick is listed as the NBA's Senior Vice President of Scheduling and Game Operations. Because the issue of venue was never litigated, the USAO's other possible reasons for establishing venue in EDNY are unknown.

[11] McMahon says at best the venue motion would have produced only a temporary victory. "You have to remember that for the defense, venue isn't necessarily a great win. It would have just meant the location would have moved from Brooklyn possibly to Manhattan [Southern District of New York] or, more likely, to Philadelphia, where the Eastern District of Pennsylvania is. It's not like the case is dismissed. To fight venue is not really that important because you have to be in a courtroom somewhere! The only difference would have been convenience, being in the Eastern District of Pennsylvania. At best, it would have put a little pressure on the government, and made it a little more difficult to move the entire case down to Philadelphia."

"Jack told [Assistant U.S. Attorney] Jeff Goldberg right after I was indicted that if I could plead guilty to illegal gambling that I'd be up there the next day," Battista says. "I wasn't denying I was a gambler, I was just denying I defrauded the NBA. Well, about a week after Tommy accepted his deal, we were scheduled to go up and fight for venue. Goldberg called Jack up just before the venue hearing and said he'd drop the wire fraud. I'd just have to say that I was a gambler and that I masterminded the scheme."

"Originally," Jack McMahon says, "when we were offered the deal for just illegal gambling, Jimmy still said, 'No. We're going to trial.' He *really* wanted to put Donaghy on the stand and expose all of his lies. It wasn't until I explained to Jimmy that it was in his best interest to plead guilty that he reconsidered his opinion of how to move forward. I told him, 'You've got kids, man. If this was just you and you wanted to rock and roll and go at this guy, I am ready for it, but you've got a wife and kids and this decision isn't just for yourself.' That's what eventually convinced him to take the plea. Besides, everyone knew he was an illegal gambler, so we weren't going to win on that charge. We'd probably beat Donaghy up and win on the wire fraud, but the government was giving us that, so why go to trial?"

The hard-charging Battista's thought process in deciding whether to take the deal was indeed preoccupied with Tim Donaghy, but he acquiesced to McMahon's sober counsel. "I think the government knew they would have had a hard time if they tried the case against me because Elvis lied so much," Battista says. "Any jury would have ripped him, and would have been like, 'This doesn't make any sense.' But, the fact of the matter is that I did gamble illegally. I was a gambler, I claimed it for a living, and I didn't deny it. I accepted that responsibility. As long as they dropped the fraud and wire fraud, the most serious offenses, I considered it a win. I never asked Elvis to fix a game. Now, in my mind did I think something was going on? *Absolutely.* He was a greedy motherfucker, and he needed to know the number we got before he went out there each game."

"Once we decided to accept the plea deal," McMahon says, "we used the court date that we had for addressing the venue issue to schedule a plea. So, obviously, we had to waive venue to accept the plea." Following some more legal haggling, on April 24, 2008, Battista formally pleaded guilty to conspiring to transmit wagering information across state lines, and faced ten to sixteen months in prison as a result.

The sentencing phase of the criminal justice process was next up for Battista and his co-conspirators, and, like the recently concluded plea negotiation phase, there was surreal drama in the offing. Tim Donaghy had played his hand skillfully until now, dating to his seminal meeting with federal authorities, but his hubris was about to come back and bite him yet again.

21

Team Donaghy's Assault on Justice

BY MAY 2008, FBI Special Agent Paul Harris had been heading the NBA betting scandal probe for approximately sixteen months, the last nine of which were in coordination with Assistant U.S. Attorney Jeffrey Goldberg, who was overseeing the prosecution of the case. Up next for Harris, Goldberg, and their colleagues was the commonly milquetoast sentencing stage. On May 8ᵗʰ, AUSA Goldberg filed a 5K letter on behalf of Tim Donaghy, explaining to the court why a downward departure from the sentencing guidelines was warranted for cooperating witness Donaghy. The eight-page letter was filed under seal, which is standard procedure and is done primarily for the protection of the cooperator. Such letters often identify the names of the parties against whom the cooperator has informed, and retaliation is of great concern. It is also true that authorities file such motions under seal so as to not affect ongoing investigations, and so that future prospective cooperators have confidence in the process.

The U.S. government's letter briefly summarized the NBA betting scandal, and offered Donaghy's version of the scheme's December 12, 2006, origins in favor of Tommy Martino's for obvious reasons, namely that Martino had perjured himself before the grand jury prior to doing an about-face and cooperating with authorities.[1] The key portion of the letter read:

---

[1] The letter also noted Donaghy had "implicated other individuals, including [Jack] Concannon and Peter Ruggieri (a professional gambler like Battista). The government

Martino eventually drove to Donaghy's hotel to pick him up. When Martino arrived, Donaghy noticed that Battista was also in Martino's car. Donaghy joined them, and they drove to a local store. While in the car, Battista and Martino confronted Donaghy with the fact that Donaghy had been providing picks to [Jack] Concannon. Battista then told Donaghy that he should provide his picks to Battista and Martino, and not to Concannon. Battista also told Donaghy that Battista 'didn't want the NBA to find out' about what Donaghy was doing. Donaghy interpreted this comment to mean that if Donaghy did not agree to deal with Battista and Martino, Battista would inform the NBA about Donaghy's prior dealings with Concannon. At a later meeting back at Donaghy's hotel, Battista also threatened harm to Donaghy's family. Battista told Donaghy that 'you don't want anyone from New York visiting your wife and kids.' Over the preceding years, Donaghy had come to believe that Battista had organized crime connections, and so he interpreted 'New York' to be the Mafia. Before the meeting concluded, Donaghy agreed to provide picks to Battista and Martino.

Importantly, prosecutors added a footnote which read, "Although Donaghy was concerned by Battista's comment regarding Donaghy's wife and children, he has never taken the position that he was anything other than a willing participant in the scheme with Battista and Martino, and, before them, with Jack Concannon."

The May 8, 2008, letter also included a passage regarding Donaghy's judgment while refereeing games that would be discussed and debated for years to come. The government

---

declines to disclose whether it is pursuing, or will be pursuing, charges against these individuals." Like Ruggieri, it was reported that Concannon was a cooperating government witness.

wrote, "There is no evidence that Donaghy ever intentionally made a particular ruling during a game in order to increase the likelihood that his gambling pick would be correct. He has acknowledged, however, that he compromised his objectivity as a referee because of his financial interest in the outcome of NBA games, and that this personal interest might have subconsciously affected his on court performance."

The government summed up Donaghy's preparation for his trial testimony by saying that Donaghy was "at all times cooperative, forthcoming, candid, and always willing to assist the government as needed." In addition to the substantive narrative regarding the NBA betting scandal, there was also a one-line mention which noted, "The government also debriefed Donaghy concerning improper conduct on the part of other NBA referees who had engaged in gambling that violated NBA rules."

Because the U.S. Attorney's Office had so many discussions with Tim Donaghy and his attorney, John Lauro, by this point, Team Donaghy had a good sense of what the government's letter would contain. Thus, it wasn't surprising when the May 8th filing wasn't contested or subjected to debate in the days that immediately followed. What happened next in the process, though, was a key flash point in the sentencing process, and was largely ignored or misunderstood by the press. The U.S. Probation Office's pre-sentence investigations of the three codefendants were taking place behind the scenes, and—just like the government's 5K letter—the resulting pre-sentence reports (PSRs) were not filed publicly. This, too, was standard procedure because PSRs contain personal information regarding things like finances (i.e., tax returns), substance use, family matters, and so on. When a PSR is submitted, the prosecution and the defense review the report and may object to, or seek to clarify, certain aspects of the PSR in writing to the court. In Donaghy's case, the amount of loss to the NBA was a hotly contested part of the PSR because there was debate as to how to calculate the league's "loss," and because the loss assessment was going to be a great driver of the sentence Donaghy received.[2] The Probation Office originally calculated loss at approximately one hundred and fifty-four thousand dollars, to which John Lauro filed an objection stating loss should be considerably less—approximately forty thousand dollars. At this point, the U.S. Attorney's Office submitted an eight-page letter on May 16th with their assessment, which yielded a loss of just over three hundred thousand dollars—*almost eight times* what Team Donaghy proposed, which would also mean a much greater enhancement to Donaghy's sentence. It is assumed that the government's "loss letter" set Team Donaghy off, resulting in a wave of hyperbole and salacious drama that filled sports talk radio airwaves for months to follow.

On Monday, May 19th, the next business day following submission of the government's loss letter, John Lauro filed two letters with the court. Unlike the government's 5K letter, each Lauro filing soon found its way into the press. The first asked for the 5K letter to be unsealed, using language that implied the government was doing something extraordinary—and being less than transparent—by placing the letter under seal.[3] The second May 29, 2008, letter included Team Donaghy's objection to the government's loss calculation—and much more.[4] The twenty-seven page diatribe took

---

[2] The issue of the NBA's "loss" involves legal arguments, including and especially the issue of Donaghy's "relevant conduct," that are not worth exploring here. Interested parties can find a good history of the arguments in the court record spawning from Jimmy Battista's appeals of restitution.

[3] Specifically, Lauro wrote, "We strongly object to this letter being filed under seal. We have been advised by the government that it has concluded its investigation into this matter, and therefore there is no reason to file this letter under seal. Moreover, the government made no showing whatsoever under established case law that such a communication should be kept from the public. Finally, we respectfully request that there be full transparency in the sentencing process."

[4] Lauro argued in the letter that the NBA's loss should have been $46,240 which, in the context of the U.S. Sentencing Guidelines, would have resulted in 6-level

after the government's May 8ᵗʰ 5K filing, arguing a host of
things that—starting with the very next day—generated
news cycles, spawned numerous legends, and muddied the
waters for anyone trying to follow the scandal. Among other
things, the letter assailed the government's plea deals with
Jimmy Battista and Tommy Martino as too lenient compared to Donaghy's agreement, and then offered two related
components of a proposed conspiracy theory in this regard.
Lauro first attempted to parse the FBI from the U.S. Attorney's Office for the Eastern District of New York (USAO),
as if they weren't collaborating throughout and in agreement
as to how to proceed with the case; and then hypothesized
that the NBA may have "pressured the USAO into shutting
down this prosecution to avoid the disclosure of information
related to Tim's conduct . . . " One has to wonder what Team
Donaghy's motivation was with such a public suggestion, since
the small universe of FBI agents and government prosecutors
working the case knew full well how they were getting along,
and given the chance would gladly debunk such inferences
before the Court. Insiders thus assumed Donaghy was simply
engaged in a publicity stunt in an effort to divert attention
away from his actions onto others, because this "argument"
would almost certainly never be a factor in court regarding
Donaghy's sentencing.

Team Donaghy's May 19ᵗʰ letter, in which it was argued
Donaghy should be a candidate for a reduced sentence because
of his "pathological" gambling addiction, went on to state that
were it not for Jack Concannon and Jimmy Battista, Donaghy
would not have bet on NBA games. Specifically, Lauro wrote,
"When Concannon lost money at casinos, he pressured Tim
to use his knowledge to help select likely basketball teams
that they could bet on. They also placed bets on games Tim

---

enhancement (compared, respectively, to the Probation Office's and U.S. Attorney's
Office's suggested 10-level and 12-level enhancements).

officiated," before turning to the claim that Battista "threatened" Donaghy to provide picks to Battista when Concannon and Donaghy supposedly stopped betting in the fall of 2006. Donaghy's version of the December 12, 2006, events spawning the NBA betting scheme were offered, and thus the public was finally introduced to it as news of the letter spread. Whereas media coverage of the betting scandal in July 2007 humored an organized crime connection, simply because of the original reporting of the scheme popping up on a Gambino wiretap, by now investigative reporters—with the help of their law enforcement sources—dismissed the supposed mob angle. This was particularly true in the Philadelphia area, where Battista was a known commodity. Various local, state, and federal investigations into the gambling industry disclosed Battista and his Delco pals repeatedly over the years. When his name was first mentioned in July 2007, local reporters—including and especially those who work the area's "mob" beat—reviewed existing files and reached out to their law enforcement and underworld sources only to confirm earlier analyses: Battista, like his longtime colleague Joe Vito Mastronardo, was one of the area's white-collar pro gamblers.[5] Furthermore, it was also clear by now that Battista, Ruggieri, Concannon, Martino, and Donaghy were all familiar with each other dating back to their high school days.[6]

Next among the sensational aspects of Team Donaghy's lengthy May 19, 2008, filing, Lauro wrote that Donaghy's "assistance expanded greatly to include NBA-related mat-

---

[5] Unfortunately and yet unsurprisingly, the further one got from hard reporting and from Philadelphia, the more likely one was to see various myths take hold. This seemed to be particularly true in sports media, and even more so in sports talk radio.

[6] Jack McMahon, Vicki Herr, Christopher Warren, and Joseph Fiorvanti, the attorneys, respectively, for Jimmy Battista, Tommy Martino, Pete Ruggieri, and Jack Concannon, each scoffed at the organized crime allegations made at various times against each man. Fiorvanti, for instance, said that Concannon had "no organized crime connections. He's just a guy who bet games with Donaghy. All of those guys were about the same age and knew each other."

ters that were of interest to law enforcement officials. These matters had nothing to do with improper activities by Tim, but involved practices well-known to NBA insiders. For example, Tim described the gambling activities of NBA officials, which were contrary to league rules." Lauro said that Donaghy "furnished information concerning circumstances that favored certain players or teams over others" and explained to authorities that "particular relationships between officials and coaches or players affected the outcome of games, and other practices prevented games from being played on a level playing field." About all of this, Lauro argued that the U.S. Attorney's Office "declined to advise the Court fully about Tim's extensive cooperation with respect [to] activities involving the NBA that had nothing to do with the instant offense" [the '06-07 betting scandal].

The NBA's president of league and basketball operations, Joel Litvin, quickly issued a statement in response to Team Donaghy's filing, which said, "The letter filed today on Mr. Donaghy's behalf contains an assortment of lies, unfounded allegations and facts that have been previously acknowledged, such as the fact that certain NBA referees engaged in casino gambling in violation of NBA rules." The statement continued, "The letter is the desperate act of a convicted felon who is hoping to avoid prison time and the only thing it proves is that Mr. Donaghy is no more trustworthy today than he was when he was breaking the law by betting on NBA games." It wasn't surprising, of course, to see the league respond in such fashion, and the NBA was joined by numerous critics who mocked Team Donaghy's various claims, especially those regarding relationships between individuals involved in NBA games. As one Philadelphia sports columnist wrote at the time, "An interesting, almost laughable section of Lauro's filing had to do with the way that players, coaches and referees get along. If Judge Amon is a sports fan, she will wad up this section and dunk it into the office wastebasket . . . His contention is that refs get along with certain players and coaches and do not get along with others. He also seems to feel this is news."

As the public processed Team Donaghy's allegations and the reactions to them, the U.S. Attorney's Office moved to unseal Donaghy's 5K letter, filing their consent to Lauro's request on May 29th. Since such letters are sealed for the privacy and confidentiality of what the cooperating witness has done, there was no reason—following Team Donaghy's May 19th lengthy filing and request—to keep the 5K letter under seal. As a result, Judge Amon ordered the letter unsealed on June 2nd, at which point Team Donaghy said in a statement: "The release today of the government's May 8, 2008, letter regarding Tim's cooperation confirms our position that Tim has been entirely truthful and credible. The letter puts a lie to the personal attacks against Tim made by the NBA." Days later, the NBA added to the drama, responding to Team Donaghy's allegations and, more importantly, offering the league's own loss estimate.[7] The latter was really the issue, because the NBA submitted a letter to the Court stating it was entitled to a million dollars in restitution from Donaghy.[8] As one legal analyst said of the unexpected and potentially significant request, "If Donaghy cannot make restitution, his jail sentence could be extended. Donaghy's plans for a reduced sentence [are] suddenly in jeopardy as a result of the NBA's demand."

---

[7] Of Donaghy's allegations, NBA executive vice president and general counsel Richard Buchanan wrote that the league had "received no information that any referee other than the defendant bet on NBA games or engaged in criminal activity with respect to NBA games." Buchanan added, "While the NBA has acknowledged that a number of referees periodically engaged in casino gaming and similar social gambling, this conduct amounted at the time only to a violation of NBA rules relating to off-the-court activities of referees, and not to any violation of criminal law."

[8] As a victim in the case, the NBA, of course, was entitled to be heard by the court. The league was represented by Lawrence B. Pedowitz and David B. Anders of the law firm of Wachtell, Lipton, Rosen & Katz. The NBA was later asked to offer a more precise figure, and thus on June 20, 2008, submitted a loss figure of $1,395,104.89 to the Court.

Not to be outdone, Team Donaghy soon responded to the NBA's filing by submitting a four-page letter of its own, ostensibly so that Judge Amon could "have complete information to determine the extent of Tim's cooperation" in consideration of Donaghy's sentencing. This time, Donaghy claimed to have given federal authorities details of game manipulation by other referees, including during the 2002 and 2005 NBA playoffs. In 2002, Donaghy alleged, two referees known as "company men" acted "in the interests of the NBA" by extending a playoff series to seven games. Donaghy also claimed that in 2005 the league gave referees instructions that benefitted the NBA because they "prolonged the series, resulting in more tickets sold and more televised games."[9] Though the filing didn't name the series being discussed, analysts quickly and easily identified them: 2002—Los Angeles Lakers vs. Sacramento Kings; 2005—Houston Rockets vs. Dallas Mavericks, two series which had already been the subject of considerable public debate and conspiracy theorizing. Depending on one's perspective, therefore, Donaghy had either consciously or coincidentally chosen as examples two series—out of the thirteen years Donaghy officiated—that just so happened to fit his claims of game manipulation by other referees but which didn't require an insider's perspective, *per se*, all the while acknowledging no influencing of games on his part.[10]

---

[9] Unsurprisingly, the NBA vehemently denied Donaghy's allegations. Commissioner David Stern said, "My reaction to Donaghy's lawyer is that clearly as the date of sentencing gets closer and the things he's thrown against the wall haven't stuck, have been given to the FBI, have been investigated, and are baseless." NBA executive vice president and general counsel Richard Buchanan released a statement, which said, "According to Mr. Donaghy, all of his allegations have previously been made to the FBI and the U.S. Attorney. They are clearly being disclosed now as part of his desperate attempt to lighten the sentence that will be imposed for his criminal conduct."

[10] As one sports columnist wrote, which was representative of many other such columns, "conspiracy theorists jumped out of the woodwork to proclaim that the Donaghy case proved their long-standing beliefs that NBA games were always fixed to produce the best outcomes for the financial benefit of the league." Beyond league executives, numerous current and former NBA coaches and players came forward to denounce Donaghy's allegations of game manipulation, etc.

The sentencing fireworks that began with the May 8, 2008, government 5K filing continued in court proceedings and, especially, in filings, with the issues of loss/restitution and cooperation clearly paramount to Team Donaghy throughout this phase of the criminal justice process. In these regards, the U.S. Attorney's Office filed two letters on June 27th, and each had implications for the former referee. Concerning the issue of loss, the government was still light years away from Team Donaghy's suggested modest figure, and regarding Donaghy's cooperation, the government was forced to offer a more critical analysis than it had earlier (when it offered the *pro forma* version). In short, prosecutors wrote that Donaghy had exaggerated his cooperation and minimized his role in the scheme. In a direct retort to Team Donaghy's assertion that the government "didn't advise the Court fully about Donaghy's extensive cooperation with respect to activities involving the NBA that had nothing to do with the instant offense," prosecutors wrote, "the activities involving the NBA that Donaghy discusses . . . are not a proper consideration [for a reduction in sentencing] because further investigation by the government of these alleged activities did not lead to evidence of prosecutable federal offenses."[11] Furthermore, prosecutors said that by the time Donaghy decided to cooperate "the government had a clear understanding of the criminal conspiracy and who was involved." The U.S. Attorney's Office, which had been careful to keep Donaghy on the hook vis-à-vis his culpability, also clarified its view of the former referee's role

---

[11] To further explain why Donaghy's allegations didn't merit consideration in his sentencing, the U.S. Attorney's Office next referenced the opening line of the relevant sentencing provision which reads, "Upon motion of the government stating that *the defendant has provided substantial assistance in the investigation or prosecution of another person who has committed an offense,* the court may depart from the guidelines" (emphasis added). Following an investigation, the Los Angeles County District Attorney's Office also dismissed Donaghy's allegations regarding the 2002 Lakers-Kings series, and the United States Attorney's Office for the Central District of California declined to investigate the matter citing a lack of evidence, among other reasons.

in the scandal. "It was only Donaghy," prosecutors wrote, "who had a duty to provide honest services to his employer, the NBA. Without Donaghy, the scheme simply could not have been carried out."

The U.S. Attorney's Office filings didn't end the back-and-forth, and the parties were soon before Judge Carol Amon's court hashing out these related issues.[12] AUSA Goldberg, who avoided discussing the case in the press throughout, publicly commented on the information Donaghy had provided to the FBI, telling Judge Amon, "A lot of it was unsubstantiated, and that's important. So, we've never taken the position that Mr. Donaghy has lied to us. But, there is a difference between telling the truth and believing you're telling the truth and finding out later that a number of allegations don't hold any water."

Tim Donaghy's co-conspirator, Jimmy Battista, remained on the sidelines awaiting his own sentencing throughout Team Donaghy's antics that began in May 2008. Battista wasn't surprised one bit to see Donaghy claim: that Jack Concannon had "pressured" Donaghy in 2003 into betting on NBA games, including games he officiated; or that Battista "threatened" Donaghy in 2006 into continuing betting on games he officiated; or, especially, that—on top of all this—Donaghy wasn't responsible for his actions, anyway, because he was a "pathological" gambler. The former gambler watched with some delight as Donaghy exhibited—again and again—the behavior patterns that Battista's lawyer, Jack McMahon, never got to illustrate to a jury. As far as Battista could tell, the notoriety and infamy Donaghy garnered as a result of his criminality hadn't changed a thing in the former ref. Team Donaghy's actions, while frustrating and problematic for federal authorities, weren't altogether surprising to them,

---

[12] Following the NBA's loss assessment submission for approximately $1.4 million, the U.S. Attorney's Office was asked to revisit the restitution issue, and on July 7, 2008, submitted a revised loss figure of $233,317.

either. Indeed, by now at least one of Donaghy's handlers had concluded the former referee was "a fucking loose cannon."

To Jimmy Battista, Tim "Elvis" Donaghy was throwing a tantrum (i.e., assailing federal law enforcement) when he didn't get his way (i.e., the government's loss letter, no prosecution of other NBA officials) and placing blame elsewhere (i.e., Concannon, Battista, the culture of the NBA, addiction) for Donaghy's own actions. Battista wasn't the only party in the process who found Donaghy's denials of responsibility without merit. AUSA Goldberg, in addition to numerous other similar comments made by prosecutors about Donaghy's culpability, told the Court that Donaghy "knew what he did when he was doing it."

By this point, Team Donaghy and the United States Attorney's Office had waged a battle that left quite a paper trail, and included some interested exchanges in court, only a hint of which made their way into the news. While the sports media, especially, focused on Donaghy's sensational NBA conspiracy claims (most, if not all, of which were already familiar to even semi-serious NBA followers), insiders were preoccupied with the merits of the legal arguments and their implications. Team Donaghy's tactics forced interested observers to more closely inspect the actual record which meant, especially, reading what little the federal government had said, and, just as importantly, what authorities had not.

With regard to Team Donaghy's allegations that the U.S. government had not sufficiently pursued the case against Jimmy Battista, John Lauro repeatedly implied that Battista had extorted Donaghy and thus Battista should have faced harsher sanctions than he received.[13] Problematically for Team Donaghy, Battista was never charged with extortion, and the

---

[13] For example, Lauro wrote, "under the plea bargain approach of the USAO, a cooperator should be punished more severely than those who engage in more serious offenses, such as perjury, extortion, and obstruction of justice."

government included Donaghy's self-serving and unsupported claims regarding Battista's threats only in consideration of Donaghy's supposed state of mind upon entering into the conspiracy.

Regarding Donaghy's claim that Battista indirectly alluded to New York mobsters in the initial meeting on December 12, 2006, Lauro discussed the unsupported Donaghy allegation no less than five times in his May 19, 2008, letter; five times more than the federal government mentioned the claim throughout the months of court filings and public utterances.[14] What was included in the government's May 8, 2008, filing vis-à-vis Battista's supposed mob ties was exclusively what Donaghy said he believed based on what he said Tommy Martino perceived and told Donaghy; nothing more. Perhaps the most succinct take on the scheme's genesis, and thus on Team Donaghy's salacious mob and extortion assertions, came from U.S. District Judge Carol B. Amon who, after almost a year of proceedings before her court, wrote (emphasis added), "In December of 2006, defendants James Battista and Thomas Martino approached Donaghy and informed him that they were aware that he had been placing bets on NBA games, including games he had refereed. *Battista proposed an arrangement* whereby Donaghy would provide picks on NBA games to Battista through Martino." The final verdict, so to speak, on the

---

[14] John Lauro thus became one of the few individuals to effectively accuse law enforcement for not sensationalizing one of their cases enough, particularly since terms like "organized crime," "mob," "mafia," "LCN," "crime family," etc. weren't mentioned a single time by the FBI or the Department of Justice in press releases and conferences relating to the case and its three co-conspirators. Any semi-serious follower of organized crime cases is intimately familiar with the Web sites of federal law enforcement agencies, which each contain their own media/press sections. The FBI and U.S. Attorney's Offices in locales such as the Eastern District of New York (Brooklyn), the Southern District of New York (Manhattan), and the Eastern District of Pennsylvania (Philadelphia) are skilled and experienced at—and notorious for—promoting their efforts and successes in organized crime cases. Indeed, critics commonly argue that federal authorities exaggerate their work in this regard.

scandal's origin characterized it simply as an illicit business transaction between three interested parties.

With respect to Team Donaghy's allegations that the U.S. government didn't sufficiently prosecute other NBA officials, FBI agents spent who knows how much time looking into Donaghy's myriad claims, all with negative results. Given Team Donaghy's repeated public accusations, perhaps it was lost on Donaghy that FBI agents and Assistant U.S. Attorneys are in the businesses, respectively, of investigating and prosecuting *crimes*. Whatever personal failings of NBA personnel and breaches of NBA protocol Donaghy described were for others beyond law enforcement authorities to concern themselves. It wasn't Donaghy's fault he was not privy to the government's findings regarding his various claims, of course; confidential information is communicated with cooperating witnesses one way, namely from the witness to the government's investigators and prosecutors. Donaghy had no clue from whom the FBI was able to obtain information, nor how or why. Former FBI Supervisory Special Agent Phil Scala, who retired just prior to the sentencing phase of the case, was privy to much of what transpired and says the FBI found no evidence of criminal wrongdoing on the part of other NBA referees. Scala told one newspaper, "If there were people that should have been indicted, they would have been, including other refs."

Throughout the back-and-forth with government prosecutors regarding Donaghy's claims against other referees, Team Donaghy seized upon the USAO's earlier statement that Donaghy had been "cooperative, forthcoming, [and] candid." Team Donaghy attempted to extrapolate from this to essentially argue that this meant *everything* Tim Donaghy told the federal government was *true*. This argument had a fatal logical flaw, however, since it is quite possible for a cooperating witness like Donaghy to *believe* something is accurate, and *believe* he is telling the truth, but his assertions are (perhaps grossly) inaccurate. Prosecutors were therefore careful not to say Donaghy lied to authorities because for all they knew Tim Donaghy believed what he told federal agents.

In sum, Donaghy's various "leads" consumed the time and resources of the FBI and, to a lesser extent, the U.S. Attorney's Office. While authorities are used to such wild-goose chases, they are far less accustomed to a criminal defendant effectively taking a bullhorn to proclaim the federal government had minimized what a quality informer he was. Perhaps it was also lost on Team Donaghy that the disclosure of confidential information could have jeopardized the hard work of numerous federal officials in other cases, directly and indirectly.[15] The last word on Team Donaghy's overhyped allegations that law enforcement authorities did not sufficiently pursue "leads" offered by Donaghy came, again, from Judge Carol Amon. Amon stated she had found "no bad faith on the part of the government in concluding that the information provided by Mr. Donaghy was not sufficient to develop further prosecution." The judge added, "The speculation of [Donaghy's] counsel in letters to this Court that the information was not pursued because of the NBA's influence on the government is just that, completely unfounded speculation."

Though gratified the judge and others saw through Team Donaghy's smokescreens, Jimmy Battista just wanted to get on with the process; the earlier he was sentenced, the quicker he could begin serving his time and start a new life. Based on what Battista had seen thus far, it was clear prosecutors

---

[15] When a cooperating witness provides information to the government, they do so confidentially. This, of course, is because the government might want to use it in other investigations. Thus, if the information becomes public without the government's permission or consent, it can hurt investigations, security, and success. This is why cooperation agreements, themselves, require confidentiality.

and Judge Amon viewed his actions, and those of his co-conspirators, as serious offenses. The former pro gambler once widely and proudly known as The Sheep had good reason to worry about the sentence he would soon receive.

22

An Hour to a Little Kid Is a Long Time

JIMMY BATTISTA FIRST heard the rumors of a federal investigation into his betting activities in the fall of 2006. In truth, he never really knew when the FBI got interested in him, but that was all trivia now as sentencing day arrived. The anxiety that consumed Battista on July 23, 2008, was aggravated by the stress induced by seeing co-conspirator Tommy Martino, his longtime friend who Battista now knew cooperated with the feds against him. Martino was to be sentenced by U.S. District Judge Carol B. Amon right after Battista.

When Battista was afforded the opportunity to make a statement, he choked back tears as he told the Court, "I'm not blaming either of my codefendants, Mr. Martino or Mr. Donaghy. I made bad choices, and I take full responsibility for what I did." After Battista publicly apologized to his wife, his kids, and his family, Judge Amon moved toward sentencing and said, 'This is a very serious wagering offense. The NBA, fans, and players depend on the integrity of the game and no single person is more important to the integrity of the game than the referee. If his interest is compromised in any way, the entire sport is compromised." Amon sentenced Battista to fifteen months in federal prison, and Tommy Martino next received a sentence of twelve months.[1] The suspense for both men was finally over, but the year-long drama involving each of their camps was not.

---

[1] Judge Amon also ruled on July 23, 2008, that the NBA was entitled to a total of $217,267 in restitution from Battista, Martino, and Tim Donaghy.

"As we were leaving the courtroom," Battista says, "Tommy wished me luck and said, 'I hope the time goes fast for you,' and I said something similar back to him. Tommy's older brother, Johnny, came up to me at that point, and his hand was trembling like crazy as he tried to shake my hand. He said, 'I'm going to be cordial at these events, but that's it. You brought my brother into this,' and I just waved Johnny off and said, 'Come on. Be serious.' We all got outside the courtroom, and there was a ton of press people waiting there for us. My lawyer, Jack McMahon, was surrounded by the media and started answering questions when Johnny said something to him. Jack just smiled and laughed at him and continued addressing the press. Johnny was trying to look like the older brother taking care of his younger brother."

"This guy, I didn't even know it was Martino's brother at first," Jack McMahon says, "said something to Jimmy about being an asshole who ought to be ashamed of himself for what he did to Tommy. I turned to the guy and told him, 'Yo. There is no need for this. This isn't the time or place for anything like that,' because I just wanted to get out of there. Well, he started in on me for defending Jimmy, he called me names, told me I should join the Hair Club for Men, and all sorts of stuff.[2] I said, 'Who the fuck are you? I don't even know who you are, and you're talking to me this way?' That's when he said that Jimmy and I fucked his brother, and I immediately stopped him and said, 'Look, pal. You're just a fucking asshole. Nobody fucked your brother. He fucked himself.' I wasn't going to let this guy come at me, and scream at me. Well, then, his father—the guy I had spent so much time helping even though his son wasn't even my client—started screaming at me. It was bizarro world."

---

[2] Jack McMahon is bald. John Martino said of the exchange with McMahon, "In the heat of the moment, you go for the first thing you see, and I saw that chrome dome."

"Jack overheard Tommy's dad saying that I corrupted his son," Battista says, "and Jack said, 'Corrupted your son? Are you kidding?!' More words were exchanged between the Martinos and Jack, and I asked Jack why he was getting into this because there didn't need to be a show there. I also felt bad for Mr. Martino, who looked like he was going to have a heart attack. I didn't like what he and Johnny were saying about me, but they didn't know the whole story about Tommy and how much drugs he sold over the years. They had no idea he was a drug dealer who was selling pounds of pot, and selling coke and stuff. I don't think Tommy was ever arrested for dealing drugs, so to Johnny and Mr. Martino, I put Tommy in prison.

"We were on the tenth floor of the building, and finally the Martinos went down the elevators. I was still waiting for Jack to finish talking to the reporters. Elvis' lawyer, John Lauro, was down the hallway with one of the NBA's attorneys looking out a window talking. I was always pissed at Lauro for saying that I threatened Timmy and his family, because that *never* happened. He came down and said, 'Good luck to you buddy. I hope everything works out.' He put his hand out for me to shake, but there was no way that was going to happen. I would rather have used my hand to knock his teeth out, so I just shook my head, turned around, and walked away. When we got out of the elevators downstairs, Johnny approached Jack, and they started at each other again."

"I thought things finally ended when we all went downstairs," McMahon says, "but when we got downstairs the father started screaming at me again! It was like something out of Alice in Wonderland. I didn't really say anything back to the father because he was just a little old Italian guy."[3] By now,

---

[3] The heated exchange made for some interesting media coverage, including one report which noted, "Downstairs in the lobby, Martino's father became infuriated at McMahon; with eyes bulging, he tried to lunge at McMahon and had to be restrained by both of his sons."

Battista just wanted to get over to the U.S. Marshal's Office to turn himself in. "Tommy looked at me like he was embarrassed by Johnny trying to look like a hero, and said, 'I'll talk to you later,' as they left the courthouse," Battista says. "Meanwhile, Jack was as red as a beet, and I was laughing and said, 'What are you doing? You are the lawyer. Why am *I* telling *you* to calm down? Shouldn't it be the other way around?!'"

Laugh as he might about the surreal scene outside the courtroom, Battista was mildly surprised and seriously disheartened about the sentence he had just received. "I was a little bit shocked at the fifteen months," Battista says, "because for just illegal gambling, that was a stiff sentence. By that point, I was down the federal building in Philadelphia every week pissing in a cup and had a clean record. The FBI agents followed me everywhere I went, like I was an operative for the French Connection or something. There have been plenty of other people who had done far worse things than me who got less time. One of the FBI agents who worked the case said he felt bad for me, because he thought fifteen months was too much.

"It bothered me that the court wouldn't recognize my drug rehab program, which would have reduced my sentence; it could have been a reduction in the sentencing guidelines. After I got clean at White Deer Run, I entered a program called 'Change or Die' at the Malvern Center where I went to meetings at least once a day. It wasn't appointed by a court, though, which is how you save time on your sentencing. I went in and got clean *before* I was ever arrested. The feds used to follow me to my meetings and even came into the meetings. My two codefendants each went into programs for their addictions *after* they got arrested. I am a drug addict and I take responsibility for the things I did, but I was upset I didn't get credit for getting clean on my own and for trying to turn my life around.

"Part of me was mad that I didn't get five to seven months, but I was relieved because at least it was closure. I was glad I didn't bring anybody else down with me, I wasn't a rat, and the only people suffering were my family. I really thought I'd get ten months, and I was hoping for five to seven. I could have lived with that for what I did. I have five kids, and fifteen months away is a long time. A day—hell, *an hour*—to a little kid is a long time. For me to be away for a year or more and miss their school, Christmas, and all sorts of activities, was going to be tough on me and on them. It was a good thing I didn't bring my wife and kids to the sentencing hearing."

Six days after Battista and Martino were sentenced, Tim Donaghy was before the same court to hear his plight. Judge Amon sentenced Donaghy to fifteen months in prison, noting, "The NBA, the players and the fans relied on him to perform his job in an honest and uncomplicated manner."[4] Amon added that Donaghy was "more culpable" than Battista and Martino, stating, "Mr. Donaghy was a central figure in the scheme, and without him, there would have been no scheme." The judge also ordered three years of supervised release and treatment for Donaghy's gambling addiction. Though harsher than the probation Team Donaghy had requested, for Jimmy Battista, Donaghy's sentence was too light and just the latest example of Donaghy manipulating others. "I was disgusted," Battista says. "I thought he would get eighteen to twenty-four months. It was a sham based on the words of a pathological liar. Part of that was my fault, though, because the feds wanted to talk to me and go against him, but I wouldn't. That could've helped me, and absolutely would have hurt Timmy. For us to get the same sentence is like saying we were equally wrong. I didn't work for the NBA, I never asked him to fix games, and he was

---

[4] Donaghy was technically sentenced to two fifteen-month sentences, one each for the two counts to which he pleaded guilty, but Judge Amon ordered the sentences to be served concurrently.

doing this before I ever got hooked up with him. How were we even close to equal? But, being the fucking egomaniac and pathological liar he is, some people are going to listen to him." Battista, a recovering drug addict, is not entirely receptive to Donaghy's claims of gambling addiction. "Timmy loved to fuck with people, going back years," Battista says. "A lot of the shit he did to people wasn't funny, and he has always been a greedy, mean-spirited motherfucker. So, he might have been addicted to gambling, but to me his betting was just the next thing with him."

* * *

On September 18, 2008, Jimmy Battista began serving his fifteen-month sentence at the federal detention center in Brooklyn.[5] The detention center was a far cry from the white-collar prison environment to which Battista assumed he would be sentenced. Battista believes he may have been sent to a general population prison because he didn't cooperate with authorities, who may also have been holding out hope the incarceration with violent criminals would compel Battista to revisit his decision not to speak with the FBI. The feds, of course, began their investigation with him, not with Tim Donaghy, and knew the spokes emanating out from Battista went far beyond the NBA betting scandal to the highest reaches of the global sports betting underworld. Less than a week after Battista entered prison, Tim Donaghy reported to the minimum-security federal prison camp in Pensacola, Florida. With the NBA betting scandal's two lead conspirators incarcerated, the sports world was now awaiting the release of the league's officiating program review.

* * *

---

[5] The facility is technically the Metropolitan Detention Center (MDC) Brooklyn, New York.

Lawrence B. Pedowitz, a partner at the law firm of Wachtell, Lipton, Rosen & Katz, formerly served as Chief of the Criminal Division in the active U.S. Attorney's Office for the Southern District of New York. In August 2007, Pedowitz was selected by the NBA to head the review of the league's officiating program. He says that when he was interviewed by the league, they focused on his prior criminal investigation experience and his appointment by a federal district court to oversee a mob-infested union for six years in the 1990s. Pedowitz also says he and his firm also have a track record of "handling internal investigations and related inquiries for major companies." As Pedowitz explained to the press:

> We were retained by the Commissioner of the NBA and the audit committee of the NBA to do a review that has had three areas of focus. First, the NBA asked us to determine if referees, other than Tim Donaghy, had bet on NBA games or had leaked confidential information to gamblers. Second, the NBA also asked us to do a forward-looking compliance review, and look at the NBA's rules, policies and procedures, and compliance systems, to see if we could recommend steps that might prevent a reoccurrence of this type of incident. Third, we were also asked to do a review of the referee program to see if we could recommend improvements.

With the assistance of a research team from his law firm, Larry Pedowitz conducted more than two hundred interviews with referees and team and NBA personnel over fourteen months, resulting in his "Report to the Board of Governors of the National Basketball Association." The one hundred and sixteen-page assessment, which also includes reviews of several game tapes, was submitted to the NBA on October 1, 2008, and released to the press the following day. The so-called "Pedowitz Report" examines numerous aspects of officiating and (often arcane) NBA policy. Its key findings regarding the referee betting scandal focus on two preeminent issues: whether other referees were involved and whether the outcomes of games were influenced by Donaghy and/or other officials. On these matters of primacy, the report respectively states:

> We have discovered no information suggesting that any NBA referee other than Tim Donaghy has bet on NBA games or leaked confidential NBA information to gamblers . . . Donaghy has denied intentionally making calls designed to manipulate games, and the government has said that it found "no evidence that Donaghy ever intentionally made a particular ruling during a game in order to increase the likelihood that his gambling pick would be correct." Based on our review, and with the information we have available, we are unable to contradict the government's conclusion.

Media observers almost universally and uncritically accepted the report's conclusions, as can be inferred from the following sample of headlines covering the report's release: "Donaghy Report Clears Other Refs" (*Washington Post*); "Probe: No evidence of other referees' misconduct" (*USA Today*); "Report confirms Donaghy was the only corrupt referee, clears NBA" (*Philadelphia Daily News*); "Review of NBA officials finds Donaghy only culprit" (ESPN.com); "NBA referees are cleared; Report: Only Donaghy guilty" (*Boston Globe*), and "Report: Donaghy fixed games alone" (*Newsday*).

Problematically, however, the Pedowitz Report notes, "Despite our repeated requests, Donaghy has declined to speak with us. The government also has declined to share any nonpublic information from its investigation with us." Combined with Battista's refusal to speak with its researchers, the Pedowitz group was confined to reviewing the public record, namely court filings. This critical weakness doomed the NBA's "study" from being anything more than a rather superficial synopsis of court activity, and kept it far from being an incisive look into the scandal.

By November 2008, with the scheme's co-conspirators in prison, and the NBA's "study" completed, for most the betting scandal story was over; public opinion had largely been formed, and was hardening. Outside of the law enforcement community and a few die-hard scandal followers, many had not considered how *necessarily* superficial the understanding was without access to Jimmy Battista, to his records, and to those in his circle who wouldn't dare cooperate in earnest with authorities.[6]

* * *

---

[6] This list of informed gambling sources includes Battista's partners, his colleagues, his clients, his adversaries, bookmakers, and those sportsbook officials who knew—or should have known—about the curiosities in betting line moves on Donaghy's games. Largely as a result of this crowd's lack of forthright cooperation with various authorities, Tim Donaghy's version of events, starting with his seminal 2007 trip to meet with the FBI in New York and running through his 2009 release from prison and beyond, remained predominant as of March 2010.

EPILOGUE

State of The Sheep

THE RESEARCH FOR *Gaming the Game* began in March 2008 with extensive interviews of Jimmy Battista, who was debating his next steps in the court process at the time (he pleaded guilty weeks after our first meeting). Interviews of Battista in March and April were augmented on occasion until Battista entered prison in September 2008. Because the plan was always to explore big-time betting and the NBA scandal, the research was never intended to cover his imprisonment or the melodrama that would likely play out for years afterward as the scandal was debated. There is thus no such narrative or analysis in that regard. I thought, however, it might be enlightening to catch up with Battista after his August 2009 release from prison to glean his perspective on certain issues after time had passed and he was no longer in the hot spotlight.[1] What follows are brief post-prison insights into the former pro gambler's views on various professional and personal matters.

---

[1] Technically, Battista was transferred to a halfway house on August 31, 2009, and was not an entirely free man until October 19, 2009. Tim Donaghy was transferred from prison camp to a halfway house in June 2009. He violated his supervised release rules, however, and was sent to a county prison. Donaghy was released a second time on November 4, 2009. Federal Bureau of Prison records show that Tommy Martino was released from the system on August 28, 2009.

On Tim Donaghy's "Extortion"/"Mob" Allegations

"The first time I heard Timmy was saying I threatened him was when it was in the news," Battista says. "I sort of knew something like that was going on because a few people close to me in the business were approached by the feds and proffered against me. Luckily for me they were men enough to let me know what they were asked and what they told the feds. The one thing they each were asked first was whether I threatened Timmy or not. These guys have all known me for, like, twenty years, and they laughed at the idea that I would threaten Timmy. They essentially told the FBI, 'Listen, that wasn't in Sheep's character, to threaten anybody. As fucked up as he was on drugs and whatever he was going through in his personal life, he was always the guy trying to help people out.' The truth is that part of my problem has always been trying to appease everyone and make them happy. Threatening Timmy, or especially his poor wife and kids, was the furthest thing from what I was like. Listen, I was a gambler. I'm not the best father in the world, but I try to be a good dad. I would never, in a million years, threaten anyone's family. It just isn't me.

"When we met at the Marriott and then went to the gas station, Tommy and Timmy were both stoned off their asses, and I had two lines of coke in me. We were in a great mood because we knew we were going to make money! It wasn't like I said {Battista says in a sarcastically dastardly tone}, 'Oh, well, you're going to fix games for me and tell me who you like or you're going to be like Luca Brasi and sleep with the fishes.' Timmy's just trying to cover up his involvement in one of the greatest scandals in sports history. Why not say, 'Well, the mob threatened me, and that's why I did it!'?

"The federal government never considered me as being a mob associate or anything like that, because I wasn't! In my eyes, I had no ties to organized crime except that they were bookmakers and we were bettors; that's the only ties I ever had to organized crime. If anything, *the mobsters were the fish and my guys were the sharks*, and anybody that knew what we were doing knows that.[2] Now, is it possible that the FBI heard on a Gambino wiretap that I was betting large amounts of money on Donaghy's games? Sure. But just because I bet with somebody in, say, Conshohocken who bets with somebody in, say, North Jersey, and somehow that gets filtered into the Gambino family or other crime groups doesn't mean I was involved in some mafia conspiracy or extortion or threats or anything like that."

On Other Possible Explanations For How The FBI Probe Into Him Began/Why The NBA Betting Scheme Popped Up On A Wiretap Of The Gambino "Crime Family"[3]

"After All-Star Sports in Curacao closed," Battista says, "Ronnie Park went back to bookmaking in New York. He was

---

[2] As another big-time pro gambler, one of the main competitors to Battista's former sharp clients, says, "The idea that 'the mob' was involved is absurd. I mean, okay, anyone who is running an illegal bookmaking operation somewhere is committing a crime and they are organized in some way. But, the idea that it's like these back room Italian guys who have decided they are going to fix NBA games, uh, this isn't like the other game-fixing scandals that went down where it was a concerted effort to seek out people and fix games. Here, you have a guy [Battista] who is already doing it on his own and they [gangsters] just happened to luck into it by way of, 'Oh, this guy's betting on games? We'll start betting on those games, too.' They weren't affiliated with Sheep in any way."

[3] As stated previously, the origins of the FBI's probe into Battista and then into the NBA betting scandal are two areas federal authorities have refused to discuss. FBI Special Agent Paul Harris, the case agent, wrote in his affidavit in support of application for arrest warrants: "In early 2007, the FBI received information that Battista was engaged in betting large amounts of money on NBA basketball games and was receiving assistance from an NBA referee in determining his bets." Retired FBI Supervisory Special Agent Phil Scala has said, "One of the case agents had come into my office and said that they had information from a wiretap stating that there was huge sums of money being made and that someone thought that a ref may be involved." According to the *New York Post*, the FBI "stumbled onto the betting scam through wiretaps being used in a massive investigation into the upper echelon of the Gambino crime family [in 2007] . . . That probe resulted in the arrest of the family's acting boss, underboss and consigliere, and five dozen lower-level gangsters in February [2008]."

pretty sharp and was good at betting NBA games. He was probably moving thirty to fifty grand a game for some of his bettors. Even though he was pretty good with NBA games, he didn't have my handicapper, Timmy 'Elvis' Donaghy, and he wound up on the other side of some of Timmy's games. Ronnie was getting destroyed on some of those games and looked like a complete moron. He started asking people who was moving these games because the lines were moving so much and they didn't make sense to him, and at some point he found out I was the one screwing with the lines. Obviously, he was pissed. Well, he got jammed up in the fall of 2006. I heard he got picked up and dimed me out to the authorities. He supposedly gave up my name, what I did, what we did together, all that."

Much like many illicit entrepreneurs, Battista has heard many rumors over the years of confederates grassing on him and others, though most often with no real evidence any such persons were engaged in cooperating with authorities. Illicit businesses, by definition, require secrecy, and paranoia of detection is a constant in this line of work. As such, it isn't surprising to hear that Battista not only questions the supposed actions of Ronnie Park, but also of his longtime colleague and friend, pro gambler Joe Vito Mastronardo— even though there is no evidence to support Battista's theories of Park or Mastronardo ratting on him. "Joe got busted in 2006," Battista says, "and they seized more than two million dollars from him and his brother. When I heard that he cut a deal and got house arrest, I assumed that Joe must have said, 'I'm gonna fuck Sheep and get him back [for the June 2006 Belmont-Paramount Sports horse racing fiasco]. I'll rat him out.'"

Jimmy Battista doesn't pretend to know which of his somewhat educated guesses about the FBI's probe is most accurate, nor if he is *even close* to understanding how the federal investi-

gation actually began.[4] He does, however, offer an alternative
explanation beyond someone matter-of-factly "ratting" on him;
one which doesn't require as much conspiracy theorizing, and
which may be the most likely.

"A *Fox News* report showed the investigation started with
Joe Vito's phone records, not my phone records," Battista says.
"Joe Vito's records have my dummy cell phone numbers calling
him, and he was my partner on a lot of stuff. He wasn't tied
into the Gambinos or anything like that anymore than I was.
He was just a bookmaker, a huge gambler, and a really sharp
business guy. We had a lot of contacts in our business, and I
am sure there were certain bookmakers who were connected
to this or that 'crime family' who were asking people like Joe
or me to move a few dimes for them, but we didn't care. It
wasn't like people approached us with their credentials, a tax
ID number, and business card and said, 'Hi, I am a bookmaker with so-and-so family, and I would like to . . . ' It was
more matter-of-fact like, 'You're a bookmaker. I'm going to
bet you, and you're going to pay me or I'm going to pay you
at the end of the week.' That was business. It isn't like *anyone
in that world* discusses things like that.

"Well, me and Bluto [the Jewish bookmaker from New York
who took large bets and whose zeal for life Battista enjoyed]
had a falling out early in the 2006-07 NBA season over one
of Timmy's picks on one of Scott Foster's games.[5] By then,
me and Joe Vito had already stopped doing business with each

---

[4] Jimmy Battista's lawyer, Jack McMahon, has no greater insights into the matter.
"My understanding is that they had a wire going against some organized crime people,"
McMahon says, "and somewhere on the wire there was discussion about somebody who
had an NBA referee who was giving them information and they were killing it, making
money. I don't know exactly what it is that they heard, but it wasn't anybody actually
connected. It was somebody just talking about it in a third-person kind of way, 'I heard
this about these guys. They got an NBA ref. They're killin' it. They're making tons of
money.' It piqued the interest of the FBI, and that was the genesis of the investigation."

[5] If Battista's guess regarding the FBI's "Gambino" wiretap picking up Bluto somehow
railing against Battista to Joe Vito is correct, there is an incredible irony: Tim Donaghy's
wager on a *non*-Donaghy game is what led to his demise, not betting on his own games.

other after we went at it about the horse. Joe Vito and Bluto were close friends and business partners, and both were really pissed at me starting in 2006. I am sure they bitched about me to each other on the phone, not to mention them copying my bets on Timmy's games and probably talking about them. I always assumed Bluto was constantly being watched because he was up in that part of the world, and supposedly knew people in the Gambino crowd. The first evidence that got turned over to me by the U.S. Attorney's Office was Joe Vito's phone records, and Bluto's phone numbers were all over the records.[6] So, maybe the feds heard, over a Gambino wiretap, Joe talking to Bluto, and that's where this whole investigation started."

On Whether He Considers Himself A Gambling Addict And, If So, If This In Part Accounted For His Downfall

"I love sports—watching sports, playing sports—and always have," Battista says. "I can't watch sports without thinking of betting. I can go to games and enjoy it, just like I always did, but I am always aware of the gambling aspect. It wasn't like I was addicted to gambling. For me, betting was the kill of getting the right number. It was like a stock broker laying Microsoft at 'X' and buying it back at 'Y.' There's an art to it, and I had gotten very good at it. I gambled socially over the years playing blackjack as a stress reliever. I loved going down to Atlantic City, having a few cups of coffee and some coke, and sitting at a table for five hours. I would usually bet a few dimes, but nothing outrageous. That was the beauty of my

---

[6] "From the time the FBI visited my house [in spring 2007]," Battista says, "I was wondering who the rat was. I was sitting in [Battista defense attorney] Jack McMahon's office one afternoon when his secretary told us the discovery evidence had come in. She brought in a box, and I opened it. The first things I pulled out turned out to be Timmy's and Joe Vito's phone records. The moment I saw Joe Vito's phone records, I thought, 'Joe's the rat. This is his way of getting back at me [for the horse racing/Paramount Sports debacle].' I was fucking furious."

business; even if I lost some money playing blackjack, I knew I could make it back with moving and betting.

"People just can't imagine all the stuff that was going through my mind when I was moving games for those four guys and dealing with Elvis. And, all of this was going on with me working out of my house with my wife and five kids around. I didn't get into debt because of a gambling addiction; I got in debt because of gambling when I was high as a kite.[7] Betting on sports and on blackjack over the course of a year while I was all fucked up, and making bad business choices, put me millions of dollars in the hole. I was so used to making good money and being able to overcome any short-term losses, that I never feared the debt. But, there just weren't enough hours in the day to fulfill all my responsibilities, from moving and betting with those guys and trying to be somewhat of a husband and a father to five kids. If I had brought on an assistant a couple of years before, maybe I could have managed everything and I wouldn't have turned to drugs. It was a very stressful life, and I would have benefitted from not being so successful. If I had stayed maybe one rung below the top echelon of gamblers, I probably would still be gambling and nobody would know who I was right now. At a minimum, I needed someone to work with me because no one person could handle what I was trying to do.

"You know, though, my drug addiction saved me—and a lot of other people. Even though it almost killed me and almost cost me my family, it saved everybody! If I didn't go into rehab, I would have continued what I was doing and the feds—no doubt—would have got me and the people I worked with on wires or something, and we'd all be doing fifteen to twenty years in federal prison right now.[8] The feds would have

---

[7] The problem of Battista gambling while stoned was made worse by his ridiculous credit lines with sportsbooks (which were the result of his established and significant wagering on behalf of his clients over the years).

[8] According to a few pro gamblers, the federal investigation into Jimmy Battista spooked them out of the sports betting business.

gone to every sharp guy, and they would have been pressed for who and what they knew. It would have been the biggest sports scandal in history. It would have gone more into the NBA, and it would have gone elsewhere. Whew. It's scary to think where the investigation would have gone."

On The Possibility Other Referees Or Officials In Other Sports Are Engaging In Activities Similar To What Transpired With Tim Donaghy

"Do I think stuff like this, involving corrupt officials, is going on in other leagues? Absolutely," Battista says. "Do I have direct evidence of other officials? No, but the money involved is too big to ignore. You have to consider the financial situation for these officials. Yeah, they're making good money, but not when you compare it to the players they are working with. Look, the officials in pro sports are traveling all the time, too, and it's a fucking grind. They're making pennies compared to the athletes, and people get jealous, not to mention how much scrutiny they're under and how much shit they have to take from players, coaches, and fans. You're gonna get a certain percentage of officials who say, 'Fuck these ungrateful people,' and do what they think they have to do. So, you can see how they would rationalize selling information and betting on games. Also, don't forget how much some people like to gamble—once somebody owes a bookmaker some cash, who knows what they'd do to pay off their debt?"

On His Addiction To Prescription Pills

"I have not had a prescription pill in my body since I entered White Deer Run in March of 2007, thank God. Even as all of that craziness post-rehab was going on [FBI investigation, grand jury, Donaghy and Martino cooperating against him, etc.], and the stress was just unreal, I never thought about going back to OxyContin. I would have lost my wife and kids if I did. There was one moment that will always stick with me, and keep me from even thinking of using drugs again. I used to pack my kids' lunches every morning when they went to school. My youngest daughter asked me if she could buy her lunch that day, and I told her she could but that I only had a quarter. I went upstairs to get two dollars from Denise's purse as she was getting ready to go to cosmetology school. This was back when my wife was facing an appearance before the grand jury, and she was furious at me over all that I had done to her and the kids. She started yelling at me about all the money I blew, and got into why I had to scrounge for two dollars. Up until then, we were pretty careful to keep everything away from the kids, even though they probably sensed things weren't all roses. Well, my daughter saw this heated exchange between us, and came up to me and said, 'Don't worry, Dad, you can have my lunch money back,' and she handed me her tiny little kiddie purse. I get emotional every time I think about that moment, and I have kept that purse with me ever since."

* * *

Not long after his release from prison, Jimmy Battista got a full-time job managing a fitness club. The money was a big step down from his heyday as one of the world's premier sports bet movers, and the hours were demanding, but it was a steady job that helped pay the bills and didn't require him to live a life of secrecy.[9] Working at a health club was a bonus for someone who wanted to get back in shape and lead a healthier lifestyle. Before trying to get back in shape, Jimmy Battista had ballooned up to roughly three hundred pounds. By March 2010, his weight was under two hundred pounds, and his daily

---

[9] For Battista, "paying the bills" includes his portion of the $217,267 in restitution he owes collectively with his co-conspirators, Tim Donaghy and Tommy Martino.

workouts and new lifestyle had him in the best shape of his adult life dating back to his rugby days. Interestingly, part of Battista's demanding regimen included a memento from the NBA betting scandal. "I actually still have the Arizona State baseball hat Tommy or Cheryl bought for me on Tommy's trip to Phoenix," Battista says, "but it's worn out. I wore it throughout the time I was exercising after rehab. I dropped at least forty pounds wearing that hat! Denise made me throw out the T-shirt they gave me from the strip club, though."

As he continues to adjust to the life of "a grinder," as he calls it, Battista says he is very appreciative for the surrounding cast of people who helped take care of him and, especially, of his family when Jimmy created so many challenges for everyone. "Luckily, my family and my wife's family have been great," Battista says. "They've helped me, my wife and kids so much. Both sets of parents have been great, and my sisters and my in-laws have been so supportive. Even our neighbors are pretty close to us, and have been helpful, too." Battista sums up his outlook on things by saying, "Overall, life is good. I'm healthy. I'm sober. Things at home with my wife and kids are great. We have two kids away at college and the younger ones are all active in sports and stuff, and we're very proud of all of them."[10]

Jimmy Battista's home is figuratively and literally different today than it was before the FBI first visited in the spring of 2007. Not only is the general feel among Jimmy and his wife and kids different now that he is drug-free and finally a part of things, his betting office is no more. The once-hyperactive room used to be filled with numerous cell phones, computer screens, and TVs, and was always bursting with energy and anxiety from the wagers being placed there. Correspondence from The Sheep's war room used to send bettors, bookmakers,

---

[10] Battista's son is enrolled at Penn State University in University Park, PA; his oldest daughter is enrolled at Millersville University in Millersville, PA (just southwest of Lancaster).

and sportsbooks into a frenzy, and betting lines around the globe were altered because of what took place in the eight-by-ten room. Now, the phones, computers and the TVs are gone, with the cherished large flat-screen taking its place in the basement. The Sheep's former betting lair, where some of the world's most consequential sports bets were placed for years, is now the province of Battista's three young daughters. One laptop remains in the "office," but at last check instead of The Sheep placing bets on it, two of Jimmy Battista's little girls and a few of their friends were using it to play a computer dress-up game.

APPENDIX

NBA Scandal Betting Analysis

*G**AMING THE GAME*** was always intended to be a nonfiction true crime read focused on the life and pro gambling career of Jimmy "Baba" Battista. Many readers, however, may be especially interested in the 2006-07 NBA betting scandal, and I thus feel obligated to offer findings from my two-plus years of research on the subject. Throughout this time, Tim Donaghy's version of events dominated the public's understanding of the scandal. This was largely because Donaghy was the first of the three conspirators to cut a deal with the federal government, and was considered a credible witness in the early stages of the investigation. Though Tommy Martino later agreed to work with the feds, this was only after he had perjured himself before a grand jury, which properly damaged his credibility. Battista, of course, never cooperated with authorities, and the investigation was therefore left with little means to corroborate Donaghy's more consequential claims, particularly since only Battista knew when, where, how much, and why he was betting. Tracking down The Sheep's computerized betting records (which are virtually unassailable) would have been a compelling way of supporting or refuting many of Donaghy's claims, and could not be conducted without Battista—if only indirectly (i.e., outlining the betting operation's machinations)—leading the way to the data.

The result of these circumstances was that Donaghy's version dictated much of the investigation, the prosecution, and the media coverage of these events. After all, short of having a court-authorized wiretap of the conspirators during the scheme, or of Battista's numerous computers being seized and searched by authorities, against what evidence could the FBI compare numerous Donaghy claims? The government simply had lesser—if any—means to determine the validity of Donaghy's assertions regarding things like: how many games were bet during the 2006-07 NBA season, especially between December 12, 2006, and March 26, 2007, and why; how and why Battista moved lines to advance his betting propositions; how much Battista was betting on games Donaghy refereed, and how the total amount wagered on those games compared to Battista's bets on NBA games not officiated by Donaghy.

Above all else, there is one unresolved question that has predictably and properly consumed interested parties: *Did Tim Donaghy influence the outcome of games to advance his betting propositions?*[1] This has been insufficiently addressed in large part because authorities (and others) were without key data to support or refute the existing record. Below, I offer insights into this area, using objective data as much as possible, and conclude with brief suggestions for further research. Some of the material below also appears in the relevant parts of the NBA betting scandal story. Because, unlike the narrative of the book, I am explicitly addressing an issue of gravity that requires all available data in one concise location, this information is revisited here. Importantly, it is augmented by data

---

[1] I am using the term "influence" as opposed to "fix" simply because one referee among three working a game may influence a game and yet still not be able to sufficiently alter (fix) the outcome because he is not in total control of the officiating or of other relevant matters (coaching decisions, injuries, etc.). Of note, it is often said that Donaghy didn't "bet" on his own games during the '06-07 scandal; he merely provided picks for them. In the gambling world, Donaghy's actions are considered "betting" because he was picking a side of a sporting event and earning winnings if his pick was correct. The fact that he didn't have to pay for losses is what confuses non-bettors regarding the definition of "betting." Gamblers call arrangements like Donaghy's betting on a "free roll," and the practice is fairly common among the world's sharps and their runners (free rolls—bets which have no cost for losses—are routinely offered as currency).

below which allow for a more comprehensive answer to the specific question of whether Tim Donaghy influenced games.[2]

---

[2] Others would likely say there is a second unresolved question (among others): Were other referees involved in the scheme (and, if so, how)? As noted earlier, Jimmy Battista claims he only bet on approximately seven games not officiated by Tim Donaghy, and that he was not privy to Donaghy's dealings with other NBA referees. Importantly, no one, including Tommy Martino, Pete Ruggieri, and other pro gamblers, is claiming that "non-Donaghy" games were of any significance in the betting scheme. I have not taken the time to investigate this issue of other referees further, and thus have little to add to the existing record beyond what already appears. Donaghy claims the other referees involved in the scandal were merely used by him for "inside information." That is, he says he routinely phoned unknowing officials to pump them for any insights regarding injuries, etc., and that he placed bets on NBA games he wasn't officiating in consideration of this information. As stated previously, no other referees were criminally charged as a result of the FBI's investigation. Of course, it is true that authorities largely followed Donaghy's lead in this regard and that they didn't have much of the information contained in *Gaming the Game* which rather seriously calls into question many Donaghy assertions. Thus, it is possible the FBI would have approached the entire investigation differently, including the particular area of other NBA referee involvement, had sources like Battista and other knowledgeable pro gamblers cooperated in earnest with authorities. I have not ruled out returning to this area of inquiry when time permits. Of note, Jimmy Battista is incredulous other officials have not been pressed further. For instance, NBA referee and former Donaghy confidante Scott Foster was the subject of considerable media attention when his phone number appeared so frequently on Tim Donaghy's phone records during the scandal's time frame. About this, Battista says, "Everybody assumed Donaghy was getting Foster's picks on Foster's games, and maybe that did happen. I would love to see Scott Foster's phone records to see who he was calling after he talked to Timmy. Why isn't anyone considering the possibility that Foster was betting on Timmy's games? And, don't forget, Timmy was getting my NFL and college football picks, before and after we hooked up in December [2006]. Well, Timmy was always on the phone with Foster back then, too, so somebody should look into that. Was Timmy giving my football picks to Foster for Foster to bet on those games?" According to media reports, the FBI questioned Scott Foster about the calls, but probably not in a manner of which Battista would approve. "They specifically asked me, 'Can you recall Tim pumping you for information?' I was thinking, 'How did I miss this? Am I a moron?'" Foster said. "I thought about everything he and I talked about and whether I knowingly gave him information or if he was using me in any way. Yes, he probably could've been doing that." In this regard, the Pedowitz Report states that "the government contacted Foster only once during its investigation—when the FBI interviewed him in August 2007. During this interview, which the FBI conducted by phone rather than in person, the FBI asked Foster about his relationship with Donaghy. Foster explained his long-term friendship with Donaghy and told the FBI that they spoke almost every day during the season. It appears that the purpose of this interview was simply to confirm that Donaghy had accurately described his relationship with his friend Foster." Foster was also cleared by the NBA. Comically, given Donaghy's allegations that federal law enforcement authorities didn't sufficiently pursue the prosecution of other NBA

When something as significant as the NBA betting scandal occurs, there are predictably any number of people who take to investigating various matters, each with his or her own focus and motivations. Given how many bettors, bookies, sportsbooks, and others had interests at stake with each Battista wager on Donaghy's games, it is not surprising to hear some have entertained their own assessments of the scandal. During the course of my work on this book, a few such individuals have approached me with accounts of their experiences and misfortunes caused by Battista's actions vis-à-vis the NBA betting scandal. One person, a renowned pro gambler known in some circles as "Louis" or "Lou," was particularly impressive when it came to his data-driven analysis of the scandal, and his conclusions—reached independently, and long before he had ever heard of me or of my work on Battista's story—mirror much of what I had discovered based on my access to Battista and others, and based on what I found when I located many of Battista's betting records. As such, I view Lou's assessment of the NBA betting scandal as credible, and offer his thoughts below where appropriate.

"If you look at a graph of my historical results," Lou says, "you can look at the dates along the bottom and see the biggest drawdown I've ever had betting sports—in other words, the most I've ever lost over any one period of time—was from December 2006 through January 2007. I do things value-based, and I'm providing data to my computer and a simulator

---

referees, there was an area of activity which could have brought criminal charges against other officials, namely if other referees were somehow part of Donaghy's 2003-07 betting on NBA games. Of course, such revelations would also have no doubt increased Donaghy's criminal liability. That is, he and his colleagues would likely be in jeopardy if other referees were: betting on their own games with or through Donaghy; getting Donaghy's picks on Donaghy's games to then place bets on these games with their own bookies or agents; and/or knowingly offering their insights and/or picks to Donaghy for him to bet in return for a fee or for winnings on bets. Donaghy, though, made no such claims against other referees, offering instead information about matters unrelated to the betting scandal.

and it's saying, 'Oh, my goodness, this game at 3.5 is really good value, the right line should be 1. Let's bet that game.' After a couple of weeks betting these games, I assumed there was something wrong with my simulator. I just figured I would stop betting sides for a while because it was obvious something was wrong with my model. I lost about $400,000–$500,000 betting these games. I was wrong about 80% of the time, compared to being wrong about 45% historically. I didn't know the games were being fixed! I had no idea what was going on. You can only beat your head against the wall for so long, so I gave up betting NBA sides for the rest of that year.

"Initially, when I heard rumblings that there was a referee that was fixing games, I put it aside. Then, when the NBA announced that the FBI was investigating one of their officials, it took me minutes—literally—to do some research, based on line movement and discrepancies in calls from one season to the next, and it was pretty clear to me what referee they were talking about. And then there were several people I spoke with who said, 'Oh, yeah, the ref they're talking about is Tim Donaghy.' I also spoke with people who were way down the food chain—in other words they weren't working with Sheep or the guys he worked for—and they had heard about these games, and even had a name for them: 'TD specials.' It turned out that *a lot* of people in the gambling world knew about this when it was going on.

"I used to do a lot of business in Asia, and in 2008 all of my [betting] limits got reduced by a large margin; they were really scared of taking bets in Asia. I had been betting there since 2004, and didn't win any more money in 2006-07 than I did in previous years. So, I talked to some people there in 2008, and asked them who won a lot the previous year. They said there was a group that did really well, and I had my guy down there do a little research to find out who had won. He couldn't really find out the names, but he could find some of the account numbers. So, we got a bunch of the bets after-the-fact, which were placed in these account numbers. Then I cross-referenced them with the games that Donaghy was reffing. That's partly how I figured out which games they bet."[3]

In addition to Lou's analyses, various referee and betting line stats were considered and analyzed during the course of the research, some of which are referenced below. Short of having a complete set of Jimmy Battista's offshore bets on NBA games for the 2006-07 season, the next best alternative are data sets of betting line activity, which are equally objective if not as compelling.[4] I was able to obtain the open and closing betting lines for Donaghy's 2006-07 season (if not more) from three sportsbooks: an influential offshore sportsbook, an influential Las Vegas sportsbook, and CRIS.[5] As mentioned previously, the federal government never researched betting line movement. In advance of the betting line analyses below, it must be noted that anything greater than a 1.5-point betting line move on an NBA game is generally considered significant.

---

[3] As the writing of this book was being completed in March 2010, Lou was still refining his master list of the games he and his researchers believe Donaghy officiated and bet. Of note, his research team's list for the 2006-07 NBA season is markedly different than the one offered by Tim Donaghy—the sides bet (and thus the bet outcomes) are different, and Lou's team claims to have found evidence of Battista's wagers on more than 40 Donaghy games they believe were part of that season's betting scandal.

[4] Regarding betting line activity, the "open" lines are their own story because some sportsbooks do not maintain records for the true opening lines. Instead, their records consider the time when the market is "full" (i.e., after the point spreads have settled, and when the sportsbooks begin taking large bets) as the "open" line. Thus, comparisons between sportsbooks regarding betting line activity are problematic, and were not undertaken. Whatever analyses were conducted and are presented here are from within a sportsbook's data (e.g., if comparing Donaghy's games versus other NBA games, each data set was from the same source and the peculiarities of that sportsbook's "open" lines are therefore consistent).

[5] Costa Rica International Sports (CRIS) describes itself as "a recognized sports betting industry leader since 1985" that "provides safe, legal, and secure sports betting on sporting events, as well as horse racing, online casino games, poker, and bingo from any location in the world, 24 hours a day 7 days a week." CRIS lines were obtained courtesy of Don Best. The Las Vegas and offshore sportsbooks would only provide data if their identities were not disclosed.

Thus, a 2-point line move is even rarer, and so on.[6] As Lou says, "No injury, no other information, a 1.5-point move is a very big move on an NBA game. That means one of two things; it means the group that's betting the sportsbook has been winning for a long period of time, because the lines don't tend to move right away, or that someone is betting an obscene amount of money. Pretty much everything I bet moves a point, because I am pretty well respected and it tends to win so you get a lot of hangers-on."

Some commentary regarding the factual record and the conventional wisdom, which are most certainly not one and the same, are offered first, followed by my related assessments.

A PRIMER

Importantly, at least as it pertains to the discussion about whether Tim Donaghy influenced games, the federal government has said very little. The U.S. Attorney's Office wrote only the following: "There is no evidence that Donaghy ever intentionally made a particular ruling during a game in order to increase the likelihood that his gambling pick would be correct. He has acknowledged, however, that he compromised his objectivity as a referee because of his financial interest in the outcome of NBA games, and that this personal interest might have subconsciously affected his on court performance." The federal government stopped considerably short of "concluding" that Donaghy didn't influence games, as some have loosely and incorrectly stated. Another related item that has unfortunately become part of the conventional wisdom about the betting scandal is that the FBI "confirmed" Donaghy's

---

[6] For example, a 3-month sample (January – March 2010 inclusive) of NBA lines from CRIS (via Don Best) shows that 21.8% of lines had equal to or greater than 1.5-point moves from open to close, and only 8.9% of moves equal to or greater than 2 points.

betting record. Since Donaghy wasn't placing the bets, and, in fact, claims to not recall precisely how many games he bet, much less specific games and betting lines and outcomes, there was very little for the FBI to "confirm" in the first place. They certainly never "confirmed" each and every one of Donaghy's dozens of bets during the 2006-07 season, let alone those in the previous three-plus seasons.

As explained earlier, Donaghy fought with authorities in making the concession that "his on court performance" may have been "subconsciously affected" by his bets, and said it was a "major, major stumbling block" in his plea negotiations. In fact, Donaghy says, "To this day, I still don't understand what 'subconsciously' meant." He has repeatedly said he didn't need to influence games because of his supposed access to "inside information."[7] Furthermore, Donaghy has carefully and consistently said that he did not make "incorrect" calls to affect the outcome of games in advance of his bets. By all accounts this is true, and even those who believe Donaghy influenced outcomes do not think he made "wrong" calls to affect games.[8] Rather, they contend that Donaghy con-

---

[7] As partly explained in Chapter 18, plenty of critics have rightly questioned Donaghy's "inside information," most of which was nothing of the sort.

[8] Officiating in many sports is subjective, with basketball a prime example, and thus quotes are necessary when using words like "incorrect" and "wrong" to describe judgment calls. I should point out that I have collected and reviewed numerous referee statistics, but require more time and expertise to conduct analyses sufficiently. I am aware of a few serious researchers who have looked into the NBA betting scandal vis-à-vis referee behavior from a statistical perspective. Most notable is the work of Indiana University business professor Wayne L. Winston in his book *Mathletics: How Gamblers, Managers, and Sports Enthusiasts Use Mathematics in Baseball, Basketball, and Football*, and of former professional gambler Haralabob "Bob" Voulgaris, whose work was featured on ESPN.com among other related internet sites. Of Voulgaris, in 2008 ESPN said, "He's one of the very few people . . . who have achieved a high level of success betting full-time on the NBA . . . He has his own massive database that would be the envy of any stat geek . . . [which] tracks the tendencies of individual referees, and factors all that and much more into forecasts. Voulgaris also watches close to 1,000 games a year." Among numerous other analyses of Tim Donaghy's officiating, Voulgaris examined the number of calls Donaghy made against each team in games he officiated. His findings regarding foul call disparities and other matters

sistently made calls for violations which are commonly not enforced. These calls would not be considered "incorrect" during reviews by various parties, and wouldn't necessarily stick out because Donaghy had a reputation for being a referee who called a lot of fouls.[9] Simply stated, Donaghy could have easily called a game "tight" against a team he bet against, and "loose" against a team on which he had wagered. None of this would have raised eyebrows, since there was no reason to question his integrity at the time. I have interviewed several basketball experts and pro gamblers who each believe Tim Donaghy influenced game outcomes, and yet these parties almost universally agree that viewing game tapes is a fruitless pursuit because there is so much subjectivity involved. Donaghy's statements on the matter, ironically, lend themselves to a compelling argument against him.

Tim Donaghy continually argues that the subjectivity of calls is a significant problem with the NBA's officiating, and says that an additional issue concerns "the friendships and hatreds between the referees and the players, coaches, and owners." In this regard, Donaghy says, "Because referees are able to make calls or ignore violations with impunity, they

---

should be researched further. Voulgaris says, for instance, that Donaghy's 2006-07 games exhibited wildly odd call disparities, meaning that whereas most games show referees call roughly the same number of fouls against each team, Donaghy's clearly favor a side. He says, "If you take the thirty-five or so games I have charted and add to those the two hundred or so games from the past two years [2009-10] and ranked the top five games in terms of greatest number of calls favoring Team A – Team B, all five spots would be owned by Donaghy." Donaghy's '06-07 season included games that had such splits between Team A and Team B as 26 – 6, and 17 – 0. At press time, Voulgaris was in the process of compiling a full data set, as well as a reference group. In advance, he says, "Donaghy has several games where the ratio is greater than fifteen. I'd lay a decent price that once we are done with [the 2009 and 2010 reference data set] there isn't one instance of another ref who has a game where he has a fifteen-call difference between Team A and Team B."

[9] According to NBA Commissioner David Stern, Donaghy was "near or at top of calls made." According to former pro gambler Bob Voulgaris, "If you track Donaghy's reffing style, you'll see he calls a lot of violations, travels, offensive fouls—as well as more than average illegal defenses and personal and shooting fouls. In short, he calls more of everything."

can hide a whole lot of love or hate for players or a team with their calls." Assuming Tim Donaghy is correct, this very logic could easily be used to illustrate why it would have been possible, indeed simple, for Donaghy to successfully influence outcomes of games. That is, if you apply Donaghy's arguments above to his particular situation vis-à-vis the possible altering of game outcomes in advance of his betting propositions, you arrive at the following statement: Because Tim Donaghy was able to make calls or ignore violations with impunity, he could—depending on which side he bet that evening—hide a whole lot of "love" or "hate" for players or a team with his calls.

* * *

THE ANALYSES

In order to assess Donaghy's explanation for his betting success during the 2006-07 scheme (i.e., exploiting "inside information"), previously unearthed and/or unexamined data is presented below to address three fundamental Donaghy claims:

- Tim Donaghy says he bet with Battista and Martino on 16 games that he officiated in the 2006-07 season, and on 14 games he did not officiate.

- Tim Donaghy says his winning percentage was the same regardless of whether he was officiating the games he was betting.

- Tim Donaghy says he often obtained "inside information" in the immediate run-up to games he was officiating, and that he placed his bets accordingly just prior to tipoff.

Donaghy vs. Non-Donaghy Games

Tim Donaghy says he bet on 30 to 40 games he officiated in each of the 2003-04, 2004-05, and 2005-06 seasons, and that he only bet on 16 of his games in the 2006-07 season. Before reviewing the evidence enumerated immediately below, I must point out that Donaghy's claim that he actually bet *less* on his own games in the 2006-07 season than he did during the prior three seasons is on its face counterintuitive. Again, he says that during each of the '03-04, '04-05, and '05-06 seasons, *when he had to pay on betting losses*, he bet on 30 to 40 games he officiated. And yet, during the '06-07 season, when Battista was covering Donaghy's betting losses, and thus *Donaghy had free license to bet on as many of his games as he liked without fear of losing money*, Donaghy says he bet only on 16 games he officiated. Put another way, the "pathological gambler" who "could not stop himself from gambling" maintains that he bet on his games roughly half as often when he didn't have to pay for losses as he did when he had to pay for his losses.

"Every game Elvis officiated in 2006-07," Jimmy Battista says on the subject, "at least through sometime in April, he bet on." Betting line analysis can shed some light on the issue on whether Donaghy's betting diminished significantly, as he claims, or if it increased as Battista, Lou, and other pro gamblers claim. As illustrated in Table A-1, 18% of Tim Donaghy's games during the three seasons prior to 2006-07 had betting line moves equal to or greater than 1.5 points. Thus, if the number of games officiated and bet by Tim Donaghy had simply remained the same as the three seasons prior (i.e., approximately 35 games), you'd expect the betting line analysis presented in Table A-1 to show that roughly 18% of games he officiated in '06-07 had betting line moves of 1.5 points or more (the highest of Donaghy's '03-05 record was 19% in 2004). If, as Donaghy claims, the number of games he officiated and bet in '06-07 was significantly reduced (to 16 games), you'd expect the analysis to show a (perhaps significantly) smaller percentage of game lines moving. Instead, what you find illustrated in Table A-1 is a demonstrable *increase* in 2006-07 over the previous three-year span (from 18% to 36%). In short, the betting line analysis supports the contentions of Battista, Lou, and other pro gamblers that Donaghy bet on far more than 16 of his games in the '06-07 season.[10]

TABLE A-1
% of Donaghy Games with ≥ 1.5 Pt Line Moves

2003–2006	2006–2007
18%	36%

Source: Offshore sportsbook

Related to the above, Tim Donaghy says he also bet on 14 NBA games he did not referee in 2006-07, and that his betting success was the same as with the 16 games he officiated. This would all make sense if "inside information," as Donaghy insists, accounted for his betting success—his bets should have been winners regardless of whether he was officiating, and there would have been no reason to wager more on his own games than others. Of course, if Donaghy's bets on his games won at a higher rate than his bets on other NBA games, it would suggest "inside info" did not account for his success, and would call into question his claim he didn't influence games.

---

[10] Recall that Battista and other pro gamblers were already betting on Donaghy's games as early as 2003. Thus, substantial money was being wagered on Donaghy's games throughout the three seasons prior to 2006-07, and line moves were taking place in these seasons as well. This must be considered when assessing the spike in betting line activity that took place in '06-07.

As noted before, Pete Ruggieri told the FBI his bets were exclusively for games Tim Donaghy officiated. In fact, Ruggieri described discovering Jack Concannon's betting pattern and betting success on Donaghy's games years before, which caused Ruggieri and Jimmy Battista to mimic the bets on Donaghy's games in the first place. According to Battista, he shared his knowledge of the bets on Donaghy's games with his main client/partner, The Chinaman, in the spring of 2005. In addition, I have identified no less than four (and believe there are at least seven) other pro gamblers who were also betting on games officiated by Tim Donaghy by the start of the 2006-07 season because of Battista's wagers, and none of them claim that "non-Donaghy" games were bet. As Battista described earlier, he experienced serious difficulties regarding the relatively few (7) non-Donaghy NBA games on which he and Donaghy bet during the '06-07 scandal (because all but one were losers), which caused him to stop taking Donaghy's bets on games Donaghy wasn't officiating. Tommy Martino, when he was cooperating against Battista without Battista's knowledge, told the FBI almost exactly the same thing.

Betting line data are of some utility here, also. If Donaghy's bets on games he wasn't officiating were approximately the same in number and won at approximately the same rate as bets on his games, the betting lines should show little difference between Donaghy and non-Donaghy games. As illustrated in Table A-2, however, there is a stark difference in the percentage of games with a 1.5-point or greater move, with games officiated by Tim Donaghy exhibiting a much greater percentage of big line moves. In short, the betting line data support the assertions of Battista and other pro gamblers that the major action was on games Donaghy officiated.[11]

---

[11] Similarly, 14.5% of non-Donaghy games had line moves of 2 points or greater versus 26% of Donaghy's games that moved 2 points or more.

TABLE A-2
% of NBA Games with ≥ 1.5 Pt Line Moves
12/12/06–3/26/07

Non-Donaghy	Donaghy
25%	43%

Source: Don Best/CRIS

One remaining item of importance in the Donaghy vs. non-Donaghy game betting assessment concerns the amount of money being wagered. Jimmy Battista bet an average of $1 to $2 million dollars on games Tim Donaghy officiated versus an average of $10,000 to $20,000 on other (non-Donaghy) NBA games. The reason for the outrageous (100 to 1) disparity in betting action is simple: Battista (just like other pro gamblers) believed Tim Donaghy was successfully influencing the outcome of games in support of his bets.[12] "The second meeting we had when he showed me his referee schedule, he said he wanted to bet other referees' games," Battista says, revisiting this subject. "We did bet a few of them, but those games sucked! In *his* games, Timmy was *so good*. He knew what he was doing. I never asked him to fix a game; I just wanted to know who he liked. But, in my eyes, as a gambler, he knew he only got paid if he won. He always called me before a game to know what number I got. There's no way a human being could have money on a game, know the number they have to beat, and not have it affect their calls in a game. Timmy was The King, Elvis, at doing what

---

[12] As Battista says of Donaghy in this regard, "He had no idea how much he was affecting the market. He was an NBA referee who was just getting his five grand a game." I should note that one respected pro gambler not prone to hyperbole believes a colleague of his was somehow privy to Battista's picks on games Donaghy was officiating as early as 2003, was wagering in the neighborhood of $2 million every game, and earned more than $200 million by the end of the scandal.

he did; what he did was incredible. Inside information *was* probably part of how he bet, but it had little to do with the final outcome of his bets." Needless to say, if Donaghy's bets on non-Donaghy games were winning greater than 70% of the time, Battista and the other pro gamblers would have bet millions on those games, too.[13]

In addition to the compelling evidence above, there is another component of Donaghy's "inside information" claim which doesn't stand up to scrutiny, namely the manner in which Donaghy says he placed bets on games he officiated.

Sociology Of The Betting[14]

One thing many observers, no doubt because they were without access to Battista's betting records (and, more

---

[13] There is another, less sophisticated way to assess Donaghy's assertion that he essentially bet equally as often on games he officiated and those he didn't during the Battista-inspired conspiracy, namely to revisit the code the three conspirators agreed upon at the start of the scheme. The reason they simply chose to use "Chuck" for home team bets and "Johnny" for away (which later became, respectively, "Mom" and "Dad") was because there was no need to discuss cities or teams since they already knew what teams were playing. Since the plan was only to bet on Donaghy's games, there was no consideration for more elaborate codes; they weren't necessary. The code would have been ineffective if they wished to distinguish between an entire slate of games on a given day. That is, if Donaghy merely phoned in to tell Martino, "I am going to visit my *Mom* this weekend" to convey his pick on the home team, Martino would not have known for which of that day's games Donaghy was picking the home team. Of course, if the parties needed to mention a city or a team's nickname as part of the "code," there was no need for the Mom/Dad or Chuck/John effort in the first place. That is, Donaghy could quite simply have said something like, "I love visiting Boston" or "The weather in Boston is great this time of year," etc. if he was picking the Celtics. It would be pointless to say, "*Chuck* says he is visiting Boston this weekend" if Donaghy simply wanted to convey his pick of the Celtics.

[14] Some parties have assumed Tim Donaghy was betting game totals, often under the assumption that it would be easier for a referee to control the points scored by a team than to influence a game outcome. About this, Jimmy Battista says, "People always say, 'The totals, the totals, the totals!' The totals were a fucking drop in the bucket compared to what money could actually be moved on the sides. You couldn't get more than a few hundred thousand down on totals. That wasn't the money. The sides were the money, and he always liked a side." It is widely acknowledged that sportsbooks have significantly lower betting limits on game total bets than they do

generally, because they are not familiar with the sociology of big-time betting), have not considered Donaghy's claim regarding how and when he placed bets on games he officiated. The former referee says that he obtained "inside information" from other referees and player personnel, often in the pregame meeting, and that he commonly called Tommy Martino from arenas just prior to game time. As former FBI Supervisory Special Agent Phil Scala says, Donaghy told the FBI that he didn't have to influence games with his calls because, Donaghy claimed, "I could pick a winner eighty percent of the time just knowing what I knew *an hour before the game*" (emphasis added).

No serious analysis of sharp sports gambling will demonstrate millions of dollars consistently being wagered in a matter of an hour or two, much less on an ongoing basis. As illustrated earlier, it takes a lot of time and effort to get that kind of money down, and the market adjusts quickly to the smart/sharp money, making it impossible to get big bets down unless there is sufficient time to manage and/or manipulate the world's markets (Asia, Europe, offshore, Vegas, etc.). Big-time bettors place wagers and manipulate betting lines on NBA games often over periods of ten or more hours in order to obtain the most favorable point spreads ("the best numbers"). As Jimmy Battista said before ever hearing Donaghy's story, and thus when it was an otherwise innocuous statement, "Starting with the very first game we bet together, Elvis bet about a third of the

---

sides bets. As Lou, the pro gambler, says regarding the issue of totals, "The reason so many people assumed Donaghy was betting on totals was that if you tracked Tim Donaghy's games you'll see a lot of his games go over the total. The reason for that isn't because Sheep was betting the totals, it's because Donaghy needed to have his fingers on so many different aspects of the game to fix a side that one of the offshoots was that the games were really high scoring because he was calling a lot of fouls." I should note that a review of Battista's wagers on Donaghy's games included bets on totals, but I have not seen enough of these bets to offer insights regarding patterns. Battista says he does not recall specifics regarding these bets and assumes they were simply for his clients.

games the night before. Most of the time he called in his bets the mornings of his games, and then I got to work."

Lou, the pro gambler, offers this analysis of what he found regarding how Battista was betting (which is remarkably similar to what Battista describes, himself). "You have places like CRIS that take $3000 or $5000 on a game and their lines are published to the world. Then you have these outlaw guys, like the little guys in Philly and everywhere taking $5000 and their lines aren't published anywhere, and sportsbooks in Asia and their lines aren't published anywhere. Well, let's say in Asia they were taking $30,000 a game, which is what they were taking at the time. The first thing Sheep was doing was faking the game in the morning, so that he could get a better line in Asia. They were betting the wrong way on purpose in the morning. You could see that by looking at their bets, and it's the same thing we do. We fake in the morning, too. Sheep wanted to do two things: bet as much money as possible but he wanted the line to move as little as possible. He also did such a good job [when Battista did want the line to move] of throwing $5000 at a book like CRIS, or $5000 here, and $3000 there, to all these books that publish their lines that everyone uses. Imagine you have 10,000 sportsbooks in the world and all of them look to these 15 sportsbooks for their lines. These little bookmakers aren't making their own lines. They don't know what the right line on a game is." Thus, with strategic, relatively small bets with the right sportsbooks, Battista influenced lines around the world until such a point he obtained the numbers he liked, at which point he bet millions on Donaghy's games, spread out in parcels with multiple outs.

Importantly, because Lou's solitary focus was to understand the scheme's betting mechanics, he didn't (and perhaps still doesn't) grasp the significance of his findings regarding Battista's early morning "head fakes" and Battista's betting in Asia. If one's motivation is to assess Tim Donaghy's claims that he placed bets just prior to game times, Lou's research findings further refute Donaghy's version of events. Instead, they support Battista's claims that Donaghy placed his bets the evening prior or early in the morning of game days, so that Battista could manipulate the market sufficiently to get the best numbers. The FBI never knew about Battista's betting pattern, however, and thus couldn't have known Donaghy's version of events flew in the face of how millions of dollars were bet on Donaghy's games.

Betting line data also support the contention that Battista was obtaining Donaghy's picks long before game times. Recall that Battista and other pro gamblers say they were betting big on Donaghy's games (often long) before Battista ever formally hooked up with Donaghy, especially including the beginning of the 2006-07 season. If—as Battista, Lou, and others claim— Battista bet earlier and more often on Donaghy's games once he consummated the deal on December 12, 2006, including manipulating the lines (which could only be accomplished over longer periods of time), betting lines on Donaghy's games would be expected to move more for those between 12/12/06 and 3/26/07 than for other Donaghy games that season. As illustrated in Table A-3, this is precisely what happened.[15]

TABLE A-3
% of Donaghy Games with ≥ 1.5 Pt Line Moves

Source	12/12/06-03/26/07	Remainder of Season 10/31/06-12/11/06 + 3/26/07-5/12/08
Offshore sportsbook	45%	23%
Las Vegas sportsbook	43%	32%
Don Best/CRIS	43%	29%

---

[15] Data for non-Donaghy games were not available from the other sportsbooks to conduct this comparison using their data as well.

The validity of Donaghy's defense against influencing games hinged largely on his story of "inside information" he was supposedly gleaning shortly before games he was officiating (i.e., overhearing other referees and player personnel in the locker rooms before games). Since Battista was betting big money long before Donaghy ever visited an arena on game day, the "inside info" explanation for Donaghy's successful wagers is further discredited.

Summing Up

As I have stated implicitly and explicitly above and elsewhere, I have yet to come across data which supports Tim Donaghy's claim that "inside information" accounted for his betting success.[16] To the contrary, I have reviewed various types of information from numerous, independent sources, and most if not all of the data suggests Donaghy influenced the outcomes of games in support of his bets. The two pro gamblers cited throughout this appendix offer the following, as I conclude this analysis. "A lot of times the lines for Donaghy's games moved four, five, six points," Battista says. "Over time, people assumed the fix was in because NBA lines just don't move that much. There was also a point in February or March 2007 when I just couldn't believe no one was looking into Donaghy's games because *so many of them* were falling right near the number [game outcomes were very close to the point

---

[16] In addition to all the other damning evidence, Tim Donaghy doesn't help his case when he says that he voluntarily took a lie detector test to prove he was telling the truth about various betting scandal matters, and yet incredibly says that he did not have the polygraph examiner ask him whether he influenced the outcome of games because, in Donaghy's mind, "that wasn't an issue." Donaghy has also made many unsupported assertions following his prison stint that are far too numerous to address in this forum. It is likely I will offer my data-driven assessments of his myriad claims at some point, which would add to an already growing body of such deconstructive works. This will especially include a critique of those made in the former referee's book and during many of his related media appearances. In advance of more on this topic, interested parties can consult my blog at http://nbascandal.blogspot.com.

spread]. If anyone was paying attention, and by then some *gamblers* were, it was obvious something was going on with his games." Pro gambler Lou voices similar sentiments, and says more pointedly, "The NBA surely has to know Donaghy was fixing games. I really wish they'd release the individual call logs, which they have for every game, that show which referee made which calls, but that would make the NBA look really bad."[17]

* * *

SOME SUGGESTED RESEARCH
FOR THE NBA

These are two things the NBA could entertain if they wanted substantive evidence of whether former referee Tim Donaghy altered game outcomes to advance his betting propositions. My first suggestion, ironically, was inspired by the NBA's own inquiry into the betting scandal. In the Pedowitz Report (pp. 113-14, under "VII. Recommendations; 4. Gambling Enforcement, Detection and Deterrence; c) Gambling Monitors; and d) Statistical Screening for Gambling and Bias"), the following is respectively discussed (**emphasis added**):

> **The League has now arranged to obtain information on a regular basis from individuals and entities involved in the gambling business who can provide the League with information about unusual movements in the betting lines,** rumors about things such as injury reports or

---

[17] Lou finds the ending to the NBA betting scandal story ironic. "The real funny part about the scandal is that here you basically have a money-printing machine," he says, "and the two guys involved are each in debt. Donaghy owes money to the NBA, and Sheep owes the NBA and a bunch of guys on the street."

referee schedules or **where the "smart money" is being wagered**. By flagging games or individuals for the League to investigate, these monitors may help the League detect gambling or misuse of confidential information. . . .

Since the 2003-2004 season, the League has been collecting data on calls and non-calls for each referee. The collection system was designed by Sibson as part of the overall effort to redesign the officiating performance program. The system itself was built by the League. Although this system was developed for training and instructional purposes, we have worked with the League and Sibson to develop **a prototype, proprietary system for screening games in an effort to help detect data patterns that may suggest misconduct by referees and others. Data—including this foul call information and the movements of betting lines—can be analyzed using various algorithms to flag patterns consistent with questionable behavior.** While this system is in development, the League has already started to actively monitor several high level data-points (such as line movements) for every game for signs of potential misconduct, and certain game and betting information is distributed to League management on a daily basis. For those games that are flagged, the League has undertaken further review. In addition, the League hired Steven Angel, a former consultant with Sibson, as Senior Vice President for League Operations and Officiating to, among other things, help **coordinate wagering intelligence and game screening** . . .

This collection of gambling and referee behavior data seems prudent, as do the related assessments. Why, though, restrict such analysis to current and future activity? If the referee/call data has been collected since the 2003-04 season (which, interestingly, is roughly when Tim Donaghy claims he first bet on NBA games), why not perform these analyses on Donaghy's games (and others) beginning with the '03-04 season? Such study would offer insights into various areas of inquiry, end much speculation, and better demonstrate for the NBA what was missed (and possibly how) during the betting scandal. There is an interesting footnote tangentially related to this suggestion. According to Kenny White, CEO and lead oddsmaker for Las Vegas Sports Consultants, the world's largest oddsmaking company, he researched betting trends involving Tim Donaghy and submitted a report to the NBA in the fall of 2007. Of this situation, White told the *Las Vegas Review-Journal*, "They never called back to discuss it or anything."

The second thing the league could do is either the most simple or the most difficult: identify and locate big-time, heavy-hitting professional gamblers, and then interview them about the NBA betting scandal. As explained and exhibited earlier, some of these individuals have done their own, remarkably sophisticated assessments, and there may be considerable wisdom to gain from speaking with them.

SOURCE NOTES

THIS BOOK WOULD have been completed a long time ago if the project simply entailed numerous interviews of former pro gambler Jimmy "Baba" Battista. Documenting as much of Battista's life story as possible, especially his involvement in the NBA betting scandal, required considerable legwork (traveling, pandering, cajoling, bartering), and data collection.[1] *Gaming the Game* is the result of numerous Freedom of Information Act (FOIA) requests, more than one hundred interviews, numerous court transcripts, and hundreds of news articles. The agencies that created the law enforcement documents include the Philadelphia Police Department and other local departments, the Pennsylvania State Police, the Federal Bureau of Prisons, the U.S. Probation Service, and especially the regional offices of the Federal Bureau of Investigation.

Beyond the consequential body of documents and betting records that are the foundation of the NBA scandal-specific portions of this work, I have interviewed dozens of people, including numerous current and former law enforcement officials at the local and federal levels. Current and former

---

[1] Needless to say, numerous relatively trivial matters—especially those that occurred ten or more years ago—were all but impossible to support or refute (considering the passing of time and lack of objective data). For instance, Battista and some of his colleagues, led by Tiger, disagree (at times considerably) on a host of dated issues. Fortunately, these divergent views are of little or no historical or sociological import, and the lack of consensus does not adversely impact our holistic understanding of the gambling underworld.

prosecutors at the local and federal levels were also interviewed, in addition to other parties of interest (e.g., betting experts, professional gamblers, sportsbook managers, Vegas casino runners) and numerous journalists who have investigated certain aspects of the story. Importantly, many of these sources have direct knowledge of the situations they describe.

In an effort to keep the book a mainstream (as opposed to a more plodding academic) read, I have tried to keep footnoting to a minimum. However, given the gravity of the subject matter, particularly in the case of the scandal, I felt obligated to offer at least some sourcing so readers can have confidence in the work. This also permits others to conduct follow-up research, and to offer informed analyses and conclusions. I have included below only those citations needed to appropriately credit sources *explicitly quoted in the narrative*. This has only been done if the citation is an author or media outlet (i.e., not a court document, a law enforcement document, or an interview I've conducted). Where applicable, I have also listed suggested readings.

Before offering the source material, I must explicitly comment on a matter some may have noticed about the work. Readers will note there are few, if any, references to former NBA referee Tim Donaghy as a direct source of information (via law enforcement files, court documents, media accounts, or interviews). The research for *Gaming the Game* began in March of 2008, with numerous and extensive interviews of former pro gambler and scandal progenitor Jimmy "Baba" Battista, known at the time throughout the betting industry mostly as "Sheep." In the more than two years of researching the scandal that followed, I vetted as many of Battista's claims and versions of events as possible. The labor-intensive and often sensitive process included interviews of Battista's former superiors, partners, colleagues, underlings, competitors, and outright adversaries (some of whom remain upset over substantial financial losses resulting from The Sheep's betting line manipulations, and others still peeved over unpaid debts following Battista's rehab stint and "retirement" from the gambling profession). Perhaps more importantly, by the time the work was done, the NBA betting scandal cases had wended their way through the criminal justice system yielding numerous documents and interview subjects that were used to further vet Battista's story.

Because I had access to interview subjects and data to which authorities and the media were never privy, my original plans to interview Tim Donaghy were eventually scrubbed.[2] Unlike my experience with Jimmy Battista, whose credibility increased with follow-up research, Donaghy's credibility decreased as the months wore on and data accumulated, and it became clear Donaghy's story was demonstrably flawed in significant ways. That is, while there are many aspects of the scandal history that will forever be "he said—he said" matters, there are, however, areas for which there is a way to critically assess how something transpired, and Donaghy's claims were repeatedly not supported by the evidence. I thus see relying on Donaghy as the basis for any matter of import as imprudent. This doesn't mean, of course, that some of what he has said isn't true, but the volume and seriousness of Donaghy's "mistaken" claims is alarming.

* * *

SOURCES

Chapter Four: The Gambling Grocer

32   Regarding the sociology of high-end professional sports betting as evidenced by Tiger's words and actions, please see the following because they each touch on the history and/or the sociology and

---

[2] This is assuming Tim Donaghy, who was alternately writing and promoting a book during the time *Gaming the Game* was being researched, would have been a willing and forthcoming interview subject in the first place. On a related note, Tommy Martino declined my request for an interview through a third party, apparently because he was in the process of selling his story to a book author.

logistics [e.g., betting line manipulation, arbitraging, off-shore betting operations, movement of money, probability science] of high-
end sports gambling (in alphabetical order by author): Steve Budin,
Bets, Drugs, and Rock & Roll (New York, NY: Skyhorse Publishing,
2007); Richard O. Davies and Richard G. Abram, *Betting the Line:
Sports Wagering in American Life* (Columbus, OH: The Ohio State
University Press, 2001); James Jeffries and Charles Oliver, *The Book
on Bookies: An Inside Look at a Successful Sports Gambling Operation*
(Boulder, CO: Paladin Press, 2000); Michael Konik, *The Smart
Money: How the World's Best Sports Bettors Beat the Bookies Out of
Millions* (New York, NY: Simon & Schuster, 2006); Chad Millman,
The Odds: One Season, Three Gamblers, and the Death of Their Las Vegas
(Cambridge, MA: Da Capo Press [Perseus], 2001); and Wayne L.
Winston, *Mathletics: How Gamblers, Managers, and Sports Enthusiasts
Use Mathematics in Baseball, Basketball, and Football* (Princeton, NJ:
Princeton University Press, 2009).

Regarding the legality of pro gambling, especially in the
internet age, the following was consulted: David G. Schwartz,
Cutting the Wire: Gaming Prohibition and the Internet (Reno, NV:
University of Nevada Press, 2005).

Chapter Six: Sharpening Up

47   *strong* and *independent*: Pennsylvania Crime Commission, *1988
      Report* (Conshohocken, PA: PCC, 1988), pp. 23-4. On Joe Vito's
      significance early in his career, see, for example, Paul Taylor,
      "Rizzo says police acted like 'KGB Agents' in son-in-law's arrest,"
      The Washington Post, April 21, 1983.

47   *The Mastronardo bookmaking*: Pennsylvania Crime Commission,
      Organized Crime in Pennsylvania: A Decade of Change: 1990 Report
      (Conshohocken, PA: PCC, 1990), p. 71.

48   *fifty thousand*: George Anastasia, *Blood and Honor* (New York,
      NY: William Morrow and Company, 1991), pp. 248-9.

48   *played a significant role*: PCC, *Organized Crime in Pennsylvania*, p.
      71. Also see Lindsey Gruson, "U.S. Accuses Shearson of Money
      Laundering," *The New York Times*, June 27, 1986.
      The case generated some fascinating legal arguments, espe-
      cially regarding money laundering laws. See, in chronological
      order, *United States of America v. Shearson Lehman Brothers, Inc.
      et al.*, Criminal Nos. 86-00293-01, 86-00293-02, 86-00293-
      03, 86-00293-04, 86-00293-05, 86-00293-06, 86-00293-07,

86-00293-08, UNITED STATES DISTRICT COURT FOR THE EASTERN DISTRICT OF PENNSYLVANIA 650 F. Supp. 490; 1986 U.S. Dist. LEXIS 16943, December 4, 1986, Decided; *United States of America v. Herbert L. Cantley, Joseph Vito Mastronardo, Jr., Joseph Vito Mastronardo, Sr., John Vito Mastronardo, John Hector,* Criminal Nos. 86-00293-02, 86-00293-03, 86-00293-04, 86-00293-05, 86-00293-06, UNITED STATES DISTRICT COURT FOR THE EASTERN DISTRICT OF PENNSYLVANIA 1987 U.S. Dist. LEXIS 6247, July 8, 1987, Decided, July 10, 1987, Filed; *United States of America v. Joseph Vito Mastronardo, Jr.,* Appellant No. 87-1525; *United States of America v. Joseph Vito Mastronardo, Sr.,* Appellant No. 87-1644; *United States of America v. John Vito Mastronardo,* Appellant No. 87-1526; *United States of America v. Herbert L. Cantley,* Appellant No. 87-1541; *United States of America v. John Hector,* Appellant No. 87-1561, Nos. 87-1525, 87-1526, 87-1541, 87-1561, 87-1644, UNITED STATES COURT OF APPEALS FOR THE THIRD CIRCUIT 849 F.2d 799; 1988 U.S. App. LEXIS 8161, May 2, 1988, Argued, June 13, 1988, Filed.

For more information on Joe Vito Mastronardo and the mob shakedowns of Philadelphia-area bookies (and related matters), see, for example, the following: George Anastasia, *Mobfather* (Philadelphia, PA: Camino Books, 1993), and *The Last Gangster: From Cop to Wiseguy to FBI Informant—Big Ron Previte and the Fall of the American Mob* (New York, NY: Regan Books [Harper-Collins], 2004); Frank Friel and John Guinther, *Breaking the Mob* (New York, NY: Warner Books, 1990); and S.A. Paolantonio, *Frank Rizzo: The Last Big Man in Big City America* (Philadelphia, PA: Camino Books, 1993).

50 *Stanfa sent me*: Susan Caba, "Transcript of a mob shakedown highlights federal bail hearings," *Philadelphia Inquirer,* March 22, 1994.

50 *I work for somebody*: Kitty Caparella and Jim Smith, "Accused mobster agrees to plead guilty, but won't sing," *Philadelphia Daily News,* June 21, 1994.

For insights into the Stanfa racketeering and extortion cases (which include Jack Manfredi), see, for example, Susan Caba, "FBI nets Stanfa in mob sweep," *Philadelphia Inquirer,* March 18, 1994; George Anastasia, "2d person guilty in Stanfa case," *Philadelphia Inquirer,* June 24, 1994, and "He took the ride, ended up in prison," November 30, 1997.

54   *Oh my God!*: Marlene DiGiacomo, "'Oh my God'—Shooting victim recalls bookmaker's final moments," *Delaware County Daily Times*, June 30, 1994.
      For insights into the Pirollo slaying, see, for example, Bill Ordine, "Norwood man accused in Darby Killing," *Philadelphia Inquirer*, December 19, 1993; Marlene DiGiacomo, "Gambler: I shot bookie," *Delaware County Times*, July 1, 1994; Nathan Gorentsein, "Bookmaker is found guilty in '93 murder," *Philadelphia Inquirer*, July 2, 1994; DiGiacomo, "Murderous gambler runs out of luck," July 3, 1994; DiGiacomo, "Gambler gets life term for murder," July 6, 1994; Gorenstein, "Man's life spared in slaying of bookie," July 6, 1994; and Charles M. Giordano, "Illegal gambling not a 'victimless crime' (letter to the editor)," *Delaware County Times*, January 9, 1995.

Chapter Seven: Go West, Black Sheep

75   For brief coverage of the charity event Jimmy Battista hosted at Marina's involving 610 WIP co-hosts Howard Eskin and Mike Missanelli, see Pauline Pinard Bogaert, "Social Scene," *Philadelphia Inquirer*, March 5, 2002.

Chapter Twelve: *There's Someone in Stripes on My Side*

130   *Vietnamese sports betting ring*: Keith Herbert, "Brothers charged in $2.7 million ring," *Philadelphia Inquirer*, June 1, 2006.
131   *who can afford to lose*: Herbert, "Brothers charged."
132   *They've been booking for*: George Anastasia, "Gambling-ring brothers are folding," *Philadelphia Inquirer*, June 11, 2006.

Chapter Thirteen: Jimmy, Tommy, and Timmy

140   *Anytime there was a*: Jack McCallum, "A retired ref believes that Tim Donaghy followed the rule book too closely for NBA's good," *SI.com*, August 1, 2007.
142   *almost adolescent in his*: Lester Munson, "Jail break? Donaghy's cooperation could make sentencing more lenient," *ESPN.com*, July 22, 2008.

142 *cars, women, working, sports*: Jana Winter, Samuel J. Goldsmith, and Dan Mangan, "Ref Pal Fears He May Be Snared in the Same Net," *New York Post*, July 27, 2007.

144 *Nobody wanted to play*: James Fanelli and Jana Winter, "Ref's hit with some bad calls," *New York Post*, July 23, 2007.

Chapter Fourteen: Trouble Shooting

161 *a divorcee . . . mother of two*: Jana Winter and Dan Mangan, "Dirty Ref's 'Sideline' Gal Eyed By Feds," *New York Post*, August 27, 2007.

Chapter Seventeen: *Gambling Investigation Rocks NBA*

195 *The FBI is investigating*: Murray Weiss, "NBA in a 'Fix,'" *New York Post*, July 20, 2007.

196 *I have been involved*: *ESPN.com*, "David Stern's Donaghy news conference transcript," July 24, 2007.

Chapter Eighteen: The Dog Days of Summer

198 *Here's the first look*: Mike Jaccarino and John Marzulli, "Ref's alleged bookie is in a foul mood," *NY Daily News*, July 27, 2007.

201 *Ruggieri noticed that Jack*: John Shiffman, "Pro gambler says Donaghy was under suspicion for lengthy period," *Philadelphia Inquirer*, July 31, 2007.

201 *Pete Ruggieri thought he*: Joseph Santoliquito and William Bender, "Lawyer says Ruggieri has no gambling connection to Donaghy," *Philadelphia Daily News*, August 1, 2007.

201 *Donaghy first partnered*: Mike Jaccarino, "Ref Changes Bet Pals to Boost Loot, Gambler Sez," *Daily News* (NY), July 31, 2007.

Chapter Nineteen: *Former N.B.A. Referee Pleads Guilty*

217 *a lot of things*: William Bender, "Donaghy's associates indicted in betting case," *Philadelphia Daily News*, February 9, 2008.

Chapter Twenty: What Characters

226 *I taught him for*: Mike Jaccarino, "Bad bounces along his way,"
     Daily News (NY), July 29, 2007.

227 *Mail carrier Charles Brogan*: Mike Jaccarino and Helen Kennedy,
     "He got his share of fouls both on and off the court," *Daily News*
     (NY), July 21, 2007.

227 *No way I'm going*: Mike Jaccarino, John Marzulli, Jonathan
     Lemire, and Rich Schapiro, "Rogue ref may blow whistle," *Daily
     News* (NY), July 22, 2007.

228 *sued Donaghy for harassment*: Associated Press, "Stern: bet probe
     'worst situation that i have ever experienced,'" July 25, 2007.

     The *Philadelphia Inquirer* article referenced which discusses the
     outcome of the Brogan (mail carrier) incident is Kathleen Brady
     Shea, "Referee out of bounds, neighbors' suit says," January 21,
     2005.

228 *In the summer of 2003*: Shea, "Referee out of bounds."

228 *We were terrorized*: Jaccarino and Kennedy, "He got his share."

229 *He was so bad*: William Bender, "Donaghy remembered locally as
     someone 'out of control,'" *Philadelphia Daily News*, July 25, 2007.

229 *as a consequence of*: Stern's Donaghy news conference.

230 *knock my . . . head off*: Bill Hutchinson, "Tim Donaghy avoids foul
     call by wife," *Daily News* (NY), March 25, 2008.

232 *Aside from former O'Hara*: Anthony J. SanFilippo, "Donaghy's
     downfall leaves many scars," *Delco Times*, July 6, 2008.

Chapter Twenty-One: Team Donaghy's Assault on Justice

240 Regarding the legal issue of the NBA's loss, see, for example,
     *United States of America, -against- Timothy Donaghy, Defendant,
     United States of America, -against- James Battista and Thomas
     Martino, Defendants*, 07-CR-587 (CBA), 08-CR-86 (CBA),
     UNITED STATES DISTRICT COURT FOR THE EAST-
     ERN DISTRICT OF NEW YORK, 570 F. Supp. 2d 411; 2008
     U.S. Dist. LEXIS 56776, July 23, 2008 Decided, July 23, 2008
     Filed; and UNITED STATES COURT OF APPEALS FOR
     THE SECOND CIRCUIT, *United States of America v. James
     Battista*, Docket No. 08-3750-cr, August 6, 2009.

243 *The letter filed today*: Michael S. Schmidt and Howard Beck,
     "Assertions by Ex-Referee Are Dismissed by N.B.A.," *The New
     York Times*, May 20, 2008.

243 *An interesting, almost laughable*: Bob Ford, "Donaghy's lawyer is fishing—and it smells," *Philadelphia Inquirer*, May 25, 2008.

244 *If Donaghy cannot make*: Lester Munson, "Donaghy's claims serious, troubling for NBA," *ESPN.com*, June 10, 2008.

244 *received no information*: Phil Jasner, "Coming to defense of NBA referees amid Donaghy allegations," *Philadelphia Daily News*, June 12, 2008.

245 *My reaction to Donaghy's lawyer*: Associated Press, "Donaghy says refs fixed playoffs; Stern says no," June 10, 2008.

245 *According to Mr. Donaghy*: Stephen A. Smith, "Dream season shaken by Donaghy nightmare," *ESPN.com*, June 11, 2008.

245 *conspiracy theorists jumped out*: John Smallwood, "NBA Surviving Donaghy scandal," *Philadelphia Daily News*, July 30, 2008.

247 *A lot of it was*: Joshua Robinson, "Prosecution plays down cooperation of Donaghy," *New York Times*, July 10, 2008.

248 *knew what he did*: Andrew Alberg, "Assisting feds cut ex-ref's jail time," *USA Today*, July 29, 2008.

250 *If there were people*: William Bender, "Do you believe disgraced ref Donaghy?" *Philadelphia Daily News*, December 10, 2009.

Chapter Twenty-Two: *An Hour to a Little Kid Is a Long Time*

253 *This is a very serious*: John Barr, "Battista sentenced to 15 months in prison; Martino gets one year," *ESPN.com*, July 24, 2008.

255 *Downstairs in the lobby*: William Bender, "Battista, Martino verdicts could be ominous for disgraced NBA ref Donaghy," *Philadelphia Daily News*, July 25, 2008.

257 *The NBA, the players*: Robin Shulman and Michael Lee, "Donaghy Sentenced to 15 Months in Prison," *Washington Post*, July 30, 2008.

259 *We were retained*: National Basketball Association, "Larry Pedowitz Teleconference Transcript," October 2, 2008.

260 *We have discovered*: Lawrence B. Pedowitz, "Report to the Board of Governors of the National Basketball Association," October 1, 2008, pp. 39, 7.

260 *Donaghy Report Clears*: Michael Lee, "Donaghy Report Clears Other Refs," *Washington Post*, October 3, 2008.

260 *Probe: No evidence*: Chris Colston, "Probe: No evidence of other referees' misconduct," *USA Today*, October 3, 2008.

260 *Report confirms Donaghy*: William Bender, "Report confirms Donaghy was the only corrupt referee, clears NBA," *Philadelphia Daily News*, October 3, 2008.

260   *Review of NBA*: "Review of NBA officials finds Donaghy only culprit, calls for change," *ESPN.com*, October 3, 2008.

260   *NBA referees are*: Marc J. Spears, "NBA referees are cleared; Report: Only Donaghy guilty," *Boston Globe*, October 3, 2008.

260   *Report: Donaghy fixed*: Ken Berger, "Report: Donaghy fixed games alone," *Newsday*, October 3, 2008.

260   *Despite our repeated*: Pedowitz, "Report to the Board of Governors," p. 7.

APPENDIX: ANALYSIS

Jimmy Battista says he does not possess betting records to support his various claims regarding his bets on Tim Donaghy's games, and obtaining these records independent of Battista has been a difficult challenge for a host of reasons.[3] When interviewed in the earliest stages of research for what became *Gaming the Game*, Battista's betting on Donaghy's games had taken place approximately 12 to 16 months prior.[4] In part because of the gap in time, and especially because his bets on Donaghy's games were such an insignificant part of his daily betting activity, Battista didn't pretend to recall each and every bet, much less the betting line movement or the wins and losses, for each and every Donaghy game that was part of the scandal.[5] As such, Battista was asked to offer his best

---

[3] I had originally intended to offer the results of an assessment of Battista's computerized betting records, many of which I have found and reviewed. Locating Battista's wagers—in numerous accounts among various sportsbooks—is ongoing as of March 2010, and the goal is to compile a full (or close to full) data set from which to draw conclusions. In advance of this analysis, I must note that the data reviewed to date supports Battista's claims regarding the significant amounts of money placed on Donaghy's games versus considerably less placed on non-Donaghy games.

[4] It is important to note that Battista's recollections regarding his bets on Donaghy's games were offered before anyone knew Tim Donaghy's detailed version of events. Thus, Battista didn't know at the time that Donaghy was/would be claiming: he stopped betting on March 18, 2007; that he only bet on 30 games with Battista, of which only 16 were games he officiated; and that his winning percentage was the same regardless of whether the bets were on games he officiated.

[5] As noted previously, Battista's gambling activity during the time period spanning the scandal involved betting multiple games for several clients and partners, monitoring minute-by-minute line changes from around the world in real time, and thus betting

recollections for the games he says made up the NBA betting scandal. Because I had just met Battista and because the issues of validity and credibility were going to be paramount in this project, I met with Battista twice for the express purpose of assessing his recollection of betting activity on Donaghy's '06-07 games.

During the first meeting, Battista was provided with a list of Donaghy's games which included only the dates of the games, the teams, and the outcomes (no betting lines were referenced). Battista was not aware that as he sat across from me, I was looking at a different version of the list of Donaghy's games— one with the open and closing betting lines. That particular interviewing experience remains a point of fascination with me because for those games Battista recalled, his recounting of betting line moves (often including the manner in which the line related to the outcome of a game) was uncanny. At a later point, after time had elapsed, after numerous other interview sessions of a range of topics had been conducted, and after much had transpired in the federal case against Battista (not to mention whatever was going on in his personal life), we revisited his memory of the betting activity for Donaghy's 2006-07 season. This was done to further assess Battista's credibility and reliability, and his recollections were virtually unchanged.[6]

282   *major, major stumbling block*: William Bender, "Donaghy reiterates he never threw games," *Philadelphia Daily News*, December 11, 2009.

---

multiple times for most games. Furthermore, he was placing his bets with dozens of outs (offshore/online, foreign markets, Vegas sportsbooks, and bookies throughout the U.S.). All of this was in addition to whatever NBA betting scandal-specific activities were taking place.

[6] Simply because his statements were the same and thus in this specific context there was *reliability*, this is distinct from the issue of *validity*. Thus, if the information from the first interview was invalid, the fact that he merely later repeated this information would mean the data was reliable but not valid.

282 *He's one of the*: Henry Abbott, "A Professional Gambler's Take on the Tim Donaghy Scandal," *ESPN.com*, June 11, 2008.

283 *near or at top*: *ESPN.com*, "David Stern's Donaghy news conference."

283 Tim Donaghy, *Personal Foul: A First-Person Account of the Scandal that Rocked the NBA* (Largo, FL: VTi Group, 2009), p. 238.

289 Regarding the belief among many NBA betting scandal observers that game totals were being bet as opposed to sides, see, for example, Justin Wolfers, "Blow the Whistle on Betting Scandals," *New York Times*, July 27, 2007; and Wayne L. Winston, *Mathletics: How Gamblers, Managers, and Sports Enthusiasts Use Mathematics in Baseball, Basketball, and Football* (Princeton, NJ: Princeton University Press, 2009), pp. 244-247. Regarding the lower betting limits on game total bets compared to sides bets, see, for example, Jon Campbell, "More answers to questions about the Donaghy scandal," *Covers.com*, July 26, 2007.

290 *I could pick*: CBS News, "60 Minutes" transcript for Sunday, December 6, 2009.

296 *They never called*: Matt Youmans, "Betting scandal cloud lingers," *Las Vegas Review-Journal*, May 23, 2008.

Glossary of Terms

"All-Star Sports"[1]—pseudonym for a now-defunct, Curacao-based offshore sportsbook in which the services of The Animals were enlisted.

"ARD"—"ARD" is short for Pennsylvania's **A**ccelerated **R**ehabilitative **D**isposition, a one-time alternative to a trial, conviction, and possible jail sentence for first offenders.

"Balloon"—one million dollars (i.e., two balloons = $2,000,000).

Betting line—"the line;" also known as the point spread; the number of points one team is favored to win over its opponent; ideally, from the perspective of bookmakers and sportsbooks, the line generates equal action on each side of a proposition, resulting in the book's profit on the juice/vig.

Bookmaker—also referred to as a "bookie;" someone who offers odds and accepts bets; the bookie's operation is often referred to as his "book."

CRIS—Costa Rica International Sports; influential offshore sportsbook.

"Crushing"—winning on betting propositions at a significantly profitable rate; not to be confused with *getting crushed* (losing money).

---

[1] The names "All-Star Sports" and "Paramount Sports" are pseudonyms. Any resemblance to real entities is purely coincidental.

"Dime"—one thousand dollars (i.e., five dimes = $5,000).

Don Best—influential subscription Web site that offers real-time odds and line moves from sportsbooks around the world; the arrival of Don Best ended the need for bettors and their crews to phone bookmakers and sportsbooks for "rundowns."

"Earner"—a bet or a sequence of bets that would likely result in financial gain. (Note: although Jimmy Battista uses the term "earner" in this fashion, other gamblers refer to these bets simply as "earns" and reserve the term "earner" for people who earn on their behalf).

"Firing"—betting rapidly, often with many outs being used simultaneously.

"First number"—the opening betting line offered by a sportsbook or bookmaker.

"Get down"—place a bet.

"Get off a game"—place bets on the opposite side of bets placed earlier in the hopes of diminishing expected losses; commonly done when information is disclosed late (e.g., injuries) or when it is discovered the line was being manipulated.

Handicapper—someone who analyzes upcoming sporting events and calculates the point spread.

"Juice"—also referred to as the "vig;" generally speaking, bookmakers and sportsbooks charge a 10% fee or tax on losing bets; a bettor must put up $110 to win $100, and bettors must win at least 52.4% of their bets over time just to break even because of the juice.

"Manipulate the line"—also referred to as "controlling the numbers;" the strategic placing of bets (at certain times and places, and in certain amounts) to cause bookmakers and sportsbooks to adjust betting lines in reaction to the wagers, often resulting in a point spread more attractive to the bettor who "manipulated the lines."

"The market"—the universe of sports betting action; pro gamblers follow the market (i.e., dozens if not hundreds of international sportsbook and bookmaker lines) looking for curiosities, weaknesses, potential earners, etc.

"Middle"—A "middle" occurs when a bettor wagers on both sides of a game at different point spreads with the intent of winning both bets (e.g., someone who bets on Penn State -4 and on Ohio State +7 wins both wagers if the final score is Penn State 27 Ohio State 21).

MLB—Major League Baseball.

"Move a game"—place bets strategically on a game.

"Mover"—one who moves games as a profession (Jimmy Battista was one of the world's most influential movers).

NBA—National Basketball Association.

"Next number"—Sharps often refer to the "next number" as the betting line that follows the "right number;" the inference is that the next number is always a weaker betting proposition than the so-called "right number" and that those who routinely take the "next number" will lose in the long run.

NFL—National Football League.

"**Offshore**"—Loosely defined term used to describe betting operations located in such locations as Santo Domingo, Curacao, Antigua, and elsewhere that rose in prominence in the mid- to late 1990s; offshore sportsbooks have proliferated in the Internet era and accommodate bettors online from around the world.

Offshore sportsbook agent—Provides various services to clients of offshore sports betting operations, including providing passcodes to betting sites and standing for the money of the bettor and the sportsbook; select agents are responsible for moving millions of dollars throughout the United States once or twice per week.

"**Off the board**"—A betting line that is either listed but not available for play at a sportsbook, or a game that has been removed from betting action.

"**Out**"—An "out" is a bookmaker or sportsbook with whom someone places a bet; one of the difficulties in wagering large sums of money is finding books to take bets, since most have tight restrictions on wager amounts, particularly if they know the bet is for a sharp bettor; the world's sharpest bettors thus employ an army of movers and an array of tactics to exploit the largest number of outs as possible to "get down" the largest amount of money on their bets.

"**Paramount Sports**"—Pseudonym for the world's largest and most consequential sportsbook; based in Curacao.

Point spread—also referred to simply as "the spread;" the betting line.

"**Queer Street**"—the wrong side of a betting proposition; oftentimes sharps (and their movers and runners) will consciously place bets on the opposite side they are actually taking, such that their hangers-on and competitors will copy the bets, thus placing them on "Queer Street."

"Right number"—Sharps, after their considerable research, refer to their opinion regarding a proper betting line as the "right number;" the right number may or may not be the same as the one posted by sportsbooks or bookmakers.

"Rundown"—Before the Internet age, bettors and their crews (runners, movers) phoned bookmakers and sportsbooks to have the day's slate of games and odds read to them over the phone; hence, what they requested and heard was a "rundown" of that day's betting lines.

"Runner"—someone who places wagers on behalf of bettors and movers; used almost exclusively to reference those in this position operating in Las Vegas (who run from casino to casino, trying to obtain the right numbers).

"Sharp"—term used within sports betting circles to describe someone who is a highly skilled handicapper or bettor; often has some combination of research teams, computer models, and inside information.

"Sharp money"—also referred to as "smart money"; bets placed by sharp bettors (often by their movers) that are often in large sums and which are often consequential enough to warrant bookmakers and sportsbook managers changing the betting line in response.

"Squares"—also referred to as suckers; uninformed bettors.

Sportsbook—legitimate, often sophisticated, bookmaking operations; can reference such entities in places such as Las Vegas and offshore; sometimes loosely referred to as a "book."

"Store"—a bookmaker or sportsbook.

"Street tax"—weekly fee extorted by organized crime organizations for operating within their territory; most often assessed to illicit entrepreneurs (e.g., bookmakers and bettors) who cannot take their grievances to law enforcement.

Suckers—also referred to as "squares"; uninformed bettors.

"Totals"—"over/under" bets on the total points scored on a game.

"Vig"—short for "vigorish;" more commonly called "juice."

ACKNOWLEDGMENTS

THIS SORT OF project requires the assistance of hundreds of people, and what follows (in no particular order) is my best attempt at a list of everyone who helped make *Gaming the Game* possible. I apologize in advance for those I no doubt forgot below.

As with much of my published research, this book would not have been possible without the unbelievable assistance of dozens of current and former law enforcement officials at the local, state, and federal levels. For obvious reasons, they do not wish to be named and I have thanked each of them personally for their various efforts. This is also true for the many members of the sports betting underworld who allowed me into their inner sanctum for, among other things, permitting me to: view betting records; accompany Vegas runners day-to-day; and sit with pro gamblers as betting lines were manipulated and money was moved electronically around the world. For a gambling novice like me, these moments—even if not explicitly referenced in *Gaming the Game*—were key to my understanding of big-time betting's sociology and thus to this project. The same is especially true for a handful of gamblers who are named in the book, especially Louie the Lump, Tiger, Bull, and Domino. Many of these folks had little to gain (and much to lose) by allowing me into their respective worlds, and I remain grateful.

Former FBI Supervisory Special Agent Phil Scala was the lone agent involved in the cases against the three NBA betting scandal conspirators who could speak on the record, and deserves thanks for offering his insights into the investigation, and for his suggested lines of inquiry. I especially need to thank attorney Jack McMahon for his generosity and accessibility throughout this project. Jack's insights went well beyond his defense of Jimmy Battista, and were key to my understanding of various legal matters. I would also like to express my gratitude to attorney Larry Pedowitz, author of the NBA's report on the scandal, who was always gracious and patient regarding various matters during the course of the research. Thanks also go to the helpful folks within the press offices of the following agencies: Montgomery County (PA) District Attorney's Office; Federal Bureau of Investigation regional offices in Philadelphia, Manhattan, and Brooklyn; U.S. Attorney's Offices in Philadelphia and Brooklyn; and the Federal Bureau of Prisons regional office in Pensacola, Florida.

The area of sports betting law and enforcement is ever-changing, as evidenced by the recent battles in various states and within the federal government regarding various proposals. I am thus indebted to two individuals above others for taking their time to walk me through the history of such laws and the enforcement of them: David G. Schwartz, Director of the Center for Gaming Research at the University of Nevada Las Vegas (UNLV); and James "Doug" Dunlap, Forensic Examiner in the FBI's Cryptanalysis & Racketeering Records Unit (CRRU).

Thanks also to: Benjie Cherniak and Angie Hart at Don Best, without whose assistance much of the betting line analysis would not have been possible; the online staff at Covers.com who also humored several of my inquiries; Wayne L. Winston, Professor of Operations & Decision Technologies at Indiana University, for his prompt replies to my questions regarding his work on sports betting; Temple University urban historian Mark H. Haller, who long ago shared his considerable insights and greatly influenced my understanding of the gambling underworld; and George Anastasia of the *Philadelphia Inquirer*, a longtime authority of the area's organized crime scene, who has always been willing to humor my requests for his time.

My academic home, Penn State Abington, is going through a promising yet challenging transition from a college more grounded on teaching to one more balanced with research. As such, faculty and staff are being pushed in multifarious ways, and the process has not been entirely harmonious. For their grace in dealing with the likes of me, 'Abington's pleasant and incredible staff members deserve at least my thanks in words, especially: Marcia Donahue, Donna Millinghausen Koenig, Phyllis Martin, Betty Mason, Eleanor Meehl, Janet Mignogno, Susan Paciolla, Joan Raudenbush, Lizanne Sarvey, and Stayce Shaffert. Penn State Abington's Chancellor, Karen W. Sandler, has never wavered in her support of my work. The same is true for Associate Dean Samir Ouzomgi and Social Science Division Head Gary S. Calore, and I thus need to thank each of them. Many of my Penn State colleagues (at 'Abington and at PSU's main campus in University Park, PA) have, as usual, lent their expertise, counsel, and time, and I owe them a great deal. This is especially true for the Criminal Justice faculty at Penn State Abington (Trish Collins, Lisa Morris, John Sullivan, and Patti Workman), who have accommodated so much of my insanity during the course of this project. 'Abington's Director of Athletics, Karen Weaver, has been a welcome addition to our campus and a great sounding board during this research, and I must especially thank her as well. Other Penn Staters of note include: Andy August, Bob Barton, Theresa Bloom, Deb Casey, Carol DeBunda, Bella Friesel, Lonnie Golden, Ellen Knodt, Kim Menard, Steve McMillan, Judy Newman, Jane Owens, Dave Ruth, Jim Smith, and Ron Zigler.

I first contacted former investigative journalist Jim Nicholson at some point in the 1990s when I was working on my Ph.D. dissertation, and he has not stopped lending his professionalism to my work ever since. I am forever indebted to him for the countless ways he has helped me with work like *Gaming the Game*. For much of my written work the past fifteen or so years, I have relied upon the editing skills of several colleagues, friends, and family members who have been rather giving of their time. Though I can't name them here, they each deserve special thanks for their great insights and criticisms; the book is better because of their comments. Similarly, I have long been surrounded by a coterie of friends who commonly offer their various (and typically unsolicited) opinions on much of my work. In the case of this particular project, their assistance, insights and criticisms were more welcome than usual, and thus I feel obligated to thank the following publicly (with the understanding I owe these fellas *nothing*, especially now): Scott Copman, Eric Hunn, Stu Revness, Andrew Senzer, Matt Spak, and Keith Traynor.

Pete Walsh, of U.K.-based Milo Books, has been a help in many ways, and was always willing to offer his insights as a publisher, author, editor, and friend. I owe you much, Pete. Pete's colleague, publisher Carole Stuart, at Barricade Books has put up with far more (I am sure!) than she ever bargained for when she took on this unwieldy project and its oft-unavailable author. I hope you are satisfied with the finished product, Carole, and that it in some way alleviates the many frustrations you experienced throughout the process. Thanks also to Barricade's print production manager, Mark Morrell, for his patience and professionalism. Entertainment attorney Judy Karfiol has continued to endure my ignorance of all things Hollywood, and I remain grateful to her for going beyond what should be expected of someone in her position (especially for *GTG*-related happenings).

Military officer, fighter pilot, and all-around good guy Kevin Kelly deserves the credit for getting this project started and, perhaps more appropriately, for seeing it through. Your yeoman, behind-the-scenes efforts were greatly appreciated, Kev. Historian/criminologist Alan A. Block had nothing—yet everything—to do with this book, and I only wish he could grasp my profound appreciation for the variegated lessons he taught me over many years. The consummate professional and mentor will never be forgotten by me or by those whose lives and careers he impacted during his time at the University of Delaware and at Penn State. Alan's wife, Constance Weaver, is always willing to lend a hand, and deserves special thanks for all she has done for Alan as his health has deteriorated. Please don't ever think your grace and your efforts have been taken for granted, Connie; you're a special person. Speaking of special people . . .

Lastly, and most importantly, I need to thank my wife and kids, who have endured much the past few years as my work has consumed me. Their friends can attest I have not been around for any number of (often consequential) events, and each has had to answer on repeated occasions questions regarding my whereabouts. To Deb, Kelly, and Connor, I hope you know your myriad sacrifices have not gone unnoticed, and that your love, patience, and understanding were treasured in a way I can't express here.

Sean Patrick Griffin
January 2011

Index

BARRICADE

OTHER BOOKS IN OUR BARRICADE *CRIME* SERIES

FOR A COMPLETE LIST OF BARRICADE TITLES PLEASE
VISIT OUR WEBSITE: WWW.BARRICADEBOOKS.COM

A Cop's Tale: NYPD The Violent Years

Jim O'Neil and Mel Fazzino
Focusing on New York City's most corrupt years, the 1960s to 1980s, this book delivers a rare look at the brand of law enforcement that ended Frank Lucas's grip on the Harlem drug trade, cracking open the Black Liberation Army case, and the author's experience as the first cop on the scene at the "Dog Day Afternoon" bank robbery.
$24,95 • Hardcover • 1-56980-372-2

Balls: The Life of Eddie Trascher, Gentleman Gangster

Scott M. Deitche with Ken Sanz
For 50 years, Eddie Trascher stole from mob-owned casinos, scammed gangsters, and was one of the top bookies in the country. He capped his career as an informant for Florida law enforcement to get inside the Trafficante Mafia family.
$24.95 • Hardcover • 1-56980-366-8

Black Gangsters of Chicago

Ron Chepesiuk
Chicago's African American gangsters were every bit as powerful and intriguing as the city's fabled white mobsters. For the first time, Ron Chepesiuk

chronicles their fascinating stories.
$22.00 • Hardcover • 1-56980-331-5

Blood & Volume

Dave Copeland
Ron Gonen, together with pals Johnny Attias and Ron Efraim, ran a multimillion-dollar drug distribution syndicate in 1980s New York. But when the FBI caught up, Gonen had to choose between doing the right thing and winding up dead.
$22.00 • Hardcover • 1-56980-327-7

Bronx D.A.: True Stories from the Domestic Violence and Sex Crimes Unit

Sarena Straus
If you dealt with violence all day, how long would it be before you burned out? Sarena Straus was a prosecutor in the Bronx District Attorney's office, working in an area of the Bronx with the highest crime and poverty rates in America. This book chronicles her experiences during her three-year stint with the Domestic Violence and Sex Crimes Unit, combating crimes against women and children. This book details how and why she finally had to stop.
$22.00 • Hardcover • 1-56980-305-6

Cigar City Mafia: A Complete History of the Tampa Underworld
Scott M. Deitche
Prohibition-era "Little Havana" housed Tampa's cigar industry, and with it, bootleggers, arsonists, and mobsters—and a network of corrupt police officers worse than the criminals themselves. Scott M. Deitche documents the rise of the infamous Trafficante family, ruthless competitors in a "violent, shifting place, where loyalties and power quickly changed."
$22.95 • Hardcover • 1-56980-266-1
$14.95 • Paperback • 1-56980-287-4

Confessions of a Second Story Man: Junior Kripplebauer and the K&A Gang
Allen M. Hornblum
From the 1950s to the 1970s, the ragtag crew known as the K&A Gang robbed wealthy suburban neighborhoods with assembly-line skills. Hornblum tells the strange-but-true story through interviews, police records, and historical research, including the transformation of the K&A Gang from a group of blue-collar thieves to their work in conjunction with numerous organized-crime families helping to make Philadelphia the "meth" capital of the nation.
$24.95 • Hardcover • 1-56980-313-7

Frank Nitti: The True Story of Chicago's Notorious "Enforcer"
Ronald D. Humble
Frank "The Enforcer" Nitti is arguably the most glamorized gangster in history. Though he has been widely mentioned in fictional works, this is the first book to document Nitti's real-life criminal career alongside his pop-culture persona, with special chapters devoted to the many television shows, movies, and songs featuring Nitti.
$23.95 • Hardcover • 1-56980-342-0

Gangster City: The History of the New York Underworld 1900–1935
Patrick Downey
From 1900 to 1935, New York City hosted more than 600 mob-land killings. No other book delivers such extensive detail on the lives, crimes, and dramatic endings of this ruthless cast of characters, including Jack "Legs" Diamond and the sadistic Dutch Schultz.
$23.95 • Hardcover • 1-56980-267-X
$16.95 • Paperback • 1-56980-361-7

Gangsters of Harlem
Ron Chepesiuk
Veteran journalist Ron Chepesiuk chronicles the life and crimes of Harlem's gangsters, including "Nicky" Barnes, Bumpy Johnson, and the notorious Frank Lucas.
$22.00 • Hardcover • 1-56980-318-8
$15.95 • Paperback • 1-56980-365-X

Gangsters of Miami: True Tales of Mobsters, Gamblers, Hit Men, Con Men and Gang Bangers from the Magic City
Ron Chepesiuk
Chronicling gangs and gangster history using profiles this book traces the notorious smugglers of the Prohibition era, famous mobsters like Al Capone and Meyer Lansky, the

Cuban mafia, the Colombian cartel, and the current street gangs that have come to plague Miami after the advent of crack cocaine.

$23.95 • Hardcover • 1-56980-368-4

I'll Do My Own Damn Killin'
Gary W. Sleeper
A detailed look into the life of notorious casino owner Benny Binion, which looks into his life in Dallas before his infamous Las Vegas days.

$22.00 • Hardcover • 1-56980-321-8

Il Dottore
Ron Felber
By day, he was Dr. Elliot Litner, respected surgeon at Mount Sinai Hospital; by night, Il Dottore, a sex and gambling addict with ties to New York's reigning Mafia Dons. But when Attorney General Rudolph Guiliani stepped in, Litner had to decide where his loyalties lay: with La Cosa Nostra, or the Hippocratic oath.

$24.95 • Hardcover • 1-56980-278-5

Jailing the Johnston Gang
Bruce E. Mowday
Pennsylvania's Johnston Gang, led by Bruce Sr. and his brothers Norman and David, ran a prolific burglary ring during the 1960s and 1970s. But in 1978, fearing that younger members of the gang were going to rat them out, the brothers killed four teenagers and nearly killed Bruce Sr.'s own son.

$22.95 • Hardcover • 1-56980-363-3
$16.95 • Paperback • 1-56980-442-1

Lucky Luciano
Hickman Powell
Written by a top investigative reporter who covered Luciano's trial from beginning to end, *Lucky Luciano* is a detailed account of Luciano's intriguing life.

$23.95 • Hardcover • 1-56980-163-0

Mala Femina
Theresa Dalessio with Patrick W. Picciarelli
Theresa "Terri Dee" Dalessio was a Mafia daughter, pregnant teenager, barkeeper, heroin addict, murder witness, and twice-divorced mother of three. For a start.

$24.95 • Hardcover • 1-56980-244-0

Rancho Mirage: An American Tragedy of Manners, Madness & Murder
Aram Saroyan
This is one of the strangest true-crime stories ever written: a story of murder, reported rape, abduction, and multiple personalities. It contains all the ingredients of a chilling page-turner. Saroyan writes nonfiction as compelling as a great novel.

$14.95 • Paperback • 1-56980-234-3

Sharon Tate and the Manson Murders
Greg King
Throughout the summer of 1969, America was transfixed by a series of brutal murders in and around Los Angeles. The victims included Sharon Tate, pregnant wife of director Roman Polanski. Greg

King unearths a trove of information on Tate while taking readers into the midst of the Manson family, profiling the killers' past, the sex and drug rites of the family, and the career of Manson himself. King unflinchingly re-creates the brutality and utter randomness of the events and includes some lucid observations on the continuing cult of Manson and the merchandising of Manson's image.

$24.95 • Hardcover • 1-56980-157-6

Stolen Masterpiece Tracker: The Dangerous Life of the FBI's #1 Art Sleuth

Thomas McShane with Dary Matera
Legendary undercover FBI agent Thomas McShane is one of the world's foremost authorities on the billion-dollar art-theft business. For thirty-six years, McShane matched wits with some of the most devious criminal masterminds of the 20th and 21st centuries. Here he presents a unique memoir that gives readers a thrilling ride through the underworld of stolen art and historical artifacts. Written with veteran true-crime author Dary Matera, this captivating account is as engaging as it is informative.

$24.95 • Hardcover • 1-56980-314-5

Terrorist Cop: The NYPD Jewish Cop Who Traveled the World to Stop Terrorists

Mordecai Z. Dzikansky with Robert Slater
Terrorist Cop is a colorful, haunting, and highly graphic tale of retired New York City Detective First Grade

Morty Dzikansky. Dzikansky first patrolled Brooklyn streets with a yarmulke on his head. A rise through the ranks would eventually result with him being in Israel monitoring suicide bombings post 9/11. It was part of Commissioner Ray Kelly's plan to protect New York from further terrorist attacks, but it led to Morty becoming a victim of post-traumatic stress disorder.

$24.95 • Hardcover • 1-56980-445-1

The Animal in Hollywood: Anthony Fiato's Life in the Mafia

John L. Smith
The Animal in Hollywood recounts in frank and chilling detail mob enforcer Anthony Fiato's explosive career in the Mafia. He grew up a tough Boston kid, good looking and a sharp dresser. By the age of 17 he moved to Hollywood and by 20 was a Mafia enforcer on both coasts. Today he lives under an assumed name as a member of the federal witness protection program.

$22.00 • Hardcover • 1-56980-126-6

The Jews of Sing-Sing

Ron Arons
Besides famous gangsters like Lepke Buchalter, thousands of Jews committed all types of crimes—from incest to arson to selling air rights over Manhattan—and found themselves doing time in Sing-Sing.

$22.95 • Hardcover • 1-56980-333-1

The Life and Times of Lepke Buchalter

Paul R. Kavieff
Lepke Buchalter had a stranglehold

on the New York garment industry, rising from small-scale push-cart terrorism to leadership of Murder Inc.'s staff of killers-by-assignment, until an obscure murder ended his reign as America's most ruthless labor racketeer.

$22.00 • Hardcover • 1-56980-291-2

The Mafia and the Machine
Frank R. Hayde
La Cosa Nostra reaches right into the heart of America. Nowhere is that more evident than in the "City of Fountains," where the Mafia held sway over the political machine.

$22.00 • Hardcover • 1-56980-336-6
$16.95 • Paperback • 1-56980-443-5

The Purple Gang
Paul R. Kavieff
This is the hitherto untold story of the rise and fall of one of America's most notorious criminal groups. The Purple Gang was a loosely organized confederation of mobsters who dominated the Detroit underworld and whose tentacles reached across the country.

$15.95 • Paperback • 1-56980-281-5
$22.00 • Hardcover • 1-56980-417-9

The Rise and Fall of the Cleveland Mafia
Rick Porrello
One of Barricade's best-selling true crime titles includes a new introduction by the author in the latest paperback print edition. This is the fascinating chronicle of a once mighty crime family's birth, rise to power, and eventual collapse. From obscurity, the Cleveland Mafia rose

rapidly to power and position, taking its place as the third most powerful operation in the country. But the city's crime syndicates nearly decimated themselves during the Sugar War—"Big Ange" Lonardo's vendetta-driven play to control the lucrative bootleg liquor production racket.

$16.95 • Paperback • 1-56980-277-7
$22.00 • Hardcover • 1-56980-058-8

The Silent Don
Scott Deitche
A follow-up to Deitche's best-selling *Cigar City Mafia*, *The Silent Don* exposes the life of one of America's most powerful and feared mob bosses, Santo Trafficante Jr.

$22.00 • Hardcover • 1-56980-322-6
$16.95 • Paperback • 1-56980-355-2

The Violent Years
Paul R. Kavieff
A follow-up to Kavieff's best-selling *The Purple Gang*, this book delves deeper into the Prohibition-Era gangs of the Detroit area.

$22.00 • Hardcover • 1-56980-210-6

Thief!
William "Slick" Hanner & Cherie Rohn
The true story of "Slick" Hanner and how he gained insider access to the Mafia, starting out as a Chicago street tough and workin his way to a friendship with Tony Spilotro, the Outfit's notorious frontman.

$22.00 • Hardcover • 1-56980-317-X